Seeking Global Justice:
Bahá'í Visions for Legal Reform

George Ronald Bahá'í Studies Series

Seeking Global Justice:
Bahá'í Visions for Legal Reform

Brian D. Lepard, Editor

GR

GEORGE RONALD

OXFORD

George Ronald, Publisher
Oxford
www.grbooks.com

A catalogue record for this book is available from the British Library

ISBN 978–0–85398–681–2

Contents

For my beloved family

Acknowledgments

This book was many years in the making. I wish to thank the contributors for their persistence, patience, and perceptive insights into the concept of global justice from a Bahá'í perspective. I could not have asked for more devoted and gracious collaborators. I also thank George Ronald for its consistent support for this project, and especially Wendi Momen and our editor, David Langness. David's excellent editorial and substantive suggestions significantly improved the book.

I furthermore appreciate the support for my research on the book of the University of Nebraska College of Law, my academic home for thirty years, and in particular of its Dean, Richard Moberly.

During the long process of writing and editing the book I relied on the love and support of my beloved wife and spiritual partner Jenina, our sons Brandon and Justin, and our daughter-in-law Alexis. Finally, I wish to pay tribute to the inspiration of my parents, Millie and David Lepard. They inculcated in me a profound concern for justice borne of love for Bahá'u'lláh and His teachings about global justice, world unity, international peace, and universal human rights. I will be forever grateful to them.

Brian Lepard

Contributor Biographies

Kiser Barnes

Kiser Barnes holds a Juris Doctor degree from the University of Maryland Law School and a Master's in the Philosophy of Law from Obafemi Awolowo University in Ife, Nigeria. He was a Senior Lecturer in the Faculty of Law at Obafemi Awolowo University. His academic experiences include Professor, Charles Hamilton Houston Lectures in Human Rights and American Law, Université du Benin, Lomé, Togo. He has authored many articles on law and the Bahá'í Faith, including 'The Principle of Justice in Religion and Law: The True Basis for Religious Harmony', 'The Nature of Bahá'í Law', and 'Human Rights and Multiculturalism'.

Aaron Emmel

Aaron Emmel works with the U.S. Government, U.N. agencies, and international organizations to develop policies that contribute to human rights protection, social and economic development, and international security. He also writes and edits books and essays and has contributed to dozens of publications. His book *Human Rights in an Advancing Civilization* has been called 'seamless and imaginative' and 'brilliant and thoroughly accessible'. He holds a Master's Degree in Security Studies, with a focus on terrorism and substate violence, from Georgetown University's School of Foreign Service. More information about him is available online at www.aaronemmel.com

Brian D. Lepard

Brian D. Lepard is the Harold W. Conroy Distinguished Professor of Law at the University of Nebraska College of Law. He has written numerous books and articles on international law, comparative law, human rights, comparative religious ethics, and tax law, including *Rethinking Humanitarian Intervention: A Fresh Legal Approach Based on Fundamental Ethical Principles in International Law and World Religions*, published by Penn State Press in 2002; *Hope for a Global*

Ethic: Shared Principles in Religious Scriptures, published by Bahá'í Publishing in 2005; *In the Glory of the Father: The Bahá'í Faith and Christianity*, published by Bahá'í Publishing in 2008; *Customary International Law: A New Theory with Practical Applications*, published by Cambridge University Press in 2010; and *Reexamining Customary International Law* (editor), published by Cambridge University Press in 2017. He is Chair of the Committee on the Formation of Rules of Customary International Law of the American Branch of the International Law Association.

Kathryn L. Moore

Kathryn L. Moore is the Stites and Harbison and Ashland-Spears Distinguished Professor of Law at the University of Kentucky College of Law, where she teaches basic federal income tax, employee benefits, state and local tax, and land use planning. She has written extensively about employee benefits law and Social Security. She is a member of the American Law Institute, the American College of Employee Benefits Counsel, and the National Academy of Social Insurance.

Emanuel V. Towfigh

Emanuel V. Towfigh holds the Chair in Public Law, Empirical Legal Research and Law & Economics at EBS University Law School in Oestrich-Winkel, Germany, where he also serves as the Vice Dean for Research. He is also a Professor of Law and Economics at the Department of Management and Economics at EBS Business School, a Max Planck Fellow and Head of the Center for Diversity in Law at the Max Planck Institute for Comparative Public Law and International Law, and a Distinguished Scholar in Residence at Peking University's School of Transnational Law. Prof. Towfigh studied Law and Economics in Münster, Germany and Nanjing, China. In 2011–12 he was a Hauser Research Scholar at New York University School of Law; in 2012–13 he was Visiting Professor of Law at the University of Virginia School of Law; and in 2015–16 he was a Visiting Professor at Humboldt University's Faculty of Law in Berlin. His research includes works on the relationship of religious law and state law, democracy and political parties, and empirical legal studies. He is a co-editor in chief of the *German Law Journal*.

PART ONE

INTRODUCTION

1

Deficiencies in the Global Legal Order and the Reformative Potential of Bahá'í Principles

Brian D. Lepard

The global legal order today exists in a state of turmoil. It has proven incapable of effectively addressing the social problems ailing humanity and securing justice for everyone. This disruption afflicts both national legal systems and the international legal order as a whole.

According to the Bahá'í teachings, the legal order of the world can only be rescued if it is transformed to reflect divinely-revealed principles, particularly those teachings of global unity and oneness brought by the Revelation of Bahá'u'lláh (1817–1892), the Prophet and Founder of the Bahá'í Faith.

This book investigates how that transformation can be brought about in various domains of law by reviewing the key features and history of the current global legal order and the many existing deficiencies of that order, weighing current debates on how to address them, and determining the potential for implementing reforms based on Bahá'í principles.

The Key Features and History of the Current Global Legal Order

What key features of the present global legal order have made it vulnerable to such turbulence today – but also may help it attain a more fruitful future? First, the current order rests on the concept of state sovereignty. This means, essentially, that each state – meaning a country or nation that is at least loosely united politically – has the authority to adopt national laws that govern its people, but also participates in creating international law that governs the global relationship between the state and other states.

The United Nations Charter, adopted in 1945, lays down key legal principles governing relations between states today, while recognizing the concept of state sovereignty. For example, it proclaims that the organization 'is based on the principle of the sovereign equality of all its Members'.[1]

---

1   U.N. Charter, art. 2, para. 1.

However, even under the doctrine of state sovereignty, states are not free to act as they please, without constraint. The story of international law is a story about how, over centuries, and even millennia, peoples and nations came to recognize that the freedom of states (and before them, various tribes, principalities, kingdoms, and nations) must be limited in the interest of preventing war, regulating conflict, fostering beneficial trade, and elevating the dignity of the human beings living within their borders, among other goals.

Early in the history of humanity groups were only loosely organized, first into tribes or clans. These tribes often evolved various customs relating to their relations with other tribes – a nascent form of international law.[2] As human civilization evolved, so did larger, more complex, and more sophisticated social entities, often unified by force, such as kingdoms and principalities. In 221 B.C.E, Imperial China became one of the world's first unified dynastic states.

The world's religions and philosophies, including Judaism, Confucianism, Hinduism, Buddhism, Christianity, and Islam, developed, either in sacred texts and traditions, or elucidations of them by religious scholars, rules regarding relations among these kingdoms and organized peoples, including on the regulation of war. These rules even addressed all-too-common wars motivated by religious differences and sought to moderate them.[3]

Political scientists generally maintain that the modern-day state was first recognized in a treaty known as the 'Peace of Westphalia' in 1648, which ended the Thirty Years' War in Europe. This devastating war, motivated in part by rival claims of Catholic and Protestant princes, resulted in a treaty that acknowledged the right of each prince and his principality to be free of external interference from other princes, including in matters of religious belief, and thus gave birth to the contemporary notion of state sovereignty.[4] The same historical period in Europe witnessed the rise of great, centralized nations such as France and England, which amalgamated disparate fiefdoms and kingdoms into powerful unitary states.

Around this time, too, jurists began to formulate theories of an international law that bound these sovereign states. These included the illustrious Dutch jurist Hugo Grotius (1583–1645), who in 1625 published his great treatise 'On the Law of War and Peace'.[5] Grotius and other jurists maintained that sovereign states were bound not only by the treaties they entered into with one another – akin to contracts, made by a meeting of the sovereign wills of the states that were parties to them – but also by customary practices that had come to be recognized as legally binding in character, referred to today as 'customary international law'.[6] Yet Grotius also recognized that states were bound by 'natural law', a law supposedly

---

2   On Indigenous law in general, see Glenn, *Legal Traditions of the World*, pp. 60–97.
3   For a discussion of such religious teachings on peace, justice, the conduct of war, and international law, see Lepard, *Hope for a Global Ethic*, pp. 145–71. See also the essays collected in Janis and Evans, eds., *Religion and International Law*.
4   See, e.g. Lyons and Mastanduno, 'Introduction', pp. 5–10.
5   Grotius, *De Jure Belli ac Pacis Libri Tres*.
6   See, e.g. Lepard, *Customary International Law*, p. 6.

ascertainable by reason, and he often gave examples from scripture to support such alleged principles of natural law.[7]

However, during the 19th century natural law and religion came to be viewed with increasing skepticism, and states generally began adhering to the 'positivist' view grounded in state sovereignty. According to this view, they were only bound by obligations to which they had explicitly assented, such as treaties, or to which they had implicitly agreed, including through their conduct, such as customary international law.

In keeping with this perspective, today states generally acknowledge three foundational sources of international law: treaties, customary international law, and general principles of law. These are now codified in Article 38 of the Statute of the International Court of Justice ('ICJ'), the principal world court that can adjudicate disputes between sovereign states – but only with their consent.[8] Treaties are analogous to contracts and bind only those states that ratify them.[9] Customary international law, by contrast, arises organically from the behavior of most states in the international system (often referred to as 'consistent state practice'), coupled with a belief that particular behavior is legally required, permitted, or prohibited (referred to as 'opinio juris').[10] In general, customary international law binds all states in the world; a state can only exempt itself from a given customary law rule if it has persistently objected to the rule from the time the rule was first recognized.[11] 'General principles of law' include principles shared by the major legal systems of the world, such as, for example, a principle that no one can be a judge in his own lawsuit, and a principle that all states must carry out their legal obligations in good faith.[12]

This nascent system of international law today is very weak, implemented only sporadically and by institutions just beginning to gain legitimacy and influence in our globalizing society. To understand why, let us briefly review the attempts to codify and implement international law during the past century.

The League of Nations, founded in 1920 in the wake of the widespread devastation of World War I, was intended in part to provide not only a forum for states to discuss solutions to global problems, but a means of enforcing a principle of 'collective security' – a commitment of all members to come to the rescue of a member state victimized by the aggression of another state. The League of Nations Covenant, the treaty that gave birth to it, also established the world's first global court, the Permanent Court of International Justice ('PCIJ'), to adjudicate disputes between state members. However, the top political organ of the League, the League

---

7   See, e.g. Janis, 'Religion and the Literature of International Law', pp. 121–6. See also Lepard, *Rethinking Humanitarian Intervention*, p. 81.
8   See Statute of the International Court of Justice, art. 38, para. 1.
9   See, e.g. Vienna Convention on the Law of Treaties, art. 34 (providing that a 'treaty does not create either obligations or rights for a third State without its consent').
10   See generally Lepard, *Customary International Law*, p. 6.
11   See ibid. p. 7.
12   See ibid. pp. 28, 164–5. On good faith as a general principle of law, see also Mattei et al. *Schlesinger's Comparative Law*, pp. 113–17.

Council, was only given the power to make 'recommendations' in case of a dispute or act of war,[13] and the League's global security system spectacularly failed to prevent World War II. That second worldwide conflagration of the 20th century, even more destructive than the first, gave birth to a new international organization, the United Nations, which was intended to put an end to aggressive war between states once and for all.

The U.N. Charter, agreed upon at the San Francisco Conference of 1945, declares that among its purposes are 'to save succeeding generations from the scourge of war'; 'to establish conditions under which justice and respect for the obligations arising from treaties and other sources of international law can be maintained'; and 'to promote social progress and better standards of life in larger freedom'.[14] The Charter created institutions, such as the U.N. Security Council, with the power to help resolve international disputes that could lead to conflicts, and to 'maintain international peace and security' – including, in the case of the Council, through the use of mandatory economic sanctions and, as a last resort, collective military measures.[15]

The U.N. Charter also emphasizes human rights. It announces that one of its purposes is to 'reaffirm faith in fundamental human rights, in the dignity and worth of the human person, [and] in the equal rights of men and women'.[16] Accordingly, in 1948 the U.N. General Assembly adopted the Universal Declaration of Human Rights, which states in Article 1 that 'all human beings are born free and equal in dignity and rights. They are endowed with reason and conscience and should act towards one another in a spirit of brotherhood.'[17] It goes on to provide for the enjoyment by all human beings of many specific rights, including, among others, the right to freedom of religion or belief, the right not to be tortured, and the rights to adequate food, clothing, housing, shelter, and health care. Many ancillary human rights treaties and declarations have been adopted since, expanding on the identification and implementation of these rights.[18]

The United Nations also reconstituted the PCIJ as the ICJ, now the principal judicial organ of the U.N., which like its predecessor is empowered to rule on disputes that states voluntarily submit for its decision – including by agreement to do so in a treaty. It can also give advisory opinions to various international bodies that request them, including the U.N. General Assembly.[19] However, the ICJ has no means to enforce its decisions, except for the hypothetical ability of the Security Council to use its enforcement powers to do so, which it has never done.[20]

---

13   See League of Nations Covenant, arts. 15, 16, available at https://www.ungeneva.org/en/about/league-of-nations/covenant
14   U.N. Charter, preamble.
15   See ibid. arts. 24, 39–42.
16   ibid. preamble.
17   Universal Declaration of Human Rights, art. 1.
18   For an overview of international human rights law and these different rights, see, e.g. Alston, *International Human Rights*.
19   See Statute of the International Court of Justice, arts. 36, 65–8.
20   See U.N. Charter, art. 94, para. 2 (providing that 'If any party to a case fails to perform the obligations incumbent upon it under a judgment rendered by the Court, the other party may have recourse to the

Alongside the U.N., scores of other intergovernmental organizations came into existence during the 20th century to help coordinate actions of states in multiple arenas. The U.N. and these organizations, including U.N. specialized agencies, facilitated the negotiation and adoption of treaties, which today regulate countless areas of relations among states, from international trade, to the rights of workers, to the coordination of international airline flights, and to respect for all human rights.[21] Influential regional institutions were created in the aftermath of World War II, including the European Union, the Council of Europe, the Organization of American States, and the African Union, among others. These led a drive toward harmonization of national legal orders at the regional level and regional political cooperation.

This nascent international legal order functions within the context of national legal institutions at the state level. Modern states have adopted a panoply of different structures of government, and national law today comes in a wide variety of forms. The story of how national legal governance and legal traditions emerged over the centuries is as fascinating as the story of the rise of international law, although its details are beyond the scope of this book.[22]

The earliest human societies were founded on certain shared 'customary' values and principles, including respecting the lives of neighbors, and coming to their aid in case of need. For example, the African concept of *ubuntu* called for respect for every person as a person. According to one African proverb based on it, 'You do not fold your hands and just look on when your neighbour's house is on fire.'[23] Indigenous societies developed these and other shared values that were most often transmitted orally rather than written down as formal 'laws'. These early societies throughout the world developed a variety of governance structures, often relying on a tribal chieftain or king, but also a 'council of elders' that advised the leader and made decisions through a process of open-minded consultation.[24]

Certain societies, of course, cultivated sophisticated legal and governance structures. Empires were founded and their leaders conquered vast swaths of territory. Leaders often treated conquered peoples ruthlessly, and exercised the same unrestrained violence against dissenters within their own cultures. Yet there were some notable exceptions that drew on the long tradition of consultation in the earliest societies. For example, the Greek city-state of Athens experimented with direct democracy, in which each Athenian citizen had the right to express his view and vote on matters affecting the populace.[25] Islamic legal scholars articulated the

---

Security Council, which may, if it deems necessary, make recommendations or decide upon measures to be taken to give effect to the judgment'). On the Council's failure in practice to use its enforcement powers to enforce a judgment of the ICJ, see Security Council Report, *The UN Security Council Handbook*, p. 87.

21 For a list of multilateral treaties deposited with the United Nations Secretary-General, organized by subject area, see https://treaties.un.org/Pages/ParticipationStatus.aspx?clang=_en

22 For a textbook that reviews the different legal systems of the world and their origins, see Mattei et al. *Schlesinger's Comparative Law*. See also Glenn, *Legal Traditions of the World*.

23 Kioko, 'The Right of Intervention', pp. 819–20.

24 See Glenn, *Legal Traditions of the World*, pp. 65–6.

25 See Held, *Models of Democracy*, pp. 13–35.

concept that rulers must not exercise power in their own self-interest, but rather rule in the interest of the people, and as trustees for their welfare, based in part on such Qur'anic verses as 'David, behold, We have appointed thee a viceroy in the earth; therefore judge between men justly, and follow not caprice.'[26] The European doctrine of the 'divine right of kings', which effectively gave them absolute power, was gradually influenced by these ideas. Great philosophers such as John Locke, Jean-Jacques Rousseau, and John Stuart Mill began to formulate theories of government that based governmental legitimacy on the will of the people and the idea of 'natural rights'.[27]

These ideas gave intellectual backing for popular revolutions that swept across Europe in the 18th and 19th centuries, including the American Revolution sparked by the Declaration of Independence from Great Britain of 1776, and the French Revolution of 1789. Those democratic revolutions paved the way for the principle of democracy to become more widely accepted. When they occurred they tended to severely constrain the powers of monarchs, even if the monarchs retained their titles as cultural symbols, as they did in the United Kingdom. Subsequently, the idea of democracy permeated various societies throughout the world, including in the Americas. Despite these progressive developments within Western countries, at the same time European powers and the U.S. during the 19th century expanded their efforts to dominate the developing world and intensified the practice of colonialism, subjugating vast regions in Africa, South America, and Asia.[28]

During the 20th century new ideologies such as communism, totalitarianism, and fascism battled against democratic ideals, contributing to the two world wars that marred that momentous century. Ideological conflicts came to dominate politics then, with the rift between the pro-democracy West and the pro-communist East, and its attendant nuclear arms race, fomenting many civil conflicts during the post-World War II period. At the same time, in the mid-20th century, colonies of the European powers, which had suffered exploitation during the era of intensifying European colonial rule in the 19th century, demanded independence, invoking Western ideas of freedom and human rights. Accordingly, a massive wave of decolonization was unleashed starting in the 1960s, leading to the proliferation of independent states. In 2024, as a result, the United Nations had 193 members, representing almost every nation on Earth – and nearly quadruple its original membership of 51 countries at its formation in 1945.[29]

Generally speaking, the legal system of a particular country today can be described as a blend of one or more legal traditions that have arisen historically, some inspired by religion. These include the civil law, which was first developed in Western Europe, and tends to emphasize written legal codes;[30] the common law

---

26 Qur'an 38.25, in Arberry, *Koran Interpreted*. See generally the discussion of the concept of a trust theory of government in Islamic law in Lepard, *Rethinking Humanitarian Intervention*, pp. 61–2.
27 See, e.g. Locke, *Two Treatises of Government*.
28 See, e.g. Fieldhouse, *Colonialism, 1870–1945*.
29 See United Nations, 'Growth in United Nations Membership', available at https://www.un.org/en/about-us/growth-in-un-membership
30 See generally Glenn, *Legal Traditions of the World*, pp. 132–79.

that evolved in England and spread throughout the British Empire, which includes the development of law inductively through case law;[31] religious law (including Jewish law, Christian law, Islamic law, and Hindu law, among others), which elevates moral rules and values;[32] and Indigenous law, which focuses on consultative decision-making and respect for communal solidarity.[33]

States today also manifest a variety of forms of government, reflecting many of the ideas about government described above that have been debated over centuries. All religious legal traditions have recognized some role for input by the people based on a trust theory of government, but also have incorporated a significant role for religious leaders. Today, many states, such as the Islamic Republic of Iran, still give broad powers to clergy.[34] The old European notion of the 'divine right of kings' has been transmuted in many states today into *de facto* autocracy, even if democratic-appearing institutions such as parliaments or consultative assemblies are employed to provide 'window dressing' to legitimate autocratic power.

Of course, one of the great achievements of the last century has been the spread of democratic ideals and the establishment of democratic institutions in many countries, especially after the fall of the Berlin Wall in 1989. Yet the decades since then have told a less optimistic story. For example, Freedom House, a nongovernmental organization that rates countries on their protections of freedom and human rights, noted in a 2023 report that for the previous 17 years the number of countries where democratic freedoms had declined exceeded the number of countries where freedoms had improved.[35]

The world's nations interact in numerous ways today, including in the fields of trade, diplomacy, cross-border business transactions, tourism, and conflict resolution. All of these interactions can create problems with determining which state's national law should apply to certain legal issues, in addition to relevant rules of international law. For example, if a citizen of one country is injured in an automobile collision while on vacation in another country, which country's national law will govern the case? These types of problems have given rise to a legal field called 'conflict of laws',[36] underscoring the increasing complexities and challenges facing the global legal order.

Deficiencies in the Global Legal Order

Unfortunately, the world's contemporary legal order is beset by many failings. At the national level, a laudable movement exists to fortify the 'rule of law' and

---

31 See ibid. pp. 236–86.
32 On Jewish law, see ibid. pp. 98–131; on Christian law, see ibid. pp. 140–1; on Islamic law, see ibid. pp. 180–235; on Hindu law, see ibid. pp. 287–318.
33 On Indigenous law, see ibid. pp. 60–97.
34 See generally various provisions of the Constitution of the Islamic Republic of Iran, including Article 4, available at https://www.wipo.int/edocs/lexdocs/laws/en/ir/ir001en.pdf
35 See Freedom House, 'Freedom in the World 2023: Marking 50 Years in the Struggle for Democracy', available at https://freedomhouse.org/report/freedom-world/2023/marking-50-years
36 See, e.g. Brilmayer et al. *Conflict of Laws*.

help nations build trustworthy governmental and legal institutions to safeguard the human rights of everyone within their borders.[37] Nevertheless, some countries struggle even to construct the rudiments of such a legal system. Furthermore, corruption afflicts many governmental systems, including those of established Western democracies.[38]

Peoples around the world frequently rise up against governments and leaders they perceive as corrupt or intoxicated with the desire for power, and against agents of law enforcement who commit criminal acts of brutality. Mass demonstrations occur regularly in many parts of the world. The world witnessed such uprisings in 2020 in response to two watershed events of that year. The first was the ferocious spread of the COVID-19 virus, which stole hundreds of thousands of lives in a matter of months, leading to a virtual planetary lockdown, in turn creating popular unrest and frustration. The second was the killing of unarmed Black people in the U.S. and other countries, typified by the vicious murder of George Floyd in Minneapolis, Minnesota in May 2020, which triggered an unprecedented mass movement in the U.S. in favor of far-reaching law enforcement reforms. As another example, students around the world, including in the U.S., organized mass protests against the war in Gaza that began in 2023.

Even when they do not face organized reform movements, governments and legal systems are handicapped by the lack of a shared conception of justice, as well as skepticism on the part of ordinary citizens, who often doubt that officials of their government and legal system will be fair-minded and exhibit high moral standards of behavior.

Scandals based on such distrust have rocked many countries. In the West, numerous governments, including that of the United States, have been haunted by allegations of partisanship and prevarication that have left publics deeply divided and suspicious of the integrity of the justice system. More generally, this has led to a growing dissatisfaction of the public in many democracies with their governments.[39]

Meanwhile, in part as a result of popular dissatisfaction with the failure to ensure an adequate standard of living and basic social and economic goods for all, populations also elect or tolerate leaders who promote exclusivist ideologies that elevate one racial, ethnic, or religious group over others. Anti-Semitism is on the rise, as is anti-Muslim sentiment.

Governments, for their part, often adopt extremist policies, sometimes in response to these prejudices and the resultant public pressure. Those policies

---

37　For example, the American Bar Association, representing U.S. lawyers, has established a 'rule of law initiative' to help countries 'promote justice, economic opportunity, and human dignity through the rule of law'. See American Bar Association, *The ABA Rule of Law Initiative 2018 Annual Report*, p. 2.

38　In this connection, the United Nations has undertaken many efforts to raise awareness of the need to battle corruption, including as a means of ensuring the more effective enjoyment of universal human rights on a basis of equality. For a summary of the U.N.'s efforts in the area of corruption and good governance, see https://www.ohchr.org/en/topic/sustainable-development-through-human-rights

39　See, e.g. Wike, Silver, and Castillo, 'Dissatisfaction with Performance of Democracy Is Common in Many Nations'.

frequently target immigrants, refugees, and other vulnerable individuals who are perceived as somehow 'inferior' or a threat to the established social order. Many racial minorities, including Black people in the U.S., believe that they are singled out unfairly by law enforcement, resulting in unwarranted detentions and deaths at the hands of police. In the U.S. this has led to the rise of such widespread movements as 'Black Lives Matter'. The U.S. government incarcerates Black people and members of racial and ethnic minorities at rates that far exceed those of the White population.[40] Both the U.S. and Canada have discriminated systematically against their Indigenous populations in many ways. One example: Canada's policy of forced removal of Indigenous children from their homes and placement in state institutions, a racially motivated practice that resulted in a major financial settlement in January 2022 between Canada and its 'First Nations' peoples.[41]

Interreligious tensions have also affected the conduct even of governments that purport to be democratic in character and welcoming to members of diverse faiths. For example, in Europe, some governments have adopted policies that may disadvantage Muslims, including implementing laws against the wearing of the Islamic headscarf.[42] In addition, using the justification of responding to Islamic extremism and terrorism committed in the name of Islam, certain governments have instituted measures of surveillance and regulation of Muslim communities that these communities believe are discriminatory and oppressive.[43]

Not only do many national legal systems fail effectively to ensure equal rights for all – and especially members of racial, ethnic, or religious minorities – but scores of others institutionalize discrimination against members of particular groups and even engage in outright persecution of them. To cite just one example, the Islamic Republic of Iran has denied members of the Bahá'í Faith the rights enjoyed by other Iranian citizens. The Iranian Constitution itself lays the groundwork for this entrenched and legalized discrimination by intentionally omitting Bahá'ís from the list of recognized religious minorities in the country.[44] Decrees at the highest governmental level have revealed a coordinated and orchestrated campaign to destroy the welfare of the Bahá'í community.[45]

Governments have also struggled to moderate growing economic inequality among citizens – and the popular unrest this inequality has spurred. Governments

---

40 See Alexander, *New Jim Crow*, p. 7 ('In some states, black men have been admitted to prison on drug charges at rates twenty to fifty times greater than those of white men.').

41 See Paperny and Shakil, 'Canada Reaches Agreement to Compensate Indigenous Children Taken from Families'.

42 See, e.g. McGoldrick, *Human Rights and Religion*.

43 See, e.g. Bisserbe, 'France's Macron Wins National Assembly Backing for "Islamist Separatism" Bill'.

44 In this connection, Article 13 of the Constitution of the Islamic Republic of Iran provides: 'Zoroastrian, Jewish, and Christian Iranians are considered the only recognized religious minorities. They may exercise their religious ceremonies within the limits of the law. They are free to exercise matters of personal status and religious education and they follow their own rituals.' Constitution of the Islamic Republic of Iran, available at https://www.wipo.int/edocs/lexdocs/laws/en/ir/ir001en.pdf. Bahá'ís do not enjoy any of these rights of other religious minorities.

45 See generally Lepard, 'The Bahá'í Faith'; Iran Human Rights Documentation Center, *A Faith Denied: The Persecution of the Bahá'ís of Iran*; Bahá'í International Community, 'Situation of Bahá'ís in Iran'.

typically turn to various modes of taxation to redress some forms of this inequality and to generate much-needed revenue to address social needs, but often siphon off these tax funds for the enrichment of rulers and favored social classes, or to strengthen their military power. Furthermore, many nations are at a loss in determining which systems of taxation are fairest. In a supposed effort to stimulate the economy, some governments resort to giving businesses and wealthy individuals large regressive tax breaks, requiring poorer individuals to pay proportionately more of their income in taxes.[46]

Many countries have seen accusations of bias in their judicial systems. In the U.S., concerns about the politicization of the judiciary intensified after the U.S. Supreme Court issued decisions in the early 2020s taking away the previously recognized right of women to terminate their pregnancies,[47] banning racial preferences in college admissions,[48] and providing partial immunity of U.S. Presidents from criminal prosecutions.[49] Many observers, and members of the general public, viewed these and other recent Supreme Court decisions as politically influenced.[50]

These fractures in domestic governmental and legal orders mirror expanding forces of disunity within national societies. The forces of disunity include rising nationalism, factionalism, and isolationism; contempt for multinational institutions; religious extremism, racial hatred and the fortification of white supremacy movements; racist and other forms of hate speech; increasing oppression of women and girls, including through human trafficking; and widening economic inequality.

As a result of these forces, extreme nationalism and neo-populism have spread rapidly, including in many countries traditionally considered 'tolerant'.[51] Nationalist and neo-fascist political parties have acquired increased influence, if not outright power, bolstered by an internet supercharged with nationalist-based hate rhetoric.[52]

At the same time, within multiple countries social fractures have deepened as governments struggle to maintain some semblance of national unity. As a result,

---

46 See, e.g. Stiglitz, *Price of Inequality*, pp. 89–93 (addressing U.S. tax policy). See especially ibid. p. 91 (noting that the net effect of lowering the capital gains tax rate in the U.S. was 'that the superrich actually pay on average a lower tax rate than those less well-off; and the lower tax rate means that their riches increase faster').

47 See Dobbs v. Jackson Women's Health Organization, 597 U.S. 215 (2022), available at https://www.supremecourt.gov/opinions/21pdf/19-1392_6j37.pdf (overruling Roe v. Wade, 410 U. S. 113 (1973) and Planned Parenthood of Southeastern PA. v. Casey, 505 U. S. 833 (1992)).

48 See Students for Fair Admissions, Inc. v. President and Fellows of Harvard College, 600 U.S. 181 (2023), available at https://www.supremecourt.gov/opinions/22pdf/20–1199_l6gn.pdf (holding that the admissions programs of Harvard University and the University of North Carolina that took race of applicants into account in certain ways violated the Equal Protection Clause of the U.S. Constitution).

49 See Trump v. United States (slip opinion), 603 U.S. ___ (2024), available at https://www.supremecourt.gov/opinions/23pdf/23–939_e2pg.pdf (holding that under the Constitution a former President is entitled to absolute immunity from criminal prosecution for actions within his conclusive and preclusive constitutional authority, to at least presumptive immunity from prosecution for all his official acts, and to no immunity for unofficial acts).

50 See, e.g. Levendusky et al. 'Has the Supreme Court Become Just Another Political Branch?'.

51 See, e.g. Snyder, 'The Broken Bargain: How Nationalism Came Back'. As Snyder observes, 'Nationalism and nativism are roiling politics on every continent.' ibid. p. 54. See also the entire March/April 2019 issue of *Foreign Affairs*, devoted to 'The New Nationalism'.

52 On the rise of nationalism, neo-populism, and neo-fascism, see Albright, *Fascism*.

the U.S. and many other Western nations find themselves politically divided and increasingly polarized. Rising nationalism and populism have created ruptures in global ties and led to such movements as 'Brexit', the withdrawal of the U.K. from the European Union, which produced unprecedented legal and social unrest in that country, and has continued to be contentious. During the late 2010s and mid-2020s the U.S. government also announced its withdrawal from many international organizations and agreements, including the U.N. Human Rights Council, the World Health Organization (WHO), and the Paris Climate Accords, and pursued policies designed to undermine the International Criminal Court. Those actions have been echoed by a number of other countries and their expressions of increasing skepticism about, if not disdain for, these and other international institutions. This hyper-nationalism, when coupled with distrust of and disengagement from international institutions, has led to trade wars and an ongoing destabilization of the world's liberal economic order, based on the ideal of free trade established in the aftermath of World War II.

The COVID-19 crisis that erupted in early 2020 illustrates one particular manifestation of these increasing strains on institutions promoting multinational action, severely testing longstanding methods of global cooperation. Members of the European Union who were committed to open borders suddenly closed them, rushing to protect their own perceived national interests and the supposed safety of their populations. Other nations scrambled to adopt policies to contain the virus, often without coordination, leading to a confusing and even deadly patchwork of laws and regulations. Some countries reopened their borders to international visitors, while others kept them locked. The U.S. withdrew funding from the WHO, and the WHO struggled to convince member countries to adhere to its recommendations and their own preexisting commitments.[53] All of these problems underscored continued tensions between nationalism and globalism.

Religious extremism, too, has continued to metastasize. One example of this extremism, as we have already seen, is the brazen oppression of religious minorities in some Islamic states, such as Iran. Another is the violence perpetrated between Muslims and Hindus in many regions of India.[54] At the same time, religious prejudice has emboldened countries with 'Western' religious traditions to adopt discriminatory policies against Muslims and other non-Christian religious groups, and sometimes to suppress various strains of secular thought.

Similarly, unabashed racial hatred has exploded out into the open in ways that were inconceivable even a decade ago. As noted above, police brutality against Black people and minorities, illustrated by the indefensible killing of George Floyd, a Black man, by police in May 2020, became a global issue that led to mass protests and a new willingness of government leaders to consider previously

---

53 See Gebrekidan, 'The World Has a Plan to Fight Coronavirus' (referring to 'the W.H.O.'s underlying weakness as an organization that by international treaty is supposed to lead and coordinate the global fight against coronavirus – yet that has, in many ways, been marginalized').

54 See, e.g. Kumar, Mashal, and Raj, '"Perpetual Violence": India's Dangerous New Pattern of Communal Tensions'.

unthinkable actions, such as defunding police departments.[55] Deaths at the hands of police in the U.S. have actually increased since 2020.[56] On 6 January 2021, a mob invaded the U.S. Capitol building in Washington, D.C.; many of the participants carried or wore symbols of racial hate.[57] The frequency of racially motivated mass shootings in the U.S. and other countries has accelerated, as exemplified by the targeting of Black customers at a grocery store in Buffalo, New York in May 2022.[58]

At the same time, in a number of countries longstanding efforts to combat racism through ensuring equal opportunities for racial minorities have come under challenge. In the U.S., for example, the Supreme Court in 2023 declared that certain college admissions programs designed to redress past racial discrimination were unconstitutional under the Equal Protection Clause of the U.S. Constitution.[59]

Racist hate speech floods the internet, mass rallies by white supremacists in many countries have energized the advocates of hate, and sympathetic governments have pursued policies that disfavor racial minorities, both in law and in fact. Indeed, racist speech is but one form of odious hate speech that has now infiltrated everyday culture. The purveyors of hate speech, emboldened by technologies such as the internet and social media apps that permit it to be spread to a potentially global audience in real time, have accelerated their activities. They increasingly propagate falsehoods and outright lies on social media in an effort to denigrate the targets of their rage – too often transforming their hate and falsehoods into acts of violence against vulnerable populations, such as immigrants and racial, ethnic, or religious minorities. One example among many is the violence against migrants by far-right groups in the United Kingdom in the summer of 2024, triggered by disinformation spread on social media falsely asserting that the perpetrator of a deadly knife attack against children was a migrant.[60] Governments struggle to cobble together an effective social and legal response to such speech and the atrocities it can motivate. Debates are intensifying about the extent to which hate speech should or must be regulated by governments or by private media platforms like X (formerly Twitter), Facebook, and TikTok.

Women's rights have also been threatened in countries around the globe, and women have responded through protests and efforts to bring about legislation to protect their freedoms. As already noted, the U.S. Supreme Court's overturning in 2022 of a nearly 50-year-old precedent guaranteeing a right of women to terminate their pregnancies before the point of viability of the fetus[61] led to many legisla-

---

55   See, e.g. 'Order Above the Law'.
56   See 'Police Are Killing More Americans Than Ever. Where's the Outrage? The Scarcity of Protests is Striking'.
57   See, e.g. Zaru, 'The Symbols of Hate and Far-Right Extremism'.
58   See, e.g. Thompson, Balsamo, and Collins, Associated Press, '10 Dead in "Racially Motivated" Mass Shooting at Buffalo Supermarket'.
59   See Students for Fair Admissions, Inc. v. President and Fellows of Harvard College, 600 U.S. 181 (2023), available at https://www.supremecourt.gov/opinions/22pdf/20–1199_l6gn.pdf
60   See, e.g. Ibrahim and Robins, 'How Anti-Immigrant Riots Flared in the U.K.'.
61   See Dobbs v. Jackson Women's Health Organization, 597 U.S. 215 (2022), available at https://www.supremecourt.gov/opinions/21pdf/19-1392_6j37.pdf

tive efforts in various U.S. states to protect women's right to make reproductive decisions.[62] To take another example, young people in Iran arose in 2022 and 2023 to protest the government's oppressive policies against women, including requirements to wear a head covering, after the killing of a young woman, Mahsa (Jina) Amini, in September 2022 while she was detained by the 'morality police' in that country for failing to wear a hijab.[63]

As violence against women has intensified, especially during the COVID-19 pandemic, women and their male supporters have also demanded more decisive action to punish perpetrators and create a culture of respect for women.[64] Human trafficking has continued to entrap and ruin the lives of countless women and girls, also prompting many efforts to thwart this odious practice.[65]

Meanwhile, economic inequality within nations has grown, as shown by many studies, creating not only grave economic injustices for billions languishing in poverty, but imperiling the health of the global economy and roiling political and social stability in many countries.[66] The COVID-19 crisis of 2020–22 only exacerbated this economic gulf and fueled greater social tensions over economic and racial injustices. Frustration over this gulf has in turn again contributed to an increasingly toxic political climate.

The gross economic disparities that persist within countries and across the globe not only contravene fundamental notions of economic justice, but also pose threats to civil peace. For example, in recent years Venezuela has been ravaged by civil unrest as economic ills deprive common people of the very basic necessities. The 'Arab Spring' of 2010–12 was fueled in large part by economic discontent. Mass protests have erupted in many countries, including Western ones, over economic injustices, including the 'yellow vest' protests in France in 2018 and 2019. The U.S., too, witnessed large economic justice movements emerge, such as 'Occupy Wall Street'. And even the 'Tea Party' movement in the U.S. during the 2010s was driven in part by concerns that a large swath of Americans had been left behind by globalization and the transfer of jobs overseas in an increasingly interdependent worldwide economy.

Governments also wrestle with how to ensure that business enterprises behave in a socially responsible way, and do not themselves help to foment widening disparities in wealth and income within national populations. At a minimum, there is growing worldwide concern that they are obsessively focused on increasing their own profits and enriching shareholders rather than benefiting their workers.[67] In the U.S., the ratio of the compensation of the top corporate officers to that of the

---

62   See, e.g. Brinkman et al. 'Two Years After Dobbs'.
63   See, e.g. Far, 'Unveiling Resistance'.
64   See, e.g. Williams and Espinoza-Wasil, 'The Power of Women's Activism'.
65   For example, the U.N. has declared 30 July each year as 'World Day Against Trafficking in Persons'.
     See https://www.unodc.org/unodc/en/endht/index.html
66   See, e.g. Stiglitz, *Price of Inequality*.
67   See, e.g. ibid. p. 77.

lowest paid workers has exploded exponentially in the last 50 years, rising to 243 to 1 in 2010.[68]

Many corporations have been accused of being complicit with gross human rights violations, for example aiding and abetting local armed forces in the massacre of minority populations.[69] Human rights observers have charged corporations with employing global supply chains that support forced labor or even modern-day slavery.[70]

There are also growing concerns that many businesses foster a patriarchal culture that facilitates the sexual harassment of female employees, as evidenced by the so-called 'Me Too' movement. This movement arose in the U.S., but has now encircled the world, empowering female victims to speak out about harassment and assault in the workplace, and leading to the resignation or firing of many business executives.[71]

Given all of these dire challenges, the realm of international law is in tumult. Much progress has been made since the founding of the United Nations in 1945 in erecting the rudiments of a system of global law that seeks to safeguard the security of each state and the well-being and rights of people residing within it.[72] However, the current system has lamentably failed to achieve these goals, as wars – both international and civil – ravage many countries.[73] Russia's invasion of Ukraine in February 2022 and the ensuing loss of life, intentional attacks on civilians, threats of the use of nuclear weapons, and disruption to world economic markets and food supplies constitutes but one example of the havoc that conflicts continue to wreak on humanity. As another example, the terrible conflict in Gaza erupted after horrendous surprise attacks by Hamas against Israel in October 2023, led to the deaths of tens of thousands of Gazans and Israelis combined as of early 2025, and threatened to plunge the entire Middle East into war.[74]

The ICJ has had the opportunity to rule on some aspects of the legality under international law of both these conflicts. For example, in a case brought by Ukraine against Russia under the Genocide Convention following Russia's invasion of Ukraine, the ICJ in provisional measures adopted in March 2022 called upon Russia to suspend its military operations in Ukraine.[75] In 2023, South Africa

---

68 See ibid. p. 4.
69 See in this connection the many cases in the U.S. brought under the Alien Tort Statute, which permits non-U.S. citizens to bring claims for violations of customary international human rights law, including, among other violations, genocide and torture. See generally, e.g. FIDH, *Corporate Accountability for Human Rights Abuses*, pp. 196–239 (discussing ATS cases).
70 See, e.g. Core Coalition, *Modern Slavery*.
71 See, e.g. Temin, 'How the Reputation Risk Of #MeToo Is Forcing Businesses to Reevaluate Their Corporate Culture'.
72 In this connection, in its letter to the world's Bahá'ís of 18 January 2019, the Universal House of Justice comments that after the founding of the U.N. 'historic advances were made relating to human rights and international law'. See Universal House of Justice, Letter to the Bahá'ís of the World, 18 January 2019.
73 For a survey of contemporary wars and conflicts, including serious criminal violence, see Council on Foreign Relations, 'Global Conflict Tracker'.
74 See, e.g. Ebrahim and Dahman, '50,000 Killed in Gaza Since Start of Israel-Hamas War'.
75 See Allegations of Genocide under the Convention on the Prevention and Punishment of the Crime of

instituted proceedings against Israel under the Genocide Convention alleging that it had committed acts of genocide in Gaza. While not ruling on the substance of South Africa's allegations, the ICJ issued provisional measures in January 2024 that, among others, called upon Israel to 'take immediate and effective measures to enable the provision of urgently needed basic services and humanitarian assistance to address the adverse conditions of life faced by Palestinians in the Gaza Strip'.[76] However, neither decision had been fully implemented by the relevant parties as of early 2025 and the rulings had had mainly a symbolic effect.

Whether due directly to armed conflict or not, human beings around the planet still suffer grievous affronts to their dignity in violation of the standards in the Universal Declaration of Human Rights and various human rights treaties. Many are victims of the most horrible atrocities, such as genocide, war crimes, and crimes against humanity. Commendably, the U.N. has in the last two and a half decades recognized the concept of an international 'responsibility to protect' (abbreviated as 'R2P') victims of such mass atrocity crimes, especially when their home governments fail to do so.[77]

In the 2005 World Summit Outcome Document, the U.N. General Assembly confirmed that while states have the primary duty to safeguard the security of their residents, the international community as a whole, through the U.N., also has a responsibility to protect populations from genocide, war crimes, ethnic cleansing, and crimes against humanity.[78] Nevertheless, despite some positive steps, states have conspicuously failed to fulfil this commitment, allowing hundreds of thousands to perish.

As a result of the world's inability to effectively protect human populations, at the end of June 2024 there were over 122 million forcibly displaced persons who had to leave their home region, often due to wars or persecution.[79] Of these, 43.7 million were international refugees who had crossed international borders to flee persecution, and 72.1 million were internally displaced persons within their own countries. An additional eight million sought asylum from persecution in another country.[80] The global community, despite tentative efforts to protect the security of states and peoples, has fallen far short in responding to these threats.

As noted above, trafficking in persons is a growing menace to their security and is usually facilitated by violence or threats of violence. As a 2011 statement by the Bahá'í International Community emphasized, 'The epidemics of sex slavery

---

Genocide (Ukraine v. Russian Federation), Request for the Indication of Provisional Measures, Order of 16 March 2022, para. 81. Available at https://icj-cij.org/sites/default/files/case-related/182/182-20220316-ord-01-00-en.pdf

76 See Application of the Convention on the Prevention and Punishment of the Crime of Genocide in the Gaza Strip (South Africa v. Israel), Request for the Indication of Provisional Measures, Order of 26 January 2024. Available at https://www.icj-cij.org/sites/default/files/case-related/192/192-20240126-ord-01-00-en.pdf

77 On the development of the R2P concept, see Evans, *The Responsibility to Protect*.

78 See United Nations World Summit Outcome Document, paras. 138–9.

79 The UNHCR reported that there were 122.6 million forcibly displaced persons at the end of June 2024. See UNHCR, 'Figures at a Glance'.

80 See ibid.

and human trafficking persist worldwide, with devastating consequences for the victims and their families.'[81] Unfortunately, many national laws are inadequate to the task of protecting victims, who are themselves often charged as criminals, and of prosecuting traffickers. Accordingly, the U.N. Office on Drugs and Crime ('UNODC') has recommended that these laws be strengthened.[82]

Transnational disputes are too frequently not resolved through consultation and collaboration, but through contentious and protracted legal proceedings, the unilateral imposition of economic tariffs or retaliatory measures, threats of the use of force, and outright military engagement and war. Internecine disputes within countries often result in fighting that claims the lives of hundreds of thousands.[83]

Nations have also struggled to create a global economic system that treats states, businesses, and individuals fairly while promoting economic growth and well-being worldwide. At a global level, states often compete to attract investment from abroad, serving as tax havens to foreign investors, leading to a 'race to the bottom' among countries that results in lower tax revenues and impoverishes social welfare programs.[84] This competition can actually result in 'zero taxation' of business income, with the income being taxed in no country. At a minimum, states jealously protect their rights to devise their own tax laws for their own ends, leading to conflicting national tax laws that can create immense complexity in the rules governing transnational transactions and investments. These conflicting laws can cause double-taxation of individuals and businesses and impede economic development and the just allocation of tax burdens.

Many nations have taken important steps to address the coordination of differing national tax laws. However, these steps have been inadequate to achieve true harmonization of tax policies and require a thoughtful reexamination at the global level.

Current Debates on Addressing Deficiencies in the Global Legal Order

As the second quarter of the 21st century opens, political leaders as well as thinkers and scholars are wrestling with how to remedy these many weaknesses in the global legal order.

Some politicians have openly advocated for 'restoring' state sovereignty and emasculating global institutions such as the United Nations.[85] Others, by contrast, have insisted on the imperative of fortifying these institutions and the international legal order they help implement to deal with the current manifold threats to the security, peace, and human rights of a global society.

---

81   Bahá'í International Community, 'Women's Health and Human Rights'.
82   See UNODC, *Global Report on Trafficking in Persons 2024*, pp. 31–2.
83   See, e.g. Rustad, 'Conflict Trends', pp. 9–12.
84   See, e.g. Stiglitz, 'Opinion'.
85   For example, a bill introduced in the U.S. Congress in 2022, entitled the 'American Sovereignty Restoration Act of 2022', would require the U.S. to withdraw from the United Nations. See H.R.7806, 117th Congress (2021–2022), available at https://www.congress.gov/bill/117th-congress/house-bill/7806/text

To give one example of the latter initiatives, world leaders have attempted to address the increasingly catastrophic impacts of climate change through new legal commitments, building on the 1992 United Nations Framework Convention on Climate Change, which came into force in 1994. They have done so at a series of global conferences of states parties to the Convention, including the 2015 'COP21' conference in Paris that resulted in the so-called 'Paris Agreement' calling for the limitation of the increase in average global temperatures to 1.5 degrees centigrade above pre-industrial levels and the 2023 'COP28' conference held in Dubai, United Arab Emirates. The latter conference assessed the success of efforts to deal with climate change under the Paris Agreement and called on governments to accelerate the transition away from fossil fuels.[86]

Alongside political leaders, scholars have also debated how to reform the existing global legal order to be more attentive to the needs of an ailing humanity. Their debates have often mirrored or supported the efforts by politicians described above. For example, some have argued unabashedly for a return to the ideals of state sovereignty that have dominated international relations since the Peace of Westphalia, and at least a partial unwinding of the program of greater global legal ordering and unification that characterized much of the 20th century. These views are sometimes referred to as the 'new sovereigntism'.[87] Others have made less dramatic and more pragmatic arguments for maintaining, and hopefully making incremental improvements to, the current system of nation-based sovereign states.[88]

Yet other scholars and thinkers have made concrete proposals, in the opposite direction, for further strengthening the global legal order and the United Nations. Many of these discussions took place at the time of the commemoration of the 75th anniversary of the United Nations in 2020. For example, a coalition of civic organizations adopted a 'UN75 Peoples' Declaration and Plan of Global Action' that contained many proposals for reform of the U.N. and more broadly of the global legal order.[89] The United Nations itself has examined ways to make its functioning more efficient and effective.[90] At the state level, scholars have devoted increasing attention to how best to implement democratic principles and international human rights standards within nations.[91]

The Potential of Reforms Based on Bahá'í Principles and Bahá'í Laws

What can we do about the many weaknesses of the existing global legal order? How can we resolve the contemporary debates about remedying them? This book

---

86   See https://unfccc.int/cop28/5-key-takeaways
87   These arguments are discussed and critiqued in Benhabib, 'The New Sovereigntism and Transnational Law'.
88   See, e.g. Mayall, *Nationalism and International Society*, pp. 145–52.
89   Available at https://www.un.org/pga/74/wp-content/uploads/sites/99/2020/05/Final-Peoples-Declaration-and-Plan-of-Global-Action-1.pdf.
90   See 'United to Reform', available at https://reform.un.org/
91   See, e.g. Held, *Models of Democracy*; Dahl, *Democracy and Its Critics*; Alston, *International Human Rights*, pp. 878–91.

explores these questions in light of the principles and laws of the Bahá'í Faith. It investigates how the transformative principles taught by the founder of the Bahá'í Faith, Bahá'u'lláh, can guide jurists and world leaders in fixing a defective legal order at the national and global levels. It suggests particular reforms to the current legal order based on these principles, in order to bring about a more just world and help alleviate many of the social problems of injustice outlined above.

Over 150 years ago, Bahá'u'lláh announced that he was the latest, but not the last, of a succession of Messengers of God whose mission is to educate humanity and bring about an ever-advancing world civilization. These Messengers of God (also referred to as 'Manifestations' or 'Prophets' of God) include, among others, Abraham, Krishna, Buddha, Moses, Christ, Muhammad, the Báb (the Forerunner of Bahá'u'lláh) and Bahá'u'lláh Himself. Bahá'u'lláh taught that all of these Messengers of God renewed and refreshed eternal spiritual verities that are detached from time and place, including the teaching to love one another and to treat others with kindness and generosity. These timeless truths also include the principle that all societies must promote and uphold justice, including through a legal system.

We find these concepts embedded in the fundamental teachings of these Messengers as recorded in revered moral texts, such as the Bhagavad-Gītā of Hinduism, the Dhammapada of Buddhism, the Hebrew Scriptures of Judaism, the Qur'an of Islam, the New Testament of Christianity, and the Bahá'í sacred writings. We have already seen that at one time these sources were turned to by great jurists of international law, but were then ignored as the law moved towards secularism and positivism.

Thus, for example, all the revered moral texts emphasize the essential unity of human beings, whether as members of a single human family or as elements of a more metaphysical single spiritual body. They also therefore call upon us to show the utmost love and kindness to one another.

To illustrate, the Bhagavad-Gītā, which is the preeminent book of Hinduism, affirms that the 'whole world' is 'united', even though it also recognizes the legitimacy of the caste system.[92] According to the Hebrew Scriptures: 'Have we not all one Father? Did not one God create us?' (Malachi 2.10)[93] Buddhist scriptures say that we should be so intimate with one another as human beings that we should take care of one another with the same affection that a mother shows toward her child.[94] Confucius teaches that everybody 'within the Four Seas' – that is, all human beings – should act toward one another as brothers.[95] Jesus urged us to love our neighbors as ourselves and, through the story of the Good Samaritan, taught that we should come to the aid of anyone who needs it.[96] According to the Qur'an, all human beings were created from a single soul and thus are members of a single

---

92   See Bhagavad Gītā 11.7, in Edgerton, *Bhagavad Gītā*.
93   From *Tanakh*.
94   See Conze, *Buddhist Scriptures*, p. 186.
95   See Analects 12.5, in Brooks and Brooks, *Original Analects*.
96   The story of the Good Samaritan is recounted in Luke 10.25–37.

human family and community; in the same spirit, a hadith says that the 'whole universe is the family of Allah'.[97] The Bahá'í writings declare: 'It is not for him to pride himself who loveth his own country, but rather for him who loveth the whole world. The earth is but one country, and mankind its citizens.'[98]

At the societal level, all the scriptures insist upon the primacy of justice in social relations among members of the single human family. They reject aggression and the rule of governors in their own self-interest. We find the theme of justice resonating in all these texts as a central principle for the ordering of society. For example, the Hebrew Scriptures admonish, 'Justice, justice shall you pursue.' (Deuteronomy 16.20). A verse in Psalms reads, 'O God, endow the king with Your judgments, the king's son with Your righteousness; that he may judge Your people rightly, Your lowly ones, justly.' (Psalms 72.1–14). The Qur'an states, regarding the obligations of both rulers and everyone to pursue justice, that: 'God commands you to deliver trusts back to their owners; and when you judge between the people, that you judge with justice' (4.61). Bahá'u'lláh urged the rulers of the planet to fulfill their God-given duty to protect the rights of all and to govern justly, declaring:

> For is it not your clear duty to restrain the tyranny of the oppressor, and to deal equitably with your subjects, that your high sense of justice may be fully demonstrated to all mankind? God hath committed into your hands the reins of the government of the people, that ye may rule with justice over them, safeguard the rights of the down-trodden, and punish the wrong-doers.[99]

Many of the scriptures, too, view law as an essential instrument for implementing justice. The revelations of each of the Messengers contain not only spiritual teachings and moral admonitions, but norms that have a more 'legal' character, some of which apparently are intended for all of society, and others of which apply only to believers who have accepted a particular revelation. For example, the Hebrew Scriptures lay down the 'Noachide laws' that apply to all the descendants of Noah – that is, every human being – while also prescribing special duties for Jews.[100] In like manner, Bahá'u'lláh has brought some laws – such as the law of justice – intended for society as a whole, and others, such as laws concerning abstention from alcohol, binding only on Bahá'ís.[101] Other laws only binding on Bahá'ís include those concerning fasting, obligatory prayer, Bahá'í marriage and divorce, and the payment of a portion of one's accumulated wealth for the common benefit, known as 'the Right of God' or 'Ḥuqúqu'lláh'.

Both categories of laws brought by the Prophets touch on such modern-day

---

97 See Qur'an 10.20, in Arberry, *Koran Interpreted*; hadith in Weeramantry, *Islamic Jurisprudence*, p. 133.
98 Bahá'u'lláh, *Tablets of Bahá'u'lláh*, p. 167.
99 Bahá'u'lláh, *Gleanings*, p. 247.
100 On the Noachide laws, see, e.g. Genesis 8:20 – 9:19.
101 On the application of the prohibition of the partaking of alcohol to Bahá'ís, see generally Hornby, *Lights of Guidance*, no. 1177.

legal subjects as the definition of crimes, the laying down of punishments for those crimes, and the implementation of procedures to ensure that criminal defendants are judged fairly and without prejudice. For example, the Hebrew Scriptures, while prescribing punishments for many crimes, such as capital punishment for murder, also provide for various protections of the rights of the accused. Thus, they require that there be more than one witness to the crime of murder as a precondition to imposing the death penalty, in order to ensure the guilt of the accused and reduce the likelihood of a miscarriage of justice.[102] The Kitáb-i-Aqdas, the Book of Laws brought by Bahá'u'lláh, empowers a democratically elected global institution, the Universal House of Justice, ultimately to decide on appropriate punishments for particular crimes when and if the Bahá'í community assumes the right to administer a system of criminal justice.[103]

Some sacred texts touch as well on the nature of legal relationships between various units of society, whether they be principalities, city-states, or what today we would consider nations or countries.[104] For example, based on teachings of the Qur'an, including those relating to treaties and the need for cooperation between Muslim nations and non-Muslim ones, classic Islamic law developed an elaborate 'law of nations'.[105]

So what unique contribution do Bahá'í principles make to the resolution of contemporary social problems and the achievement of global justice through law?

First, the Bahá'í Faith puts front and center the principle of the unity of the entire human family. While this principle has been expressed previously in various religions, the Bahá'í writings announce it forthrightly and emphatically as the necessary organizing principle for transforming the global legal order.

Second, the writings of the Bahá'í Faith have renewed, but also expanded upon, other fundamental spiritual verities of all religions. For example, 'Abdu'l-Bahá, the eldest son of Bahá'u'lláh and the authorized interpreter of His teachings, reaffirms the virtue of love, and expressly makes it an overarching global principle, counseling that:

> The fundamental truth of the Manifestations is peace. This underlies all religion, all justice. The divine purpose is that men should live in unity, concord and agreement and should love one another.[106]

In pursuit of this goal of human oneness, Bahá'u'lláh calls upon all rulers to govern justly – a common teaching of the world's faiths.

Third, in addition to revitalizing these ageless principles – principles that Bahá'ís

---

102 See Numbers 35.30, and Deuteronomy 17.6, 19.15.
103 See, e.g. Bahá'u'lláh, *Kitáb-i-Aqdas*, n. 87 (indicating that with regard to penalties for murder, and in particular the choice Bahá'u'lláh permits between capital punishment and life imprisonment, 'it remains for the Universal House of Justice to legislate on the matter in the future').
104 See, e.g. Lepard, *Hope for a Global Ethic*, pp. 149–53 (reviewing religious teachings on respect for treaties and the obligation to promote international law and cooperation).
105 See, e.g. Khadduri, *Islamic Law of Nations*.
106 'Abdu'l-Bahá, *Promulgation of Universal Peace*, p. 32.

believe emanate from the Divine will – Bahá'u'lláh has brought new social principles and laws uniquely adapted to the needs of a globalized human society. Indeed,
Bahá'u'lláh teaches that along with providing a refreshing of spiritual verities,
each revelation of God annunciates social laws that vary with the requirements of
their particular epoch and place. Differences in these social laws account for the
perceived disparities between the teachings of various religions, and lamentably,
have resulted in believers themselves creating divisions and barriers between
themselves and adherents of other faiths. Avowed believers have promoted a self-
oriented vision that at times has resulted in horrific violence perpetrated in the
name of perpetuating and expanding a particular religious community or defending
it against ostensible enemies. In this connection, 'Abdu'l-Bahá said:

> The essential purpose of the religion of God is to establish unity among
> mankind. The divine Manifestations were Founders of the means of fellowship
> and love. They did not come to create discord, strife and hatred in the world.
> The religion of God is the cause of love, but if it is made to be the source of
> enmity and bloodshed, surely its absence is preferable to its existence; for then
> it becomes satanic, detrimental and an obstacle to the human world.[107]

'Abdu'l-Bahá explains that one reason for the strife between the followers of
different religions, which is against their own teachings, is the existence of differences in social laws. He wrote:

> Briefly, the foundation of the divine religions is one eternal foundation, but the
> laws for temporary conditions and exigencies are subject to change. Therefore,
> by adherence to these temporary laws, blindly following and imitating ancestral
> forms, difference and divergence have arisen among followers of the various
> religions, resulting in disunion, strife and hatred.[108]

The Bahá'í writings give a number of examples of these changing social laws. For
example, at the time of Moses, the law of '*lex talionis*' – 'an eye for an eye and a
tooth for a tooth' – represented a great advance over prior social practices, for it
imposed a proportionality limitation on punishments.[109] However, Jesus abolished
this law.[110] By the time of Jesus's ministry, humanity was ready for a law that went
beyond mere reciprocity.

'Abdu'l-Bahá again elaborates on this concept that each religion renews fundamental laws and principles of past revelations, while also bringing new social laws
to meet the requirements of an evolving society:

---

107 ibid. p. 202.
108 ibid. p. 339.
109 See, e.g. Lepard, *Hope for a Global Ethic*, p. 84.
110 See ibid. p. 45.

Each one of the divine religions has established two kinds of ordinances: the essential and the accidental. The essential ordinances rest upon the firm, unchanging, eternal foundations of the Word itself. They concern spiritualities, seek to stabilize morals, awaken intuitive susceptibilities, reveal the knowledge of God and inculcate the love of all mankind. The accidental laws concern the administration of outer human actions and relations, establishing rules and regulations requisite for the world of bodies and their control. These are ever subject to change and supersedure according to exigencies of time, place and condition. For example, during the time of Moses, ten commandments concerning the punishment of murder were revealed in His Book. Divorce was sanctioned and polygamy allowable to a certain extent. If a man committed theft, his hand was cut off. This was drastic law and severe punishment applicable to the time of Moses. But when the time of Christ came, minds had developed, realizations were keener and spiritual perceptions had advanced so that certain laws concerning murder, plurality of wives and divorce were abrogated. But the essential ordinances of the Mosaic dispensation remained unchanged. These were the fundamental realities of the knowledge of God and the holy Manifestations, the purification of morals, the awakening of spiritual susceptibilities – eternal principles in which there is no change or transformation.[111]

In accordance with the concept of evolving social laws, Bahá'u'lláh brought new laws for society in this age, some of which apply to all humanity, and some of which apply only to Bahá'ís. Those far-reaching Bahá'í laws and principles intended for all humanity include:

- the elimination of all forms of prejudice, including racial prejudice and religious prejudice;
- the recognition and implementation of universal human rights for all;
- the promotion of fellowship among members of all religions;
- the provision of universal education for every human being, rich or poor;
- the right of each individual to investigate truth for herself or himself, free of compulsion to accept a particular religion or belief;
- the full social and spiritual equality of women with men;
- the need for a global system of collective security and a global commonwealth of nations to address problems with worldwide ramifications;
- the institution of democratic procedures in global governance;
- the choice by world authorities of a common universal language, either new or existing, to allow free and effective communication among people of all nations;
- the creation of a global economic system that permits free trade while assuring that everyone enjoys a minimal, dignified standard of living;

---

111 'Abdu'l-Bahá, *Promulgation of Universal Peace*, p. 338.

- the implementation of a just, equitable tax system;
- the unity of science and religion; and
- the principle of open-minded consultation as a potent method of reaching solutions to vexing problems, whether familial, local, national, or international.[112]

This list includes just a few of the many social laws and principles brought by Bahá'u'lláh, and elaborated upon by 'Abdu'l-Bahá and Shoghi Effendi, the Guardian of the Bahá'í Faith. For members of the Bahá'í Faith, any reform of the global legal order must be anchored in these sorely-needed laws and principles to adequately address the urgent challenges we collectively face.

How can we understand the currently vexed state of the global legal order in light of these enlightened Bahá'í teachings? First of all, the Bahá'í writings make clear that we live in an age in which society is undergoing changes akin to those experienced by an adolescent; we see evidences of growing maturity, but also the turmoil created by clinging to more immature patterns of behavior developed in childhood, including an ingrained selfishness. At the collective level, our growing human maturity is evidenced by the development of new mechanisms, including legal ones, to promote and foster cooperation and unity and bring about global peace. Yet humanity's collective immaturity remains in evidence, characterized by the tenacious grip of ideologies based on competition, hate, and conflict in the minds of many individuals and in the laws, practices, and policies of governments.

Shoghi Effendi emphasized the turbulence in the contemporary world associated with these simultaneous integrative and disintegrative forces, stating:

> Humanity is now experiencing the commotions invariably associated with the most turbulent stage of its evolution, the stage of adolescence, when the impetuosity of youth and its vehemence reach their climax, and must gradually be superseded by the calmness, the wisdom, and the maturity that characterize the stage of manhood.[113]

Unfortunately, as the Universal House of Justice, the global governing body of the Bahá'í Faith, pointed out in 2020, 'furious storms [are] lashing humanity'.[114] The turmoil of humanity's youth is indeed reaching a climax, with potentially dire consequences. Bahá'u'lláh Himself warned:

> Witness how the world is being afflicted with a fresh calamity every day. Its tribulation is continually deepening . . . neither hath the world been tranquillized, nor have the hearts of its peoples been at rest. At one time it hath

---

112 For an explanation of many of these principles and how they will help build the Kingdom of God on earth, see Lepard, *In the Glory of the Father*, pp. 155–81.
113 Shoghi Effendi, *World Order*, p. 202.
114 Universal House of Justice, Message to the Bahá'ís of the World, 25 November 2020.

been agitated by contentions and disputes, at another it hath been convulsed by wars, and fallen a victim to inveterate diseases. Its sickness is approaching the stage of utter hopelessness, inasmuch as the true Physician is debarred from administering the remedy, whilst unskilled practitioners are regarded with favor, and are accorded full freedom to act.[115]

Indeed, humanity now faces a stark choice as to which of those adolescent forces – integrative or disintegrative – will prevail. The Universal House of Justice affirmed in *The Promise of World Peace*, written to the world's leaders in 1985:

Whether peace is to be reached only after unimaginable horrors precipitated by humanity's stubborn clinging to old patterns of behaviour, or is to be embraced now by an act of consultative will, is the choice before all who inhabit the earth.[116]

More recently, in a letter on the achievement of world peace of 18 January 2019, the Universal House of Justice soberly recounted the rise of destructive forces during the previous 20 years, after a period of greater optimism about international cooperation. It warned again that these forces may seem to briefly gain the upper hand, leading to extreme social and political turmoil, but also reaffirmed Bahá'u'lláh's promise that in the final analysis the constructive forces of global unity will prevail:

Thus do the forces of disintegration regroup and gain ground. So be it. The unification of humanity is unstoppable by any human force; the promises made by the prophets of old and by the Author of the Cause of God Himself testify to this truth. Yet the course humanity takes to achieve its destiny may very well be tortuous. The tumult raised by the contending peoples of the earth threatens to drown out the voices of those noble-minded souls in every society who call for an end to conflict and struggle. As long as that call goes unheeded, there is no reason to doubt that the world's current state of disorder and confusion will worsen – possibly with catastrophic consequences – until a chastened humanity sees fit to take another significant step, perhaps this time decisive, towards enduring peace.[117]

When chastened world leaders do take that next step, Bahá'ís understand that it will be towards creation of a primarily political peace, one not firmly grounded in spiritual precepts. The Bahá'í writings refer to this tentative, fragile peace as 'the Lesser Peace'. They contrast it with a later, future time, in which humanity will have recognized its organic wholeness at a spiritual level, and become willing to create institutions necessary to reflect in its material life this unified spiritual

---

115 Bahá'u'lláh, *Gleanings*, pp. 39–40.
116 Universal House of Justice, *Promise of World Peace*, p. 1.
117 Universal House of Justice, Letter to the Bahá'ís of the World, 18 January 2019.

reality. The Bahá'í writings refer to this long-awaited period as the 'Most Great Peace'. The Most Great Peace is also associated with more widespread recognition of Bahá'u'lláh's Revelation, and the exercise of peace-making functions by the institutions of the Bahá'í Administrative Order. Bahá'u'lláh says to the leaders of the world: 'Now that ye have refused the Most Great Peace, hold ye fast unto this, the Lesser Peace, that haply ye may in some degree better your own condition and that of your dependents.'[118] Shoghi Effendi explains these two concepts in the following way, as described by the Universal House of Justice:

> We are told by Shoghi Effendi that two great processes are at work in the world: the great Plan of God, tumultuous in its progress, working through mankind as a whole, tearing down barriers to world unity and forging humankind into a unified body in the fires of suffering and experience. This process will produce in God's due time, the Lesser Peace, the political unification of the world. Mankind at that time can be likened to a body that is unified but without life. The second process, the task of breathing life into this unified body – of creating true unity and spirituality culminating in the Most Great Peace – is that of the Bahá'ís, who are laboring consciously, with detailed instructions and continuing divine guidance, to erect the fabric of the Kingdom of God on earth, into which they call their fellowmen, thus conferring upon them eternal life.[119]

We are now experiencing those 'fires of suffering and experience' that are 'forging humankind into a unified body', which will, as Shoghi Effendi promises, lead to 'the political unification of the world' as part of the Lesser Peace. The Bahá'í writings specifically refer to the importance of giving legal form to that unification, and creating institutions of global governance that help humankind combat the injustices that threaten global stability.

Clearly, consistently, and boldly, the Bahá'í teachings call for the establishment of a global federation of nations. In this connection, Shoghi Effendi writes:

> The unity of the human race, as envisaged by Bahá'u'lláh, implies the establishment of a world commonwealth in which all nations, races, creeds and classes are closely and permanently united, and in which the autonomy of its state members and the personal freedom and initiative of the individuals that compose them are definitely and completely safeguarded.[120]

The organs of that federation include an international court able to take binding decisions without the specific consent of states, a global legislature elected through democratic procedures, and a world executive.[121]

---

118 Bahá'u'lláh, *Gleanings*, p. 254.
119 Universal House of Justice, *Wellspring of Guidance*, pp. 133–4.
120 Shoghi Effendi, *World Order*, p. 203.
121 See ibid.

Bahá'u'lláh clarified that a key element of this new legal order must be a system of collective security designed to ensure that all nations commit to protect the security of each against attacks by another, thus ensuring a minimal degree of global peace between nations. Bahá'u'lláh wrote:

> The time must come when the imperative necessity for the holding of a vast, an all-embracing assemblage of men will be universally realized. The rulers and kings of the earth must needs attend it, and, participating in its deliberations, must consider such ways and means as will lay the foundations of the world's Great Peace amongst men. Such a peace demandeth that the Great Powers should resolve, for the sake of the tranquillity of the peoples of the earth, to be fully reconciled among themselves. Should any king take up arms against another, all should unitedly arise and prevent him. If this be done, the nations of the world will no longer require any armaments, except for the purpose of preserving the security of their realms and of maintaining internal order within their territories. This will ensure the peace and composure of every people, government and nation.[122]

Because a global commonwealth including this system of collective security will be associated with the Lesser Peace, this commonwealth will still be political in character rather than having a spiritual foundation. The Bahá'í teachings say that a future stage of human evolution will occur when 'true unity and spirituality' are established as part of the Most Great Peace.

The Bahá'í writings ask Bahá'ís to labor intentionally to build the Most Great Peace, understanding that the Lesser Peace must precede it. Nevertheless, the Universal House of Justice in many communications has made clear that Bahá'ís can contribute to the process of global unification through three specific lines of action: community building; engagement in social action; and participating in the discourses of society. It has stated:

> The expansion and consolidation of the Bahá'í community itself can be regarded as one area of action, the approach, methods and instruments of which are now well understood. Social action can be considered another . . .
>
> Efforts to participate in the discourses of society constitute a third area of action in which the friends are engaged. Such participation can occur at all levels of society, from the local to the international, through various types of interactions – from informal discussions on Internet forums and attendance at seminars, to the dissemination of statements and contact with government officials. What is important is for Bahá'ís to be present in the many social spaces in which thinking and policies evolve on any one of a number of issues – on governance, the environment, climate change, the equality of men and women, human rights, to mention a few – so that they can, as occasions permit, offer

---

122 Bahá'u'lláh, *Tablets of Bahá'u'lláh*, p. 165.

generously, unconditionally and with utmost humility the teachings of the Faith and their experience in applying them as a contribution to the betterment of society.[123]

Accordingly, the essays collected in this book offer a humble contribution to discourses on the global legal order, including how to reform it to achieve justice and address many of the challenges identified by the Universal House of Justice. The authors hope that these essays will foster social action for the well-being of humanity. The chapters in these pages seek both to make a helpful contribution to current discourses that will lead in time to the Lesser Peace, as well as offer reflections on the longer-term goal of establishing the Most Great Peace, when a new infusion of spiritual life will be breathed into the body of humankind. Furthermore, the purpose of this volume is not to persuade others of the truth of the Bahá'í Faith, but to offer a contribution to current discourses on law in a spirit of mutual learning.

To this end, Part Two, the heart of the book, reflects on the implications of the Bahá'í teachings for some aspects of the national and international legal orders and sketches visions for their reform. It explores how the application of Bahá'í principles can help solve vexing international legal problems relating to relations among states and the protection of the well-being of the entire global community of individuals.

Part Two begins with Kiser Barnes' chapter on 'Rendering Service to the Oneness of Humanity and the Quest for Justice in the Global Legal Order'. Mr Barnes investigates the intimate relationship between the quest for justice in the national and international law orders, on the one hand, and the effort to uphold the oneness of humanity, the pivotal teaching of Bahá'u'lláh, and to exemplify various personal virtues, on the other. The chapter shows that the Bahá'í writings enable believers to answer questions that seem important for a deeper appreciation of humanity's troubling spiritual condition: What kind of people are needed to build a just civilization? What virtues and qualities are called for? What is the purpose of justice? What is the prevailing role of religion in fostering individual and social transformation? In particular, the chapter focuses on 'spiritual prerequisites' required for success in all Bahá'í endeavors – moral rectitude, nobility, chastity, and freedom from all forms of prejudices – set down by the Guardian of the Bahá'í Faith, Shoghi Effendi, in his book *The Advent of Divine Justice*. The chapter explores his assertions that rectitude of conduct is a 'sublime standard', of which 'justice is so essential and potent an element', that Bahá'ís should serve humanity with 'an abiding sense of undeviating justice', and that 'the purpose of justice is the appearance of unity among men'. The chapter considers the implications for the global legal order of the spirit of learning and action that the Guardian advanced in *The Advent of Divine Justice* by immersing Western Bahá'ís in scriptures regarding justice, service, administrative requirements, and practical methods needed to

---

123 From a letter written on behalf of the Universal House of Justice to the National Spiritual Assembly of the Bahá'ís of Australia, 4 January 2009.

achieve success in their undertakings. It also investigates how the Universal House of Justice's direction that all believers reflect on the implications of the Guardian's observations should motivate them to think about the global legal order and how it can be reformed to address the social problems of injustice today.

The next chapter, by Prof. Emanuel V. Towfigh, which is entitled 'Religious Plurality in Society: Some Preliminary Thoughts Pertaining to Legal Policy from One Bahá'í's Perspective', explores the implications for law of religious plurality. Prof. Towfigh observes, as noted above, that one of the most insistent and smoldering conflicts in Western societies is associated with the increasing degree of religious diversity. He points out that latent antagonisms flare up with grim regularity, serving as a painful reminder of this unresolved conflict and preventing our societies from attaining real peace and stability. He posits how worldly law and religious ordinances often conflict – which means that our ability to secure social stability in the long term will very much depend on implementing a satisfactory solution to this problem. His chapter seeks to find a way of dealing with religious plurality that allows and promotes a peaceful social order. It explores whether the teachings of the Bahá'í Faith, with their recognition of the secular nature and decision-making authority of the state, on the one hand, and the principle of unity, on the other hand, can help to balance the different interests and beliefs at stake. In this way it seeks to find a Bahá'í perspective on reconciling, in part through law, the disharmony now afflicting relations between many religious communities.

In the following chapter, entitled 'Exploring the Unique Character of Ḥuqúqu'lláh: Insights from a Comparison with U.S. Tax Laws', Kathryn L. Moore, a distinguished professor of law, explores the implications of the law of Ḥuqúqu'lláh, which Bahá'u'lláh lays down in His Book of Laws, the Kitáb-i-Aqdas. She attempts to understand it as a unique and significant socio-economic and spiritual law, underscoring that Ḥuqúqu'lláh is a spiritual law that applies to the material resources Bahá'ís possess. She notes that, at least superficially, Ḥuqúqu'lláh resembles a well-known material law, the U.S. federal income tax code. At the same time, she observes that because Ḥuqúqu'lláh is a spiritual law, it profoundly differs from the U.S. federal income tax. Her chapter compares and contrasts basic aspects of Ḥuqúqu'lláh and the U.S. federal income tax. In discussing Ḥuqúqu'lláh's spiritual purpose, the chapter explains how and why the law has the potential to transform society as well as rectify many economic injustices.

In Aaron Emmel's chapter on 'Equality and Security' he posits that a policy of ensuring equality before the law, anchored in a recognition of the oneness of humanity, is essential for societies to achieve peace and stability. He observes that, unfortunately, many leaders today emphasize artificial divisions between people instead of equality, using these feigned divisions to foment social discord and maintain their power. He points out that these cynical leaders argue, wrongly, that ensuring security requires violation of equal protection of the law. Drawing on Bahá'u'lláh's teachings on oneness, equality, and global and national security, he maintains that equality before the law promotes our actual security, properly under-stood. He gives several examples of this intimate relationship between equality and security, and, in light of Bahá'í principles, offers a number of solutions to the problems of inequality, social division, and social instability.

The next chapter, written by the editor, is entitled 'Implementing International Law on Combating Systemic Racism in the United States: Legal, Psychological, and Spiritual Insights from the Bahá'í Teachings'. The chapter first emphasizes the problem of pervasive racism, focusing on its permeation of the legal system and culture in the U.S., but also observing its deep roots in other countries. It reviews key international legal norms adopted under the auspices of the United Nations to combat racism and racial discrimination and highlights some of the accomplishments of the global community in implementing these norms, but also examines major shortcom-ings in implementation, particularly in the United States. The chapter asserts that full implementation of those norms will require far-reaching changes in national legal orders and in the behavior of individuals at all levels of society, grounded in a practical, moral, and spiritual recognition of the unity of all people. It maintains that only such a multi-faceted approach can extirpate the tenacious cancer of racism. It shows how Bahá'í principles suggest particular legal reforms as well as psycho-logical transformations, and makes specific recommendations for changing laws, legal institutions, and the personal outlook and behavior of individuals to achieve the global community's goal of eliminating racial discrimination.

The final chapter of Part Two, entitled 'Toward a New World Tax Order: A Bahá'í Vision for International Tax Law and Policy', also written by the editor, points out that current features of the international tax system have often resulted in huge inefficiencies, loss of revenue, and either zero taxation or double taxation of taxpayers. It reviews some recent, significant reform efforts that governments and international organizations have undertaken as well as their weaknesses. It argues that some basic principles of the Bahá'í Faith – including the elimina-tion of extremes of wealth and poverty, prioritizing common global interests, and instituting a fair system of taxation – highlight the importance of greatly increased cooperation between governments in reforming the international tax system. It suggests some possible directions for reform in light of Bahá'í principles to create a fairer global tax and economic order.

The final chapter of the book, which comprises Part Three and is written by the editor, evaluates the larger prospects for reforming the global legal order at both the national and international levels so that it reflects Bahá'í ideals of justice. Based on the insights of all the contributors, it suggests various ways in which Bahá'í principles can help global law address the contemporary social problems highlighted above more effectively and justly.

Bibliography

'Abdu'l-Bahá. *The Promulgation of Universal Peace: Talks Delivered by 'Abdu'l-Bahá During His Visit to the United States and Canada in 1912*. Compiled by Howard MacNutt. 2nd ed. Wilmette, IL: Bahá'í Publishing Trust, 1982.

Albright, Madeleine (with Bill Woodward). *Fascism: A Warning*. New York: HarperCollins, 2018.

Alexander, Michelle. *The New Jim Crow: Mass Incarceration in the Age of Colorblindness*. Rev. ed. New York: The New Press, 2012.

Alston, Philip. *International Human Rights*. New York, NYU Law, 2024.

American Bar Association. *The ABA Rule of Law Initiative 2018 Annual Report*. https://abaruleoflaw.blogspot.com/2019/05/2018–annual-report.html

Arberry, A.J., trans. *The Koran Interpreted*. New York: Simon and Schuster, 1955.

Bahá'í International Community. 'Situation of Bahá'ís in Iran'. https://www.bic.org/focus-areas/situation-iranian-bahais

— 'Women's Health and Human Rights: The Case for Comprehensive and Sustainable Development'. The Bahá'í International Community's Contribution to the 44th Session of the UN Commission on Population and Development, 18 January 2011. https://www.bic.org/statements/womens-health-and-human-rights-case-comprehensive-and-sustainable-development

Bahá'u'lláh. *Gleanings from the Writings of Bahá'u'lláh*, trans. Shoghi Effendi. 2nd rev. ed. Wilmette, IL: Bahá'í Publishing Trust, 1976.

— *The Kitáb-i-Aqdas: The Most Holy Book*. Wilmette, IL: Bahá'í Publishing Trust, 1993.

— *Tablets of Bahá'u'lláh Revealed after the Kitáb-i-Aqdas*, trans. Habib Taherzadeh. Haifa: Bahá'í World Centre, 1978.

Benhabib, Seyla. 'The New Sovereigntism and Transnational Law: Legal Utopianism, Democratic Scepticism and Statist Realism'. *Global Constitutionalism*, vol. 5, issue 2, pp. 109–44 (2016).

Bisserbe, Noemie. 'France's Macron Wins National Assembly Backing for "Islamist Separatism" Bill: The Proposed Legislation Heads to the French Senate Amid Criticism that It Stigmatizes Muslims'. *The Wall Street Journal*, 16 February 2021. https://www.wsj.com/articles/frances-macron-wins-national-assembly-backing-for-islamist-separatism-bill-11613501154?st=mleey2tom69pl0a&reflink=article_email_share

Brilmayer, R. Lea, Jack L. Goldsmith, Erin O'Hara O'Connor, and Carlos Vázquez. *Conflict of Laws: Cases and Materials*. 8th ed. Frederick, MD: Aspen, 2019.

Brinkman, Emily L., Rachel L. Zacharias, and Aneliese Castro. 'Two Years After Dobbs: The Complex Landscape of Reproductive Health Care'. *Reuters*, 11 June 2024. https://www.reuters.com/legal/litigation/two-years-after-dobbs-complex-landscape-reproductive-health-care-2024-06-11/

Brooks, E. Bruce and A. Taeko Brooks, trans. *The Original Analects: Sayings of Confucius and His Successors*. New York: Columbia University Press, 1998.

Conze, Edward, trans. *Buddhist Scriptures*. London: Penguin Books, 1959.

Core Coalition. 'Modern Slavery: Top Companies Fail to Name Supply Chain Risks'. *European Coalition for Corporate Justice*, 5 October 2017. https://corporatejustice coalition.org/wp-content/uploads/2017/10/Top-companies-fail-to-name-supply-chain-risks-PR_Oct-3.pdf

Council on Foreign Relations. 'Global Conflict Tracker'. https://www.cfr.org/global-conflict-tracker

Dahl, Robert A. *Democracy and Its Critics*. New Haven and London: Yale University Press, 1989.

Ebrahim, Nadeen and Ibrahim Dahman. '50,000 Killed in Gaza Since Start of Israel-Hamas War, Health Ministry Says'. *CNN*, 24 March 2025.

Edgerton, Franklin, trans. *The Bhagavad Gītā*. Cambridge: Harvard University Press, 1972.

Evans, Gareth. *The Responsibility to Protect: Ending Mass Atrocity Crimes Once and for All*. Washington, D.C.: Brookings Institution Press, 2008.

Far, Tara Sepehri. 'Unveiling Resistance: The Struggle for Women's Rights in Iran'. *Human Rights Watch*, 26 June 2023. https://www.hrw.org/news/2023/06/26/unveiling-resistance-struggle-womens-rights-iran

FIDH. *Corporate Accountability for Human Rights Abuses: A Guide for Victims and NGOs on Recourse Mechanisms*. 3d ed. 2016. https://www.fidh.org/IMG/pdf/corporate_accountability_guide_version_web.pdf

Fieldhouse, D.K. *Colonialism, 1870–1945: An Introduction*. New York: St. Martin's Press, 1981.

Gebrekidan, Salam. 'The World Has a Plan to Fight Coronavirus. Most Countries Are Not Using It'. *The New York Times*, 12 March 2020. https://www.nytimes.com/2020/03/12/world/coronavirus-world-health-organization.html

Glenn, H. Patrick. *Legal Traditions of the World*. 5th ed. Oxford: Oxford University Press, 2014.

Grotius, Hugo. *De Jure Belli ac Pacis Libri Tres*. Translated by Francis W. Kelsey. New York: Oceana; London: Wildy and Son, 1964.

Held, David. *Models of Democracy*. 2nd ed. Stanford: Stanford University Press, 1996.

The Holy Bible Containing the Old and New Testaments: New Revised Standard Version. New York: Oxford University Press, 1989.

Hornby, Helen Bassett, comp. *Lights of Guidance: A Bahá'í Reference File*. 6th ed. New Delhi: Bahá'í Publishing Trust, 1999.

Ibrahim, Nader and Peter Robins. 'How Anti-Immigrant Riots Flared in the U.K'. *The New York Times*, 8 August 2024. https://www.nytimes.com/2024/08/08/world/europe/uk-riots-southport-timeline.html?smid=nytcore-android-share

Iran Human Rights Documentation Center. *A Faith Denied: The Persecution of the Bahá'ís of Iran*. Published on 3 February 2011. https://iranhrdc.org/a-faith-denied-the-persecution-of-the-bahais-of-iran/

Janis, Mark W. 'Religion and the Literature of International Law: Some Standard Texts', in Janis, Mark W. and Carolyn Evans (eds.). *Religion and International Law*, pp. 121–43. The Hague: Kluwer Law International, 1999.

Janis, Mark W. and Carolyn Evans (eds.). *Religion and International Law*. The Hague: Kluwer Law International, 1999.

Khadduri, Majid, trans. *The Islamic Law of Nations: Shaybānī's Siyar*. Baltimore: The Johns Hopkins Press, 1966.

Kioko, Ben. 'The Right of Intervention under the African Union's Constitutive Act: From Non-Interference to Non-Intervention'. 85 *International Review of the Red Cross* 807 (2003).

Kumar, Hari; Mujib Mashal and Suhasini Raj. '"Perpetual Violence": India's Dangerous

New Pattern of Communal Tensions'. *The New York Times,* 11 May 2022. https://www.nytimes.com/2022/05/11/world/asia/india-hindu-muslim-violence.html

Lepard, Brian. 'The Bahá'í Faith', in Forsythe, David P. (ed.). *The Oxford Encyclopedia of Human Rights.* New York: Oxford University Press, 2009.

— *Hope for a Global Ethic: Shared Principles in Religious Scriptures.* Wilmette, IL: Bahá'í Publishing, 2005.

— *In the Glory of the Father: The Bahá'í Faith and Christianity.* Wilmette, IL: Bahá'í Publishing, 2008.

Levendusky, Matthew et al. 'Has the Supreme Court Become Just Another Political Branch? Public Perceptions of Court Approval and Legitimacy in a Post-*Dobbs* World'. *Science Advances*, vol. 10, no. 10 (2024). https://www.science.org/doi/full/10.1126/sciadv.adk9590

Locke, John. *Two Treatises of Government.* New York: Cambridge University Press, 1960.

Lyons, Gene M. and Michael Mastanduno. 'Introduction: International Intervention, State Sovereignty, and the Future of International Society', in Lyons, Gene M. and Michael Mastanduno (eds.). *Beyond Westphalia? State Sovereignty and International Intervention*, pp. 1–18. Baltimore and London: The Johns Hopkins University Press, 1995.

Mattei, Ugo A.; Teemu Ruskola, and Antonio Gidi. *Schlesinger's Comparative Law: Cases-Text-Materials.* 7th ed. New York: Thomson Reuters/Foundation Press, 2009.

Mayall, James. *Nationalism and International Society.* Cambridge: Cambridge University Press, 1990.

McGoldrick, Dominic. *Human Rights and Religion – The Islamic Headscarf Debate in Europe.* Oxford: Hart Publishing, 2006.

'Order Above the Law: How to Fix American Policing'. *The Economist*, 6 June 2020, pp. 17–20.

Paperny, Anna Mehler and Ismail Shakil. 'Canada Reaches Agreement to Compensate Indigenous Children Taken from Families'. *Reuters*, 5 January 2022. https://www.reuters.com/world/americas/canada-reaches-agreements-compensate-indigenous-children-over-discriminatory-2022-01-04/

'Police Are Killing More Americans Than Ever. Where's the Outrage? The Scarcity of Protests Is Striking'. *The Economist*, 24 August 2024. https://www.economist.com/united-states/2024/08/22/police-are-killing-more-americans-than-ever-wheres-the-outrage.

Rustad, Siri Aus. 'Conflict Trends: A Global Overview, 1946–2023'. *Peace Research Institute Oslo Paper.* Oslo: PRIO, 2024.

Security Council Report. *The UN Security Council Handbook: A User's Guide to Practice and Procedure.* New York, NY: Security Council Report, 2019.

Shoghi Effendi. *The World Order of Bahá'u'lláh: Selected Letters.* Wilmette, IL: Bahá'í Publishing Trust, 1991.

Snyder, Jack. 'The Broken Bargain: How Nationalism Came Back'. *Foreign Affairs*, March/April 2019, vol. 98, no. 2, pp. 54–60.

Stiglitz, Joseph E. 'Opinion: The Race to the Bottom on Corporate Taxation Starves Us of the Resources We Need to Solve Our Biggest Problems'. *Market Watch*, 8 October 2019. https://www.marketwatch.com/story/the-race-to-the-bottom-on-corporate-taxation-starves-us-of-the-resources-we-need-to-solve-our-biggest-problems-2019-10-07

— *The Price of Inequality: How Today's Divided Society Endangers Our Future.* New York: W.W. Norton and Co., 2013.

Tanakh: A New Translation of the Holy Scriptures According to the Traditional Hebrew Text. Philadelphia: The Jewish Publication Society, 1985.

Temin, Davis. 'How the Reputation Risk Of #MeToo Is Forcing Businesses to Reevaluate Their Corporate Culture'. *Forbes*, 14 May 2018. https://www.forbes.com/sites/daviatemin/2018/05/14/how-the-reputation-risk-of-metoo-is-forcing-businesses-to-re-evaluate-their-corporate-culture/#7dd1c68d7c58

Thompson, Carolyn; Michael Balsamo, and Dave Collins, Associated Press. '10 Dead in "Racially Motivated" Mass Shooting at Buffalo Supermarket'. *Los Angeles Times*, 10 May 2022. https://www.latimes.com/world-nation/story/2022-05-14/supermarket-shooting-buffalo-new-york

U.N. Charter. 1945. https://www.un.org/en/charter-united-nations/

U.N. Office on Drugs and Crime ('UNODC'). *Global Report on Trafficking in Persons 2024*. New York: United Nations, 2024. https://www.unodc.org/unodc/data-and-analysis/glotip.html

UNHCR. 'Figures at a Glance'. https://www.unhcr.org/en-us/figures-at-a-glance.html

United Nations World Summit Outcome Document. G.A. Res. 60/1 (2005). https://digitallibrary.un.org/record/556636/?v=pdf

Universal Declaration of Human Rights. G.A. Res. 217A (III) (1948).

Universal House of Justice. Letter to the Bahá'ís of the World, 18 January 2019. https://www.bahai.org/library/authoritative-texts/the-universal-house-of-justice/messages/20190118_001/1#276724432

— Message to the Bahá'ís of the World, 25 November 2020. https://www.bahai.org/library/authoritative-texts/the-universal-house-of-justice/messages/20201125_001/1#300076430

— *The Promise of World Peace.* https://www.bahai.org/documents/the-universal-house-of-justice/promise-world-peace

— *Wellspring of Guidance: Messages of the Universal House of Justice 1963–1968.* Wilmette, IL: Bahá'í Publishing Trust, 1976.

Vienna Convention on the Law of Treaties (1969). 1155 U.N.T.S. 331.

Weeramantry, C. G. *Islamic Jurisprudence: An International Perspective.* New York: St. Martin's Press, 1988.

Wike, Richard; Laura Silver, and Alexandra Castillo. 'Dissatisfaction with Performance of Democracy Is Common in Many Nations'. Pew Research Center, Global Attitudes and Trends, 29 April 2019. https://www.pewresearch.org/global/2019/04/29/dissatisfaction-with-performance-of-democracy-is-common-in-many-nations/

Williams, Loui and Anduriña Espinoza-Wasil. 'The Power of Women's Activism: Protests Against Gender-Based Violence During COVID-19'. *UN Women*, 12 December 2022. https://data.unwomen.org/features/power-womens-activism-protests-against-gender-based-violence-during-covid-19

Zaru, Deena. 'The Symbols of Hate and Far-Right Extremism on Display in Pro-Trump Capitol Siege: Some Rioters Displayed Extremist Symbols of White Supremacy and Anarchy'. *ABC News*, 14 January 2021. https://abcnews.go.com/US/symbols-hate-extremism-display-pro-trump-capitol-siege/story?id=75177671

BAHÁ'Í VISIONS FOR REFORMING SOME ASPECTS OF THE NATIONAL AND INTERNATIONAL LEGAL ORDERS

2

Rendering Service to the Oneness of Humanity and the Quest for Justice in the Global Legal Order

Kiser Barnes

In recent years, serious discussions about the establishment of a just and united world order have evolved. However, uncertainties persist about the very nature of justice, the implications of various kinds of justice, and the conditions necessary for just governments, just individuals, and a just international order to exist, in relation to the notion of the oneness and wholeness of humankind.

Today the human species seems unsure about the role of national and global legal systems in bringing about these diverse conceptions of justice.

It is generally agreed that human beings' understandings of the concept of the progressive unification of humankind have developed through the course of time in connection with divine revelations. The Bahá'í teachings affirm this reality and emphasize human unity and the quest for a just world order in this way:

> All the divine Manifestations [Prophets] have proclaimed the oneness of God and the unity of mankind. They have taught that men should love and mutually help each other in order that they might progress. Now if this conception of religion be true, its essential principle is the oneness of humanity.[1]

Thus, the idea of the unity of humankind, and the moral responsibility placed upon individuals to help achieve it, is not new. However, it does seem new that the Bahá'í Dispensation places this idea at the center of an evolving ethical and legal order. Thus, the writings of Shoghi Effendi, the Guardian of the Bahá'í Faith, affirm that of all the principles enshrined in the writings of Bahá'u'lláh, the Prophet and Founder of the religion:

> the most vital of them all is the principle of the oneness and wholeness of the human race, which may well be regarded as the hallmark of Bahá'u'lláh's

---

1   'Abdu'l-Bahá, *Promulgation of Universal Peace*, p. 31.

Revelation and the pivot of His teachings. Of such cardinal importance is this principle of unity that . . . He unreservedly proclaims it as the central purpose of His Faith.[2]

What appears new is that Bahá'u'lláh has revealed teachings about these related elements that directly apply to the needs and conditions of the modern world. What is also undoubtedly new is that, in the words of Shoghi Effendi, it is toward a 'new World Order, Divine in origin, all-embracing in scope, equitable in principle . . . that a harassed humanity must strive'.[3]

For the first time in human history, according to the Guardian, the Bahá'í teachings present a new perspective:

> The principle of the Oneness of Mankind, as proclaimed by Bahá'u'lláh, carries with it no more and no less than a solemn assertion that attainment to this final stage in this stupendous evolution is not only necessary but inevitable, that its realization is fast approaching, and that nothing short of a power that is born of God can succeed in establishing it.[4]

Bahá'u'lláh has uniquely implanted at the very core of His revelation the spiritual responsibility of rendering service to the ancient quest for a just and united world. The Bahá'í writings disclose that this phenomenon conforms with the spiritual precepts of former revelations. In the words of the Universal House of Justice:

> The scriptures of all religions have always taught the believer to see in service to others not only a moral duty, but an avenue for the soul's own approach to God. Today, the progressive restructuring of society gives this familiar teaching new dimensions of meaning. As the age-old promise of a world animated by principles of justice slowly takes on the character of a realistic goal, meeting the needs of the soul and those of society will increasingly be seen as reciprocal aspects of a mature spiritual life.[5]

Strikingly, Bahá'u'lláh regards the 'love of mankind' and 'service to its interests as the worthiest and most laudable objects of human endeavor'.[6]

According to the Bahá'í writings, law must play a key role in such service to the whole of humankind. They indicate that the 'moral duty' to render service to humanity in relation to a realistic quest for global justice involves the unifying role of law, toward what has been termed by some observers 'Law and the Idea of Mankind'.[7] Law is an essential instrument in achieving divine justice in our present

---

2   Shoghi Effendi, *God Passes By*, pp. 216–17.
3   Shoghi Effendi, *World Order*, p. 34.
4   ibid. p. 43.
5   Universal House of Justice, 'To the World's Religious Leaders', April 2002, p. 5.
6   Shoghi Effendi, *God Passes By*, p. 217.
7   Jones, *Law and the Idea of Mankind*, p. 752.

age, an age in which, according to 'Abdu'l-Bahá, 'divine justice will become manifest in human conditions and affairs'.[8]

In the words of Shoghi Effendi, this realization of justice is 'the goal of a new World Order' that the writings of the Bahá'í Faith envision. In connection with the 'progressive restructuring of society', he also makes clear that a:

> . . . universal fermentation . . . in every continent of the globe and in every department of human life, be it religious, social, economic or political, is purging and reshaping humanity in anticipation of the Day when the wholeness of the human race will have been recognized and its unity established.[9]

Although the future order conceived by Bahá'u'lláh goes far beyond what we might perceive today, this chapter explores the idea that rendering service to humanity and pursuing justice, including through law, comprise interrelated elements of a process toward world unity set in motion by the revelation of Bahá'u'lláh. According to that revelation, every individual has a responsibility in the search for and creation of a united world. It explores this theme in the writings of Shoghi Effendi – that moral rectitude, nobility, and freedom from all forms of prejudice are 'prerequisites' for Bahá'í undertakings related to serving the cause of oneness. Shoghi Effendi elaborated on this theme in his important and influential 1939 book *The Advent of Divine Justice*.

This chapter reflects on Shoghi Effendi's designation of rectitude of conduct as a 'sublime standard', of which 'justice is so essential and potent an element'.[10] It also explores his affirmation that service to humanity is a moral duty that must be pursued with 'an abiding sense of undeviating justice'.[11] It considers the prevailing influence of religion and the valuable contributions of certain philosophers to human progress. This chapter also discusses Shoghi Effendi's statement that the course set forth by Bahá'u'lláh for the establishment of global unity and justice is 'the double task of simultaneously building an ideal society and perfecting the behavior of individuals'.[12] It reviews the concept of the oneness of humanity, the nature, character and purpose of justice, and perspectives regarding the status of the quest for justice itself. It also examines the approach of the Bahá'í Faith to the establishment of a new world order, animated by principles of justice, with a focus on the Faith's conception of law and how the idea of the oneness of humanity relates to international law, including international human rights law.

The Force of Unity and the Quest for Justice

Regarding the concept of unity, Shoghi Effendi proclaims:

---

8   'Abdu'l-Bahá, *Promulgation of Universal Peace*, p. 132.
9   Shoghi Effendi, *World Order*, p. 170.
10 Shoghi Effendi, *Advent of Divine Justice*, p. 29.
11 ibid. p. 23.
12 Universal House of Justice, 'Issues Related to the Study of the Bahá'í Faith', 10 December 1992.

Of such cardinal importance is this principle of unity that . . . He (Bahá'u'lláh) unreservedly proclaims it as the central purpose of His Faith. 'We verily', He declares, 'have come to unite and weld together all that dwell on earth.' 'So potent is the light of unity', He further states, 'that it can illuminate the whole earth.' . . . Unity, He states, is the goal that 'excelleth every goal' and an aspiration which is 'the monarch of all aspirations'. 'The world', He proclaims, 'is but one country, and mankind its citizens.' He further affirms that the unification of mankind, the last stage in the evolution of humanity towards maturity is inevitable . . . He deplores the defectiveness of the prevailing order . . . in human society, and regards the 'love of mankind' and service to its interests as the worthiest and most laudable objects of human endeavor.[13]

As to the scope and purpose of the principle, Shoghi Effendi further explains:

Let there be no misgivings as to the animating purpose of the world-wide Law of Bahá'u'lláh. Far from aiming at the subversion of the existing foundations of society, it seeks to broaden its basis, to remold its institutions in a manner consonant with the needs of an ever-changing world. It can conflict with no legitimate allegiances, nor can it undermine essential loyalties. Its purpose is neither to stifle the flame of a sane and intelligent patriotism in men's hearts, nor to abolish the system of national autonomy so essential if the evils of excessive centralization are to be avoided. It does not ignore, nor does it attempt to suppress, the diversity of ethnical origins, of climate, of history, of language and tradition, of thought and habit, that differentiate the peoples and nations of the world. It calls for a wider loyalty, for a larger aspiration than any that has animated the human race. It insists upon the subordination of national impulses and interests to the imperative claims of a unified world. It repudiates excessive centralization on one hand, and disclaims all attempts at uniformity on the other. Its watchword is unity in diversity.[14]

Viewed in their most fundamental context, these statements envisage an emerging global society where the consciousness of human oneness, serving the 'principle of unity', and the quest for justice all function as interrelated elements. The theme of rendering service to humanity is expressed in this way by Bahá'u'lláh:

That one indeed is a man who, today, dedicateth himself to the service of the entire human race . . . Blessed and happy is he that ariseth to promote the best interests of the peoples and kindreds of the earth . . . It is not for him to pride himself who loveth his own country, but rather for him who loveth the whole world. The earth is but one country, and mankind its citizens.[15]

---

13   Shoghi Effendi, *God Passes By*, p. 217.
14   Shoghi Effendi, *World Order*, pp. 41–2.
15   Bahá'u'lláh, *Gleanings*, p. 250.

Bahá'u'lláh further states:

> Is there any deed in the world that would be nobler than service to the common good? Is there any greater blessing conceivable for a man, than that he should become the cause of the education, the development, the prosperity and honor of his fellow-creatures? . . . The highest righteousness of all is for blessed souls . . . to arise and energetically devote themselves to the service of the masses, forgetting their own worldly advantage and working only to serve the general good.[16]

He also teaches that: 'Everyone should have some trade, or art or profession, be he rich or poor, and with this he must serve humanity. This service is acceptable as the highest form of worship.'[17]

The Role of Religion in the Quest for a Just Society

Although skepticism reigns in many parts of the world about the value of religion, the teachings of the Manifestations of God have contributed much to the advancement of the quest for a just society. The contributions made by certain philosophers to the search for the meaning of justice in relation to the progress of humanity, as commended in the writings of the Bahá'í Faith, have also advanced the quest.

The contemporary philosopher Sun Libo has observed that:

> Since the beginning of civilization, humankind has been pursuing justice as a form of ideal state and countless philosophers and thinkers and sages have proposed theories on justice. These thoughts have inspired generations of people in their striving after justice, and this quest has contributed much to civilization as we know it today. This eternal pursuit of justice is, in fact, the spiritual force motivating social, political and cultural advances.[18]

In connection with the influence of religious teachings on the pursuit of justice and the search for unity, in 1625 the great Dutch humanist, Huig de Groot, or Grotius, a devout man of letters aroused by the savagery of religious wars, published his treatise on war and peace – a general theory of law that he hoped would bring order out of the chaos of international conflict. Based on Judeo-Christian teachings on humility, love, and charity, Grotius' appeals to religious and moral sentiments permeated the text. He argued that the entire field of international relations was subject to principles of morality, and that political leaders should not take account only of persons entrusted to their care – instead, they should consider the interests of the whole human race. Cornelius Murphy comments, 'It is thought that the

---

16 'Abdu'l-Bahá, *Secret of Divine Civilization*, p. 103.
17 'Abdu'l-Bahá, *'Abdu'l-Bahá in London*, p. 93.
18 Libo, *Morality, Law and Religion*, p. 57.

emphasis [Grotius] put on the personal responsibility of those holding sovereign power for war gives the work a permanent value.'[19] John Huddleston observes in his book *The Search for a Just Society*:

> Although there is widespread skepticism today about the value of religion, especially in Western society, there is undeniable historical evidence that much of what has been achieved in moving towards the just society should be attributed to the direct or indirect impact of the world's great religions. They have immensely broadened man's vision of the universe and provided a sense of meaning, purpose and direction in life, encompassing such themes as brotherhood of man and noble ethical standards of behavior and thought.[20]

The Nature of Justice as a Universal and All-Encompassing Concept

What is justice? What does it encompass? Thinkers throughout the millennia have reflected on these challenging questions, and the Bahá'í writings also address them.

While the Bahá'í teachings on the spiritual prerequisites required for human progress indicate 'new dimensions of meaning' and applications of the concept of justice, the philosophical investigations of some Western philosophers over the centuries have concluded that justice is, *inter alia*: 'The Queen of virtues'; God's 'favours and commands'; the 'synthesis of every virtue'; 'the virtue par excellence, sovereignty amongst all (the virtues) and all-comprehensive'; 'an architect of all virtues, the aim of the law'; 'a virtue of social institutions'; 'the whole of social virtue . . . in relation to your neighbor'; 'the virtue which disposes the just man to act just as a matter of habit'; 'the most public and legal of virtues'; 'the idea where all virtues are gathered together'; 'the fruitful mother' and the 'nurse of the other virtues'; 'total or perfect virtue'; 'love of the highest good and/or of God'; 'the supreme virtue which directs love to the goal of the universal good'; 'a disposition of the soul'; 'the actions which man performs in himself but also those which he performs in relation to others'; 'the virtue which rules and harmonizes the acting both of individuals and of congregated multitudes'; 'a principle regulative of the whole of life – individual and social'; 'an ethical or deontological form'; 'the catalyst in the quest of personal and group harmony'.[21]

While these ancient and credible descriptions open the way for promising reflections on the spiritual, social, legal, and practical character of justice, the Bahá'í writings explicate the concept of justice both individually and collectively, emphasizing that members of the Bahá'í Faith should:

> . . . be living examples of justice! So that . . . the world may see in your actions that you manifest the attributes of justice and mercy . . . become just, and

---

19   Murphy, *Search for World Order*, p. 8.
20   Huddleston, *Search for a Just Society*, p. 395.
21   Del Veccio, *Justice – An Historical and Philosophical Essay*, pp. 5–22.

direct your thoughts towards the unity of mankind . . . Justice is not limited, it is a universal quality. Its operation must be carried out in all classes, from the highest to the lowest. Justice must be sacred, and the rights of all the people must be considered. Desire for others only that which you desire for yourselves. Then shall we rejoice in the Sun of Justice, which shines from the Horizon of God. Each man has been placed in a post of honour, which he must not desert. A humble workman who commits an injustice is as much to blame as a renowned tyrant. Thus we all have our choice between justice and injustice.[22]

The Essential Role of Religion in Achieving Global Justice

From a Bahá'í perspective, religion has an essential role to play in advancing the ultimate meaning and purpose of the interrelated elements of rendering service and the search for justice. In this connection, 'Abdu'l-Bahá affirms that 'religion serves the world of morality . . . Religion impels men to achieve praiseworthy deeds.'[23] He underscores that the religion of God remains 'that fixed foundation which insures the progress and stability of the body politic and the illumination of humanity'.[24] He further says:

The real bond of integrity is religious in character, for religion indicates the oneness of the world of humanity. Religion serves the world of morality . . . Religion becomes the cause of love in human hearts, for religion is a divine foundation, the foundation ever conducive to life. The teachings of God are the source of illumination to the people of the world. Religion is ever constructive, not destructive.[25]

Shoghi Effendi clarified that 'the fundamental purpose of all religions . . . is to bring man nearer to God, and to change his character, which is of the utmost importance'.[26] According to 'Abdu'l-Bahá, 'Even the minutest details of civilized life derive from the grace of the Prophets of God. What thing of value to mankind has ever come into being which was not first set forth either directly or by implication in the Holy Scriptures?'[27]

With these truths in mind, the idea that humankind can create for itself a process of establishing global justice and world order without the influence of religion is untenable. John Huddleston puts it well:

There has been a tendency in recent decades to downplay the importance of religion . . . The fact is that religion has been an extremely powerful force in

---

22 'Abdu'l-Bahá, *Paris Talks*, pp. 159–60.
23 'Abdu'l-Bahá, *Promulgation of Universal Peace*, p. 344.
24 ibid. p. 404.
25 ibid. p. 344.
26 Letter on behalf of Shoghi Effendi, *Compilations of Compilations*, vol. 2, p. 16.
27 'Abdu'l-Bahá, *Secret of Divine Civilization*, p. 96.

human history . . . [I]t has played a very significant part in the evolution of the idea of the just society . . . The contribution of religion to the evolution of the concept of the just society has been its role in the development of ethics: the basic motivations of the individual and the community, and a sense of distinction between right and wrong. Ethics drawn from the great religions of the past have moderated human greed, selfishness, violence and destruction – all characteristics of the unjust society.[28]

The Futility of the Quest for Justice without Guidance from Religion or Spirituality

Without religion, humanity remains rudderless in navigating its way to a common understanding of justice. Many observers have commented on the need for humanity to agree on such a conception, but also on its failure to do so. For example, R. K. Ramazani has written: 'Seldom in the historical past have individuals and collectivities everywhere been so profoundly concerned with the quest for justice, a concept that is, indeed, elusive but not by any means illusive.' He lamented that:

> The so-called realists, or pessimists [contend] that the search for common universal standards of law and justice is doomed because, despite the processes of modernization, primordial loyalties, values, attitudes, and ethnic and linguistic particularities continue to undermine the new elements of communality.[29]

More than three centuries ago the great philosopher Leibniz regretted that 'the notions of right and justice are still far from clear despite the fact that the clearest writers have written about them'.[30] Otto Bird notes in an extensive exploration of the concept of justice in his essay 'The Idea of Justice' that 'Good and learned men, seriously concerned about justice, have dismissed the search for the meaning of justice as a hopeless task and a waste of time and effort.'[31]

Some observers have blamed religious divisions for this failure to agree on the meaning of justice. For example, the historian Yuval Noah Harari asserts that 'Our [humanity's] sense of Justice might be out of date.' He wonders: 'Should we call it quits, then, and declare that the human quest to understand the truth and find justice has failed? Have we officially entered the post-truth era?' He answers that while 'religious dogma' and 'firm commitment to scientific truth' provide people 'with intellectual comfort and moral certainty it is debatable whether they provide justice'.[32]

Others have agreed that it is not possible for human beings to arrive at a

---

28   Huddleston, *Search for a Just Society*, p. 3.
29   Khadduri, *Islamic Conception of Justice*, p. ix.
30   Quoted in Bird, *Idea of Justice*, p. 5.
31   ibid. p. 8.
32   Harari, *21 Lessons for the 21st Century*, p. 235.

definitive answer to the question, 'what is justice?' Hans Kelsen, an Austrian-American jurist, legal philosopher, and political philosopher, asserted:

> The important question, the eternal question of mankind: What is justice? No other question has been discussed so passionately; no other question has caused so much precious blood and so many bitter tears to be shed; no other question has been the object of so much intensive thinking by the most illustrious thinkers from Plato to Kant; and yet, this question is today as unanswered as it ever was. It seems that it is one of those questions to which the resigned wisdom applies that man cannot find a definitive answer, but can only try to improve the question.[33]

From a Bahá'í point of view, the conclusions of such commentators that the noble search for justice has 'failed', that it constitutes 'a hopeless task, a waste of time and effort', is 'elusive', and 'doomed', or that there can never be a 'definitive answer' to the question 'what is justice?' are erroneous. Whatever disagreements persist about the meaning of justice, they have not removed the deep yearning in the hearts of people everywhere for a just world.

Many philosophers have long recognized that a shared conception of justice must be based on spiritual principles. In this connection, several influential Greek philosophers recognized that the basis of ethics and morality has a spiritual foundation, which must undergird the quest for justice. Bahá'u'lláh Himself praised the contributions of Socrates, Plato, and Aristotle, who devoted their philosophical inquiries to both natural and spiritual phenomena, studied the basis of ethics and morality, and rendered praiseworthy service to humanity by fostering understanding of the virtue of justice. Bahá'u'lláh writes:

> Consider Hippocrates, the physician. He was one of the eminent philosophers who believed in God and acknowledged His sovereignty. After him came Socrates who was indeed wise, accomplished and righteous. He practiced self-denial, repressed his appetites for selfish desires and turned away from material pleasures . . . He dissuaded men from worshipping idols and taught them the way of God . . . What a penetrating vision into philosophy this eminent man had! He is the most distinguished of all philosophers and was highly versed in wisdom. We testify that he is one of the heroes in this field and an outstanding champion dedicated unto it . . . After Socrates came the divine Plato . . . He acknowledged his belief in God and in His signs which pervade all that hath been and shall be. Then came Aristotle, the well-known man of knowledge . . . These men who stand out as leaders of the people and are pre-eminent among them, one and all acknowledged their belief in the immortal Being Who holdeth in His grasp the reins of all sciences.[34]

---

33 Kelsen, *What is Justice?*, p. 1.
34 Bahá'u'lláh, *Tablets of Bahá'u'lláh*, pp. 144–7.

Other philosophers in recent times have also argued that justice must have a spiritual foundation. For example, the prominent 20th century Italian legal philosopher Giorgio De Vecchio declared:

> It would be a mistake to think that one can fulfill every duty and be abundantly 'just' only by abstaining from violating positive juridical laws and by observing them so as to gain the greatest possible profit. These laws are often rigid and narrow, and in no case do they avail, by themselves alone, to point the way that leads to the supreme good. Beyond our earthly Justice let us aim at that which is eternal, and from it let us take our standard; only so shall we find salvation for our souls.[35]

The great Greek philosophers Bahá'u'lláh praised, as well as more contemporary philosophers such as Del Vecchio who have paid attention to the teachings of religions regarding justice, all had a glimpse of the Divine – and thus could begin to appreciate the true meaning of justice. However, according to the teachings of Bahá'u'lláh, full agreement on the answer to the question 'what is justice?' can only come about through humanity's collective turning to the teachings of God's Prophets, which can be referred to as the 'Word of God'. Thus, Bahá'u'lláh revealed that:

> The Word of God is the king of words and its pervasive influence is incalculable. It hath ever dominated and will continue to dominate the realm of being . . . The Word is the master key for the whole world, inasmuch as through its potency the doors of the hearts of men, which in reality are the doors of heaven, are unlocked.[36]

Bahá'u'lláh further affirms: 'O ye discerning ones! Verily, the words which have descended from the heaven of the Will of God are the source of unity and harmony for the world.'[37] He states: 'Every thing must needs have an origin and every building a builder. Verily, the Word of God is the Cause which hath preceded the contingent world.'[38] Bahá'u'lláh also asserts:

> As the body of man needeth a garment to clothe it, so the body of mankind must needs be adorned with the mantle of justice and wisdom. Its robe is the Revelation vouchsafed unto it by God. Whenever this robe hath fulfilled its purpose, the Almighty will assuredly renew it. For every age requireth a fresh measure of the light of God. Every Divine Revelation hath been sent down in a manner that befitted the circumstances of the age in which it hath appeared.[39]

35 Del Vecchio, *Divine Justice and Human Justice*, p. 157.
36 Bahá'u'lláh, *Tablets of Bahá'u'lláh*, p. 173.
37 Bahá'u'lláh, quoted in Shoghi Effendi, *Advent of Divine Justice*, para. 55.
38 Bahá'u'lláh, *Tablets of Bahá'u'lláh*, p. 141.
39 Bahá'u'lláh, *Gleanings*, p. 81.

Bahá'u'lláh's utterances express the reality that the teachings of the Prophets reveal the standard of truth and justice, and that in this age His revelation provides the standard against which all questions about the meaning of justice and the quest for a new world order can be measured. At the same time, however, members of the Bahá'í Faith understand, in the words of Shoghi Effendi, that:

> . . . the Revelation identified with Bahá'u'lláh . . . unhesitatingly acknowledges itself to be but one link in the chain of continually progressive Revelations, supplements their teachings with such laws and ordinances as conform to the imperative needs . . . of a fast evolving and constantly changing society . . . functioning within the framework, and in accordance with the precepts, of a divinely conceived, a world-unifying, a world-redeeming Order.[40]

Indeed, the quest for justice involves every soul turning toward all the Revelations of God, but especially the most recent Revelation of God's guidance. In the time of the Revelation of the Báb, for example, this meant that all devout followers of Muhammad should have turned to the new Prophet. This truth was demonstrated by Bahá'u'lláh in His dialogue with His brother Musa. 'Musa, what have you to say?' Bahá'u'lláh asked after reading aloud passages from a scroll of inspired writings sent Him from someone He knew nothing about (the Báb), who lived 425 miles (684 kilometers) away, and who had publicly declared in Shiraz, Persia, three months earlier in 1844, that the promised 'days of the Advent of Divine Justice' had broken upon the world. Before the startled brother could answer, Bahá'u'lláh declared:

> Verily I say, whoso believes in the Qur'án and recognizes its Divine origin, and yet hesitates, though it be for a moment, to admit that these soul-stirring words are endowed with the same regenerating power, has most assuredly erred in his judgment and has strayed far from the path of justice.[41]

Today, Bahá'ís believe that agreement on the universal meaning of justice ultimately will require humanity's recognition of the twin Revelations of the Báb and Bahá'u'lláh. These Revelations explicate both the personal and societal dimensions of justice, to which we will now turn.

The Spiritual Prerequisites for Success in Bahá'í Undertakings and the Role of Personal Virtues in Achieving Justice

According to the Bahá'í teachings, justice has two major dimensions – one personal and the other societal. Law plays a critical role in achieving both facets.

---

40   Shoghi Effendi, *God Passes By*, p. 100.
41   Zarandí, *Dawn-Breakers*, p. 107.

For example, Bahá'í law prescribes the inner spiritual virtues that each individual should cultivate, as well as the elevated conduct that should characterize every believer, both of which contribute to justice in personal relationships. Yet the Bahá'í teachings also give law a central place – both religious and secular – in achieving justice at the larger level of human society.

This relationship between justice and personal virtues links directly to the 'prerequisites' Shoghi Effendi identified in *The Advent of Divine Justice*. Shoghi Effendi made it clear that Bahá'ís should manifest in all their undertakings, in their 'own individual and inner lives', in their 'administrative activities, and social relationships':[42]

> A rectitude of conduct, an abiding sense of undeviating justice . . . a chaste, pure, and holy life, unsullied and unclouded by the indecencies, the vices, the false standards, which an inherently deficient moral code tolerates, perpetuates, and fosters; a fraternity freed from that cancerous growth of racial prejudice, which is eating into the vitals of an already debilitated society – these are the ideals which the . . . believers must, from now on, individually and through concerted action, strive to promote, in both their private and public lives, ideals which are the chief propelling forces that can most effectively accelerate the march of their institutions, plans, and enterprises, that can guard the honor and integrity of their Faith, and subdue any obstacles that may confront it in the future.[43]

A subsequent letter from Shoghi Effendi affirmed that:

> These standards of Bahá'í conduct . . . should be the paramount duty of every loyal and conscientious believer to endeavour to uphold and promote . . . The principles and methods . . . of Bahá'í ethics should indeed prove of valuable inspiration and guidance to all and thus prepare them to better appreciate the privileges, and more adequately discharge the responsibilities, of their citizenship in the World Order of Bahá'u'lláh.[44]

Bahá'ís understand that all the Prophets of God have summoned humanity to cultivate and practice virtues in their relationships with others. Bahá'u'lláh declares:

> The purpose of the one true God in manifesting Himself is to summon all mankind to truthfulness and sincerity, to piety and trustworthiness, to resignation and submissiveness to the will of God, to forbearance and kindliness, to uprightness and wisdom. His object is to array every man with the mantle of a saintly character, and to adorn him with the ornament of holy and goodly deeds.[45]

---

42   Shoghi Effendi, *Advent of Divine Justice*, p. 21.
43   ibid. p. 23.
44   From a letter written on behalf of Shoghi Effendi to an individual, 20 May 1939, in *Compilation of Compilations*, vol. 1, p. 224.
45   Bahá'u'lláh, *Gleanings*, p. 299.

Additionally, 'Abdu'l-Bahá writes: 'The purpose of the Manifestation of God and the dawning of the limitless lights of the Invisible is to educate the souls of men, and refine the character of every living man.'[46]

As explored by Shoghi Effendi in *The Advent of Divine Justice*, the Bahá'í teachings elaborate on the importance of a virtuous life, including a personal commitment to justice. Bahá'u'lláh declares:

> A good character is, verily, the best mantle for men from God. With it He adorneth the temples of His loved ones. By My life! The light of a good character surpasseth the light of the sun and the radiance thereof.[47]

He further counsels: 'Be fair to yourselves and to others, that the evidences of justice may be revealed, through your deeds.'[48] Again, Bahá'u'lláh writes: 'Beautify your tongues, O people, with truthfulness, and adorn your souls with the ornament of honesty.'[49] According to 'Abdu'l-Bahá, 'The most vital duty, in this day, is to purify your characters, to correct your manners, and improve your conduct.'[50] Bahá'u'lláh counsels us to practice truthfulness:

> Truthfulness is the foundation of all human virtues. Without truthfulness progress and success, in all the worlds of God, are impossible for any soul. When this holy attribute is established in man, all the divine qualities will also be acquired.[51]

Shoghi Effendi emphasizes the importance of each individual rendering service to humanity and to the Faith, drawing on the writings of Bahá'u'lláh:

> The entire community must, as one man, arise . . . [to] teach the Cause of God, to proclaim its truths, to defend its interests, to demonstrate, by words as well as by deeds, its indispensability, its potency, and universality . . . 'God,' Bahá'u'lláh Himself has unmistakably revealed, 'hath prescribed unto everyone the duty of teaching His Cause.' 'Say,' He further has written, 'Teach ye the Cause of God, O people of Bahá, for God hath prescribed unto everyone the duty of proclaiming His Message, and regardeth it as the most meritorious of all deeds.'[52]

Bahá'u'lláh also counsels, as quoted by Shoghi Effendi:

> The companions of God are, in this day, the lump that must leaven the peoples of the world. They must show forth such trustworthiness, such truthfulness and

---

46   'Abdu'l-Bahá, *Selections*, p. 10.
47   Bahá'u'lláh, *Tablets of Bahá'u'lláh*, p. 36.
48   Bahá'u'lláh, *Gleanings*, p. 278.
49   ibid. p. 297.
50   'Abdu'l-Bahá, *Selections*, p. 10.
51   Bahá'u'lláh, quoted in Shoghi Effendi, *Advent of Divine Justice*, p. 26.
52   ibid. p. 45.

perseverance, such deeds and character that all mankind may profit by their example.[53]

The Universal House of Justice has stated that these standards set out by the Guardian initially for believers in North America now apply to 'the entire Bahá'í [world] community, both in its collective life and the lives of its individual members'.[54] These standards are, of course, established within the framework for ethics and justice set out by Bahá'u'lláh Himself. Bahá'u'lláh, writing about this framework, defines justice as giving to each person what he or she deserves, saying that justice 'consisteth in rendering each his due'. He also affirms that justice:

. . . dependeth upon and is conditioned by two words: reward and punishment. From the standpoint of justice, every soul should receive the reward of his actions, inasmuch as the peace and prosperity of the world depend thereon.[55]

Each prerequisite for success in Bahá'í undertakings identified by Shoghi Effendi represents an 'essential requirement', a vital component of an ethical framework for thought and behavior. Each demonstrates that the challenge to attain community harmony and justice is a personal one. Each offers an opportunity to grow spiritually and to engage in a process of establishing a new world order. Each inspires consciousness of the importance of voluntarily accepting responsibility for both moral development and promoting the welfare of others.

This individual dimension of justice, while furthered by Bahá'í law, springs from the heart and conscience of each individual rather than fear of punishment or sanctions. In this connection, Shoghi Effendi clarifies:

The Bahá'í Faith, like all other Divine religions, is thus fundamentally mystic in character. Its chief goal is the development of the individual and society, through the acquisition of spiritual virtues.[56]

While the importance of virtuous behavior and deeds flows through the selected Bahá'í writings, the counsels of these writings do not take the form of overbearing instructions – instead, they gently raise human consciousness. They increase understanding and aspirations for upholding divine standards. In an important sense, they affirm that these divine virtues must be practiced for the unification of the human race. Shoghi Effendi urges believers:

. . . to ponder in their hearts the implications of this moral rectitude, and to uphold, with heart and soul and uncompromisingly, both individually and

---

53   Quoted in ibid. p. 23.
54   Universal House of Justice, 'To the Believers Gathered for the Events Marking the Completion of the Projects on Mount Carmel', 24 May 2001.
55   Bahá'u'lláh, *Tabernacle of Unity*, p. 40.
56   Shoghi Effendi, in *Compilation of Compilations*, vol. 2, p. 238.

collectively, this sublime standard – a standard of which justice is so essential and potent an element.[57]

He thus identifies justice as an essential component of personal virtue and rectitude. Shoghi Effendi further describes the unique rank and exaltation of rectitude:

This rectitude of conduct, with its implications of justice, equity, truthfulness, honesty, fair-mindedness, reliability and trustworthiness, must distinguish every phase of the life of the Bahá'í community.[58]

This direct and remarkable Bahá'í association of the universal virtue of rectitude of conduct with justice – with standards of behavior governing inter-personal and institutional behavior – gives our conception of justice new meaning.

Regarding the broad application of this 'great and transcendental principle of Divine justice', Shoghi Effendi pointed out that it should extend even to how Bahá'ís elect their leadership, run their businesses, and conduct their daily lives:

Such a rectitude of conduct must manifest itself . . . in every verdict which the elected representatives of the Bahá'í community . . . may be called upon to pronounce. It must be constantly reflected in the business dealings of all its members, in their domestic lives, in all manner of employment, and in any service they may . . . render their government or people . . . It must constitute the brightest ornament of the life, the pursuits, the exertions, and the utterances of every Bahá'í teacher, whether laboring at home or abroad.[59]

Regarding the spiritual obligation of the individual in striving to manifest divine principles, including justice, for living today in an evolving new world order, 'Abdu'l-Bahá counsels:

The most vital duty, in this day, is to purify your characters, to correct your manners, and improve your conduct. The beloved of the Merciful must show forth such character and conduct among His creatures, that the fragrance of their holiness may be shed upon the whole world . . . inasmuch as the purpose of the Manifestation of God and the dawning of the limitless lights of the Invisible is to educate the souls of men, and refine the character of every living man . . .[60]

It is possible to find, in these prerequisites relating to personal conduct, some support for the suggestion, in the words of the legal scholar Julius Stone, that 'justice is best seen as a positive ethical social [interpersonal value]'. Stone observes that if justice:

57   Shoghi Effendi, *Advent of Divine Justice*, p. 29.
58   ibid. p. 23.
59   ibid. p. 26.
60   'Abdu'l-Bahá, *Selections*, p. 10.

. . . has some definite distinctive meaning, this must lie in precepts or values addressing themselves to men generally and prescribing what kinds of behavior and procedures are worthy of acceptance as governing their inter-personal relations.[61]

As a number of these quotations indicate, and in keeping with Stone's observation about the intimate relationship between justice and interpersonal ethics, the Bahá'í writings explicitly call upon everyone to develop justice and equity as inner virtues. Shoghi Effendi writes:

> Justice and equity are two guardians for the protection of man. They have appeared arrayed in their mighty and sacred names to maintain the world in uprightness and protect the nations.[62]

Bahá'u'lláh Himself writes:

> Equity is the most fundamental among human virtues. The evaluation of all things must needs depend upon it . . . Observe equity in your judgment, ye men of understanding heart! He that is unjust in his judgment is destitute of the characteristics that distinguish man's station.[63]

He further affirms: 'The canopy of existence resteth upon the pole of justice, and not on forgiveness, and the life of mankind dependeth on justice and not on forgiveness.'[64] He also says: 'The light of men is Justice . . . The purpose of justice is the appearance of unity among men,'[65] and, 'No radiance can compare with that of Justice . . . That which traineth the world is Justice, for it is upheld by two pillars, reward and punishment.'[66] He further clarifies concerning justice: 'The organization of the world and the tranquility of mankind depend upon it.'[67]

Shoghi Effendi develops these teachings of Bahá'u'lláh on the personal dimension of justice as a virtue by also drawing a connection with the virtue of moral uprightness, stressing that rectitude in our conduct:

> . . . must be made the controlling principle in the behavior and conduct of all Bahá'ís, both in their social relations with the members of their own community, and in their contact with the world at large. It must adorn and reinforce the ceaseless labors and meritorious exertions of those whose enviable position is to propagate the Message, and to administer the affairs, of the Faith of Bahá'u'lláh.[68]

---

61   Stone, *Human Law and Human Justice*, p. 322.
62   Shoghi Effendi, *Advent of Divine Justice*, p. 28.
63   Bahá'u'lláh, *Gleanings*, pp. 203–4.
64   Bahá'u'lláh, quoted in Shoghi Effendi, *Advent of Divine Justice*, p. 28.
65   Bahá'u'lláh, quoted in ibid.
66   Bahá'u'lláh, quoted in ibid. p. 27.
67   Bahá'u'lláh, quoted in ibid. p. 28.
68   ibid. p. 29–30.

The Bahá'í writings devote particular attention to this theme, especially where it concerns the importance of each individual resolving to uphold racial equality as an essential element of interpersonal justice. Drawing upon the Bahá'í writings for his guidance on the abolition of racial prejudice, Shoghi Effendi brought together in *The Advent of Divine Justice* the following counsels from Bahá'u'lláh and 'Abdu'l-Bahá:

> Close your eyes to racial differences, and welcome all with the light of oneness . . . [A]ll men [should become] . . . as brothers; that the bonds of affection and unity between the sons of men should be strengthened . . . differences of race be annulled . . . [T]he various races of humankind lend a composite harmony and beauty of color to the whole. Let all associate, therefore, in this great human garden even as flowers grow and blend together side by side without discord or disagreement between them . . . God maketh no distinction between the white and the black. If the hearts are pure both are acceptable unto Him . . . All colors are acceptable unto Him, be they white, black, or yellow . . . all were created in the image of God . . . In the estimation of God . . . all men are equal. There is no distinction or preference for any soul, in the realm of His justice and equity. God did not make these divisions[;] these divisions have had their origin in man himself. Therefore, as they are against the plan and purpose of God they are false and imaginary. In the estimation of God . . . all are one in the color and beauty of servitude to Him . . . He whose morals and virtues are praiseworthy is preferred . . . One of the important questions which affect the unity and the solidarity of mankind is the fellowship and equality of the white and colored races . . . The diversity in the human family should be the cause of love and harmony, as it is in music where many different notes blend together in the making of a perfect chord.[69]

These represent just some of the counsels in the Bahá'í writings that would enable individuals to demonstrate a concern for justice – in this case, for racial equality – in every aspect of their personal lives. The Bahá'í writings also contain counsels to pursue other important aspects of justice, including upholding the equality of women and men.

Social Justice, the Oneness of Humanity, and the Role of Law

The other dimension of justice articulated in the Bahá'í writings relates to society. The Bahá'í conception of social justice uniquely anchors it in the pivotal principle of the oneness of humanity. Yet another precept of the Bahá'í conception of social justice is that such justice, and the principle of human unity, should be carried into action through the development of a global legal order that incorporates international law as well as national and local law. The Bahá'í writings contain original,

---

69   ibid. p. 37–8.

explicit teachings on some key features of this global legal order. Still, the Bahá'í conception of social justice intimately relates to the conception of interpersonal justice – Bahá'u'lláh inextricably links the two.

In this connection, numerous possible implications for the global legal order relate to the spirit of learning and action that Shoghi Effendi advanced in *The Advent of Divine Justice* by immersing Western Bahá'ís in the Bahá'í writings regarding justice.

Although different views exist as to what law is and what it ought to be, most observers generally agree that the operation of a legal order – local, national, or international – is inseparably tied to ethical conceptions. Racism, for example, clearly contravenes the spirit of a just international rule of law. The idea of human oneness also challenges the idea of national sovereignty, the central pillar of traditional international law.

Members of the Bahá'í Faith appreciate that there have been remarkable developments in the rudiments of a law of international relations, the law of treaties, the law of international organizations, the law of international trade and finance, the law of diplomacy, conflicts of law, and other branches of public and private international law. The existence of a common legal language, in which nations of the world regulate their affairs, and the emergence of world institutions of a political, economic, and cultural character, are also noteworthy.

The American diplomat and scholar Henry Kissinger points out that the order of national sovereignty devised at the peace conference in the German region of Westphalia nearly four centuries ago was conducted 'without the involvement or even the awareness of most other continents or civilizations'. The negotiators never imagined they were laying a foundation for an applicable global system. He writes: 'It was applied to the geographic extent known to the Western European statesmen at the time.'[70]

Kissinger observes that China had its own universal concept of order, 'based on the presumed boundlessness of the Emperor's reach, who held sway over "All under Heaven."' The version of a universal order under Islam was imposed by Muslim rulers after unifying the Arab world, taking over remnants of the Empire, subsuming the Persian Empire, and governing the Middle East, North Africa, and large portions of Asia and of Europe. This vision of a global order was not based on the idea of the sovereign equality of states. Rather, it was grounded in the belief that Islam was destined to expand over all regions populated by unbelievers, until the whole world became a unitary system brought into harmony by religion.[71] Clearly, each one of these conceptions provides a recipe for conflict and contention.

In contrast to these more limited visions, Shoghi Effendi described the Bahá'í view of global order in this way:

---

70   Kissinger, *World Order*, pp. 3–5.
71   ibid.

Unification of the whole of mankind is the hall-mark of the stage which human society is now approaching. Unity of family, of tribe, of city-state, and nation have been successively attempted and fully established. World unity is the goal towards which a harassed humanity is striving. Nation-building has come to an end. The anarchy inherent in state sovereignty is moving towards a climax. A world, growing to maturity, must abandon this fetish, recognize the oneness and wholeness of human relationships, and establish once for all the machinery that can best incarnate this fundamental principle of its life.[72]

The Bahá'í writings suggest that the inevitable curtailment of unfettered national sovereignty must occur as an indispensable preliminary to the formation of a future Commonwealth of all the nations of the world. This Commonwealth will include a supreme tribunal whose judgment will be binding even where the parties concerned did not voluntarily agree to submit their case to its consideration.

Kissinger observed that when the doctrine of the sovereignty of states was established 'the then prevailing technology did not permit the operation of a single global system'.[73] 'Abdu'l-Bahá makes a similar point, stating:

In cycles gone by, though harmony was established, yet, owing to the absence of means, the unity of all mankind could not have been achieved. Continents remained widely divided, nay even among the peoples of one and the same continent association and interchange of thought were well nigh impossible. Consequently intercourse, understanding and unity amongst all the peoples and kindreds of the earth were unattainable. In this day, however, means of communication have multiplied, and the five continents of the earth have virtually merged into one . . . In like manner all the members of the human family, whether peoples or governments, cities or villages, have become increasingly interdependent. For none is self-sufficiency any longer possible, inasmuch as political ties unite all peoples and nations, and the bonds of trade and industry, of agriculture and education, are being strengthened every day. Hence the unity of all mankind can in this day be achieved. Verily this is none other but one of the wonders of this wondrous age . . . Of this past ages have been deprived . . . Hence the miraculous unfolding of a fresh marvel every day. Eventually it will be seen how bright its candles will burn in the assemblage of man.[74]

This emphasis on a perspective anchoring global law and justice in the oneness of humanity has another benefit – it contributes to diminishing the lingering parochialism underlying legal thinking, that the English or the French way, or the Buddhist or the Muslim way, is the only true way of law. Those limited conceptions often regard all others as misguided, primitive, or worse.

---

72 Shoghi Effendi, *World Order*, p. 202.
73 Kissinger, *World Order*, p. 32.
74 'Abdu'l-Bahá, *Selections*, pp. 31–2.

Identifying an accrediting source for the concept and practice of justice requires a major original source, be it 'nature', 'utility', 'the categorical imperative', 'human interests', or the 'original position in a social contract'. Bahá'u'lláh identifies the divine source of justice, which in turn is served by law, in this way:

> Know verily that the essence of justice and the source thereof are both embodied in the ordinances prescribed by Him Who is the Manifestation of the Self of God amongst men.[75]

According to His writings, justice is 'The best beloved of all things' by God, and His 'gift' to mankind.[76]

The Bahá'í International Community (BIC), which represents the worldwide Bahá'í community at the United Nations and in other global forums, has consistently shared perspectives regarding the goal of world unity, principles of the oneness of the human family, unity in diversity, and service to humankind. In connection with the overarching principle of the oneness of humanity, it has stated:

> The bedrock of a strategy that can engage the world's population in assuming responsibility for its collective destiny must be the consciousness of the oneness of humankind. The human species is an organic whole, the leading edge of the evolutionary process. What the people of the world are experiencing . . . is their collective coming of age, and it is through this emerging maturity of the race that the principle of unity in diversity will find full expression.[77]

The Importance of Protecting Universal Human Rights in a Global Legal Order

One key element of a new global legal order based on recognition of the principle of the unity of the human family is the creation of laws and institutions to protect universal human rights. The Bahá'í writings explicitly teach, in the words of 'Abdu'l-Bahá, that 'an equal standard of human rights must be recognized and adopted'.[78] Bahá'u'lláh warned: 'They that perpetrate tyranny in the world have usurped the rights of the peoples . . . and are sedulously pursuing their selfish inclinations.'[79] Bahá'u'lláh advised the world's rulers not to 'connive at injustice', to set their hearts 'firmly upon justice',[80] to 'be the emblems of justice' amongst men, to 'tread . . . the path of justice'. He counseled rulers: 'Be vigilant, that ye

---

75   Bahá'u'lláh, *Gleanings*, p. 175.
76   Bahá'u'lláh, *Tablets of Bahá'u'lláh*, pp. 36–7.
77   Bahá'í International Community, *Bahá'í World, 1995–1996*, p. 289.
78   'Abdu'l-Bahá, *Promulgation of Universal Peace*, p. 182.
79   Bahá'u'lláh, *Tablets of Bahá'u'lláh*, p. 85.
80   Bahá'u'lláh, *Gleanings*, p. 230.

may not do injustice to anyone',[81] and He praised the leader who 'preferreth justice and fairness to injustice and tyranny.'[82]

The principle of the oneness of humanity aligns entirely and consistently with the idea of universal human rights, and indeed, provides critical support for it. This empowering principle represents, from the perspective of the Bahá'í Faith, and in the words of Shoghi Effendi, 'the consummation of human evolution'.[83]

The primary Bahá'í principle of human oneness can anchor a broader conception of human dignity, which in turn forms a foundation for the idea of human rights. In this connection, the contemporary legal philosopher Ronald Dworkin writes: 'Anyone who professes to take rights seriously . . . must accept, at the minimum . . . the vague but powerful idea of human dignity.'[84] Dworkin's reliance for this view on ideas associated with Kant prompted Richard Harries to ask in his paper on secular and religious perspectives of human rights:

> One wonders why Kant is singled out rather than the framers of the Old Testament's legal codes, [or] Jesus, or Aquinas, to suggest a few of the thousands of pre-Kantian alternatives. The worth and dignity of the human person is basic to the Jewish, Christian and Muslim traditions and could be illustrated in hundreds of different ways, of which the preeminent is the sense that human beings are made in the image of God, endowed with rationality, choice, a capacity to pray and love, and endowed with moral consciousness.[85]

As the holy scriptures of all religions do, the Bahá'í writings extol the dignity of the human person. Bahá'u'lláh writes: 'Man [is] the noblest and most perfect of all created things'[86]; 'His is the loftiest station, and his influence educateth the world of being.'[87] This vision of the dignity of every person as a noble being created by God to fulfil a divine purpose can lead to a new commitment to upholding universal human rights, and a broader perspective on the essential role of international law in securing those rights.

Conclusion

Under the guidance of the Universal House of Justice, the Bahá'í world community strives to advance divine principles for living in a just world order. Its members endeavor to manifest spiritual prerequisites and to advance the reality of the oneness of the human family. Service to humanity plays an integral part in their lives. In this connection, the Universal House of Justice wrote:

81   ibid. pp. 250–1.
82   Bahá'u'lláh, *Tablets of Bahá'u'lláh*, p. 65.
83   Shoghi Effendi, *World Order*, p. 43.
84   Dworkin, *Taking Rights Seriously*, p.198.
85   Harries, 'The Complementarity Between Secular and Religious Perspective of Human Rights', p. 19.
86   Bahá'u'lláh, *Gleanings*, p. 179.
87   Bahá'u'lláh, *Tablets of Bahá'u'lláh*, p. 220.

Bahá'ís all around the world share with their family, friends, neighbours, and co-workers their belief in the oneness of humanity and invite them to participate in activities aimed at community building and increasing the capacity of individuals to contribute to the betterment of the world. This includes programmes for . . . the systematic study of the Creative Word and the exploration of its implications to develop individual capacity to serve the spiritual and material needs of humanity.[88]

Exposure to such holy writings puts in sharp focus the interrelationship of rendering service to the human family, manifesting moral virtues, and pursuing the quest for a global legal order animated by principles of justice, as expressed in this passage from 'Abdu'l-Bahá:

God has chosen you for the worthy service of unifying mankind; God has chosen you for the purpose of investigating reality and promulgating international peace; God has chosen you for the progress and development of humanity, for spreading and proclaiming true education, for the expression of love toward your fellow creatures and the removal of prejudice; God has chosen you to blend together human hearts and give light to the human world. The doors of His generosity are wide, wide open to us; but we must be attentive, alert and mindful, occupied with service to all mankind, appreciating the bestowals of God and ever conforming to His will.[89]

Bibliography

'Abdu'l-Bahá. *'Abdu'l-Bahá in London.* London: Bahá'í Publishing Trust, 1982.

— *Paris Talks.* Oakham, Rutland: U.K. Bahá'í Publishing Trust, 1972.

— *The Promulgation of Universal Peace: Talks Delivered by 'Abdu'l-Bahá During His Visit to the United States and Canada in 1912.* Wilmette, IL: Bahá'í Publishing Trust, 1982.

— *The Secret of Divine Civilization.* Translated from the Persian by Marzieh Gail in consultation with Ali-Kuli Khan. Wilmette, IL: Bahá'í Publishing Trust, 1990.

— *Selections from the Writings of 'Abdu'l-Bahá.* Haifa: Bahá'í World Centre, 1978.

Bahá'í International Community. *The Bahá'í World, 1995–1996.* Haifa: Bahá'í World Centre, 1997.

Bahá'u'lláh. *Gleanings from the Writings of Bahá'u'lláh.* Wilmette, IL: Bahá'í Publishing Trust, 1983.

— *The Tabernacle of Unity: Bahá'u'lláh's Responses to Manikchi Sahib and Other Writings.* Haifa: Bahá'í World Centre, 2006.

— *Tablets of Bahá'u'lláh Revealed after the Kitáb-i-Aqdas.* Translated by Habib Taherzadeh. Compiled by the Research Department of the Universal House of Justice at the Bahá'í World Centre. Wilmette, IL: Bahá'í Publishing Trust, 1998.

Bird, Otto. 'The Idea of Justice', in Brooks, Richard O. (ed.) *Plato and Modern Law*, pp. 575–618. London: Routledge, 2017.

---

88   Universal House of Justice, Letter to a National Spiritual Assembly, 28 March 2010.
89   'Abdu'l-Bahá, *Promulgation of Universal Peace*, pp. 334–5.

Compilation of Compilations. Prepared by the Universal House of Justice, 1963–1990, vols. 1 and 2. Victoria: Bahá'í Publications Australia, 1991.

Del Vecchio, Giorgio. 'Divine Justice and Human Justice'. *Juridical Review* 1, part 2 (August 1956), p. 157.

— *Justice: An Historical and Philosophical Essay.* Edinburgh: University Press, 1952.

Dworkin, Ronald. *Taking Rights Seriously*. Cambridge, MA: Harvard University Press, 1978.

Harari, Yuval Noah. *21 Lessons for the 21st Century*. New York: Random House, 2018.

Harries, Richard. 'The Complementarity Between Secular and Religious Perspectives of Human Rights', in Ghanea-Hercock, Nazila; Alan Stephens, and Ralph Walden (eds.), *Does God Believe in Human Rights?*, pp. 19–28. Leiden, Netherlands: Brill, 2007.

Huddleston, John. *The Search for a Just Society*. Oxford: George Ronald, 1989.

Jones, Harry W. 'Law and the Idea of Mankind'. 62 *Columbia Law Review* 752 (1962).

Kelsen, Hans. *What is Justice? Justice, Law, and Politics in the Mirror of Science; Collected Essays*. Berkeley: University of California Press, 1957.

Khadduri, Majid. *The Islamic Conception of Justice*. Baltimore: Johns Hopkins University Press, 2001.

Kissinger, Henry. *World Order*. New York: Penguin Press, 2015.

Libo, Sun. 'Morality, Law and Religion', in Lerche, Charles O. (ed.). *Towards the Most Great Justice: Elements of Justice in the New World Order*, pp. 57–73. London: Bahá'í Publishing Trust, 1996.

Murphy, Cornelius F. *The Search for World Order: A Study of Thought and Action*. Hingham, MA: Kluwer Academic Publishers, 1985.

Shoghi Effendi. *The Advent of Divine Justice*. Wilmette, IL: Bahá'í Publishing, 2006.

— *God Passes By*. Wilmette, IL: Bahá'í Publishing Trust, 1974.

— *The World Order of Bahá'u'lláh*. Wilmette, IL: Bahá'í Publishing Trust, 1982.

Stone, Julius. *Human Law and Human Justice*. Palo Alto: Stanford University Press, 1965.

Universal House of Justice. 'Issues Related to the Study of the Bahá'í Faith', 10 December 1992.

— 'To the Believers Gathered for the Events Marking the Completion of the Projects on Mount Carmel', 24 May 2001.

— 'To the World's Religious Leaders', April 2002.

— Letter to a National Spiritual Assembly, 28 March 2010.

Zarandí, Nabíl. *The Dawn-Breakers: Nabíl's Narrative of the Early Days of the Bahá'í Revelation*. Wilmette, IL: Bahá'í Publishing Trust, 1953.

3

Religious Plurality in Society: Some Preliminary Thoughts Pertaining to Legal Policy from One Bahá'í's Perspective

Emanuel V. Towfigh

Introduction

One of the most insistent smoldering conflicts in Western societies revolves around the question of how to deal with the increasing degree of religious plurality. In many European countries – in which I will include Turkey in this context – the conflict becomes manifest in, and in fact is symbolized by, discussions about the wearing of headscarves by Muslim women, the controversy over the slaughter of animals in accordance with religious rites, and concern about Islamic religious education. In other countries the same discussions take place, but focus on different religious symbols and customs. In France it is the wearing of headscarves (by schoolgirls); in Turkey it is the same issue (at universities, for example); in Finland it is the obligation of health insurance companies to cover the costs of circumcision carried out for religious reasons; in the Netherlands it is the law under which the public expression of disapproval of homosexuality is a criminal offense.[1]

The subject remains – especially, but by no means only, in regards to Islam – quite literally a 'burning issue'. Latent antagonisms flare up with grim regularity, serving as painful reminders of the unresolved conflicts and preventing multiple societies from attaining real peace and stability. This complex of themes relating to plurality in society, to the state, and to religion, will undoubtedly concern societies at large, and especially politics and religious communities, for some time to come. Ultimately, the ability to secure social stability in the long term will very much depend on finding a satisfactory solution to this fundamental problem. To solve the

---

1 See Oebbecke, 'Das "islamische Kopftuch" als Symbol', in particular pp. 600 and 606. Oebbecke also points out the difficulties concerning the use of symbols. See also Hildebrandt, Brocker, and Behr, 'Säkularisierung und Resakralisierung', p. 24; Langenfeld, 'Die Diskussion um das Kopftuch verkürzt das Problem der Integration', pp. 4, 7 et seq.; Magen, 'Staatskirchenrecht als symbolisches Recht?'; Schavan, 'Das Kopftuch ist ein politisches Symbol', p. 5.

conflict, societies, as in other cases of conflict, draw on the law for coordinating and balancing the different interests at stake.

Against this background I would like, in the following pages, to give very preliminary and indeed limited consideration from a Bahá'í perspective to the question of how religious plurality in society should be dealt with legally – even though the Bahá'ís themselves have neither a clergy nor special items of obligatory clothing such as a *kippa* or headscarf. I will seek to point out ways of dealing with religious plurality that promote a peaceful social order. The Bahá'í teachings may be able to make a particularly valuable contribution to this inquiry, since Bahá'ís do not have any vested interests in the current conflicts, and may thus be seen as 'honest brokers' contributing to the current academic and societal discourses.

In this chapter, I shall address the issue in four main parts:

- First, a description of the current situations of social conflict from the point of view of legal policy.
- Second, a brief attempt to develop abstract legal approaches to seeking a solution from a Bahá'í perspective.
- Third, I will try to bring these elements together. And
- Fourth, we will apply the conclusions to a specific problem, the wearing of the Islamic headscarf.

Analysis of Situations of Social Conflict

The principal driving force behind the pluralization of human society, including the growth of religious plurality, emerges from the now all-encompassing process of globalization,[2] along with the political, economic, and cultural changes it has brought about. This phenomenon originated in developments that took place in the mid-20th century and was given new impetus by the ending of the Cold War. Globalization – together with the concomitant phenomena of multiculturalism and multi-polarity – has dramatically increased the complexity of world politics and hence the insecurity of both governments and the governed,[3] which Habermas described as 'new complexity' (*neue Unübersichtlichkeit*).[4] The complexity of the challenges arising from pluralization makes it impossible to deal with all its aspects

---

2   The late former German Federal President Roman Herzog rightly treated globalization as a fact and therefore preferred to use the term 'globality'. In this connection, see his speech at the opening of the World Economic Forum in Davos on 28 January 1999, available at https://www.bundespraesident. de/SharedDocs/Reden/DE/Roman-Herzog/Reden/1999/01/19990128_Rede.html (last visited on 27 March 2025). He stated: 'When I addressed this Forum in 1995, the subject was still globalization. Today we already speak of globality. The process has developed into a state of affairs. Globality is shaping our transition to the next century. Its effects are evident in politics, the economy, culture, and society.'

3   See Mahmoudi, 'Obligation and Responsibility in Constructing a World Civilization', p. 147; Walter, 'Religiöse Toleranz im Verfassungsstaat', p. 77; Lepard, 'Deficiencies in the Global Legal Order and the Reformative Potential of Bahá'í Principles'.

4   Translation of the title of a work by Jürgen Habermas, 'Die Neue Unübersichtlichkeit'.

here. By analyzing specific, manageable problems in a series of small steps, as is typical of a jurist's approach, I shall seek to draw attention to two issues that might well be regarded as fundamental in dealing with the question of religious plurality.

The Conflict Between Legal Systems

The first of these issues touches on the conflict between state and religious legal orders. This conflict arises where different and often contradictory forms of behavior are required under religious law, on the one hand, and state law, on the other. Because part of this conflict arises in law, at least a part of the solution to the overall conflict needs to be delivered by law.

A few examples may illustrate this conflict:

1. The law of some of the German *Länder* (states) prohibits the wearing of a headscarf (or any other religious symbol) by a female teacher, even if the wearing of such a symbol is required under religious law. In France, the wearing of a headscarf is even forbidden to pupils, as it is in Turkey for university students. In society, particularly in Germany, France, and Turkey, the question of how to deal with the headscarf worn in public is discussed with great passion. One of the two main factions in the argument calls for the establishment of a 'primary culture' that everyone living in the respective country should adopt or with which they should at least comply, while the second faction advocates a form of multiculturalism largely disregarding a need for social cohesion. I will come back to both views – and to an approach inspired by the Bahá'í teachings – later in the chapter.

2. Potentially, states could pass a law establishing sexual equality, under which men and women must be granted equal access to all occupations. With such a law in place, the restriction of the priesthood to men would undoubtedly become problematic. This example may sound contrived, but there have been discussions in German law journals as to whether the occupation of 'female Catholic priest'[5] has in effect been introduced by European Union law.

3. However, there can even be problems at a more mundane level. If Jews and Muslims were forbidden (as they in fact are in Switzerland) to slaughter animals in accordance with religious rites to ensure that the meat is *kosher* or *halal*, the logical consequence is that they have to adopt a vegetarian diet. Pointing out that the eating of meat is not a religious duty would not seem to present a very convincing argument.

Conflicts between different legal systems represent a familiar problem (particularly in private international law), but in the given context they have only become viru- lent as a result of the religious pluralization of society. That is because, in European

---

5   Compare Waldhoff, 'Kirchliche Selbstbestimmung und Europarecht'.

legal culture, state and religious law have traditionally been finely tuned to one another. Whereas in the past the state was based on a more or less uniform culture and, at least for a time in Europe, on an undivided church, we now have pluralist states with a plurality of religions. Historically, the legal principles governing the laws relating to religion, in particular, had the status of special law in view of their relevance for one or two Christian churches.[6] As a result of its historical development, the state law governing religion is specifically tailored to suit the Christian churches, and both State and Church have adapted themselves accordingly.

However, this legal garment does not really fit new customers such as Muslims or Bahá'ís.[7] Even so-called secular or laical countries such as France and Turkey have manifold and coordinated relations with the traditional religious systems (in the case of Turkey, with Islam) that call for rearrangement in an increasingly pluralistic society. The questions arising with regard to the non-Christian faith communities, such as the Muslim community, are, in the words of one scholar, 'an expression of divergent coordinate systems'.[8] In order to ensure the equal treatment of faith communities, the law must take their peculiarities into account, so that the character of the law is necessarily required to change, in the same way that a chamber quartet has to be conducted differently than a symphony orchestra.

At the same time, the new faith communities (like all other new cultural factors) present a challenge for the established institutions and large sections of society. For example, in a Christian environment, the crucifix does not antagonize anyone, but today some people find the crucifix disconcerting, while for others the Islamic headscarf can be equally discomforting.

Religion as a Factor in Identity Formation

This leads us to a second area of conflict, and to the next set of issues I will discuss here: namely, the fact that crucifixes and headscarves represent religious symbols that can play a powerful role in personal identity formation. Moreover, religion – like state order – claims to influence all aspects of human life, so it also has a public effect (as have its symbols), the extent of which differs in the various religions and faith communities. This public aspect of religion often generates social tensions.

The majority of what may, in a broad sense, be described as 'cultural' conflicts actually arise from religion – for example, when people speak of a *Leitkultur* ('primary culture'), or when we discuss questions of integration and migration. Even when cultural and religious conflicts can be differentiated, their issues often intermingle. This demonstrates itself particularly clearly in countries such as Greece and Italy, where religion completely pervades the national identity of the

---

6   Leisner, 'Das kirchliche Krankenhaus im Staatskirchenrecht', p. 13. See also Loschelder, 'Der Islam und die religionsrechtliche Ordnung des Grundgesetzes', pp. 150, 156, 173; Weiler, *Ein christliches Europa*, passim; Czermak, 'Das Religionsverfassungsrecht im Spiegel der Tatsachen', p. 570.

7   Oebbecke, 'Tua res agitur', p. 115.

8   Loschelder, 'Der Islam und die religionsrechtliche Ordnung des Grundgesetzes', p. 150.

population. Although Feuerbach once said that the Enlightenment had turned the Christian into the human being, the absoluteness of this assertion is doubtful.[9]

The significance of religion for the formation of cultural identity means that the newly appearing faith communities with their divergent systems of beliefs and values – Islam in all its different variants as well as other religions such as Buddhism, Hinduism, or the Bahá'í Faith – must necessarily present a challenge to the cultural identity of those around them. The conflicts mentioned above, such as the headscarf issue, demonstrate this dynamic. Religious pluralization, in turn, leads to general cultural pluralization. This pluralization intensifies still further when religious pluralization derives at least in part from immigration, and when the immigrants come from cultural environments where their religion closely relates to national identity. The problem of divergent values resulting 'exclusively' from religious differences is further complicated by the difficulties associated with immigration and integration, which makes it impossible to draw a clear distinction between the two.

Certainly, the discussions in Europe are not concerned merely with Islam or immigration and Islam's adaptation to existing systems; rather, the issues raised act as a catalyst for religious and political discussion of how liberal democracies can deal with socio-cultural conflicts brought about by religious and cultural plurality. In view of the complexity and confusion of the attendant issues, the motives of those participating in such discussions are often unclear – even when the arguments dress themselves in merely legal garments. That, too, creates potential for conflict.

Sections of society, the political establishment, and official institutions ignore this reality for various reasons, not all of which can be completely resolved. These reasons include the fear of being swamped by foreign influences, existing or anticipated problems with integration, the possible future problem of redistribution, or simply critical attitudes towards religion in general.

Against this background new questions arise, such as: Can religion be displaced as a factor in cultural identity? How much cultural divergence (i.e. diversity) can the state afford to allow, and how much convergence (i.e. unity) must it call for or even demand? Let's consider those questions, which hold the key for a possible solution to these conflicts, in more detail from a perspective inspired by the Bahá'í teachings.

Approaches to Finding a Solution from a Bahá'í Perspective

Broadly speaking, human conflicts regarding religion seem to be just as much a part of the problem as a part of the solution. According to one scholar:

> There are problems that cannot be solved within the terms set by modernity, for the simple reason that they are not procedural, but rather valuational or, to use

---

9   See Armstrong, *Battle for God*, pp. ix et seq., xii, and 364 et seq.

the simple word, moral . . . The human project is inescapably a moral project. That is one reason why the great faiths, with their history of reflection on moral issues, must be part of the conversation.[10]

Speaking of the purpose of religion, 'Abdu'l-Bahá said:

> Religion should unite all hearts and cause wars and disputes to vanish from the face of the earth, give birth to spirituality, and bring life and light to each heart. If religion becomes a cause of dislike, hatred and division, it were better to be without it, and to withdraw from such a religion would be a truly religious act. For it is clear that the purpose of a remedy is to cure; but if the remedy should only aggravate the complaint it had better be left alone. Any religion which is not a cause of love and unity is no religion. All the holy prophets were as doctors to the soul; they gave prescriptions for the healing of mankind; thus any remedy that causes disease does not come from the great and supreme Physician.[11]

It must therefore be in the interests of religion to contribute to meeting the challenges associated with religious pluralization and to seek a solution to the problems. What conclusions can be drawn from the Bahá'í teachings regarding the issues raised here?

Resolving Conflicts Between Legal Systems

To begin with, then: how does the Bahá'í Faith deal with the conflict between state and religious order? It is an entirely unresolved question, and currently a controversial one, whether – and if so in what form – secularity will play a part in a potential future Bahá'í political theory. While it remains speculative to say today what kind of political order the Bahá'í teachings envisage, Bahá'u'lláh did reveal clear statements that set the standard for encountering worldly authority. He writes:

> The one true God, exalted be His glory, hath ever regarded, and will continue to regard, the hearts of men as His own, His exclusive possession. All else, whether pertaining to land or sea, whether riches or glory, He hath bequeathed unto the Kings and rulers of the earth.[12]

> It is not Our wish to lay hands on your kingdoms. Our mission is to seize and possess the hearts of men.[13]

---

10   Sacks, *Dignity of Difference*, p. 195. See also Bogner, 'Säkularisierung als Programmierungswechsel'; Arani, 'Religion als Medium der Integration: die Bahá'í in Deutschland'.
11   'Abdu'l-Bahá, *Paris Talks*, p. 130.
12   Bahá'u'lláh, *Gleanings*, p. 206.
13   Bahá'u'lláh, *Kitáb-i-Aqdas*, para. 83.

The Primacy of State Authority

With those words, the Bahá'í teachings reinforce and legitimate the imperative for state power and its primacy over religious law in worldly affairs.

Bahá'u'lláh declares from the outset that He does not raise any claims of profane or political power: He claims nothing but the human heart. He even teaches that along with state power, the:

> . . . instruments which are essential to the immediate protection, the security and assurance of the human race have been entrusted to the hands, and lie in the grasp, of the governors of human society.[14]

In Bahá'u'lláh's terms, these 'governors' are responsible for establishing the 'reign of justice'[15] in the world. Bahá'u'lláh's expression of respect for just rulers in general – He refers to them as 'God's shadow on earth'[16] – and the duty of the believers to display loyalty and obedience[17] towards the authorities in whichever country they live,[18] reinforce this interpretation. So also does the injunction not to 'contend with those who wield authority over the people'[19] and not to 'stir up mischief in the land'.[20] Also, Bahá'u'lláh's utter condemnations of tyranny[21] and anarchy[22] fully concur with this view; in fact, they are only necessary because of the primary role accorded to state authority throughout the Bahá'í teachings.

Hence, for Bahá'ís the state possesses the authority to make final legal decisions – not religion. This means one implication of the Bahá'í teachings is that the right to lay down ultimate and authoritative rulings – for example, in the case of a conflict between state and religious law – is the prerogative of the state.

Limits of State Authority

However, the statements by Bahá'u'lláh cited above also indicate the immanent

---

14 Bahá'u'lláh, *Gleanings*, p. 207.
15 ibid. p. 218.
16 ibid. p. 237; Bahá'u'lláh, *Summons of the Lord of Hosts*, Suriy-i-Haykal, para. 217.
17 See, for example, Bahá'u'lláh, *Gleanings*, p. 102; Bahá'u'lláh, *Epistle to the Son of the Wolf*, p. 86.
18 Irrespective of the ruler's person. In this connection, see Bahá'u'lláh, *Summons of the Lord of Hosts*, Suriy-i-Haykal, para. 217: 'A just king is the shadow of God on earth. All should seek shelter under the shadow of his justice, and rest in the shade of his favour. This is not a matter which is either specific or limited in its scope, that it might be restricted to one or another person, inasmuch as the shadow telleth of the One Who casteth it.'
19 Bahá'u'lláh, *Kitáb-i-Aqdas*, para. 95.
20 ibid. para. 64.
21 Bahá'u'lláh, *Tablets of Bahá'u'lláh*, para. 11:11; see also Bahá'u'lláh, *Gleanings*, pp. 232–40.
22 Compare Bahá'u'lláh, *Kitáb-i-Aqdas*, para. 123: 'Liberty must, in the end, lead to sedition, whose flames none can quench. Thus warneth you He Who is the Reckoner, the All-Knowing. Know ye that the embodiment of liberty and its symbol is the animal. That which beseemeth man is submission unto such restraints as will protect him from his own ignorance, and guard him against the harm of the mischief-maker. Liberty causeth man to overstep the bounds of propriety, and to infringe on the dignity of his station. It debaseth him to the level of extreme depravity and wickedness.'; Schaefer, 'Ficicchia's Presentation of Bahá'í Doctrine', p. 306 (with further references).

limits of state authority. These limits are to be found at the point where secular powers attempt to wield authority over the hearts of individuals, for example when they affect human dignity, freedom of religion, and freedom of conscience, or human rights more generally.[23] The state cannot claim control of a person's 'innermost being'; it must not interfere with the conscience of the individual. According to the Bahá'í teachings, citizens do not have to put up with such interference.[24] Therefore, Bahá'ís in Iran do not recant their faith – and rather accept severe persecutions or death – even though ordered to do so by the government; they are, in some sense, 'disobedient' to the government, but in this case their refusal to recant is justified by Bahá'u'lláh's teaching that worldly rulers must not interfere in what touches men's hearts.

But when does such interference take place, and who has the right to decide whether the state has overstepped the bounds of its sphere of authority? The boundaries are undoubtedly fluid and cannot be clearly defined. However, it is logical that the final decision in this sphere belongs to the individual and not to the state, because the latter can never judge what – allegorically speaking – is in the heart of the former; moreover, it would then be too easy to undermine the fundamental human right of a person not to have his or her innermost thoughts and feelings subjected to interference. Indeed, according to the Bahá'í teachings, this is a right of God, not of governments.

It therefore follows that guaranteeing human liberty also entails prohibiting the investigation of peoples' motives; the state is obliged to accept the limits defined by the individual subject. Otherwise the state would arrogate to itself the competence to authoritatively define by interpretation the 'true meaning' of religious teachings. Conversely, however, the individual cannot be permitted constantly to appeal to his or her conscience and thus incessantly undermine the decision-making authority of the state.

The solution arrived at by the German Federal Constitutional Court in evaluating whether the performance of a certain action falls within the sphere of religious freedom seems to constitute a similar, and prudent, approach.[25] According to the principle adopted by the Court, the decision as to whether something is an integral aspect of religious practice and is therefore absolutely binding is left to the individual, but it may be subjected to a plausibility test by the state. Thus, the prohibition on the investigation of motives is upheld, while the possibility of abuse is largely ruled out. From this it follows that, in cases of conflict between the different legal orders, the individual believer will be obliged to consider the hier-

---

23   Thus, in *A Traveler's Narrative*, p. 119, 'Abdu'l-Bahá states: 'Convictions and ideas are within the scope of the comprehension of the King of kings, not of kings; and soul and conscience are between the fingers of control of the Lord of hearts, not of [His] servants.' See also 'Abdu'l-Bahá, *Promulgation of Universal Peace*, pp. 91, 197, 390; Shoghi Effendi, Letter 11 February 1934, in Shoghi Effendi, *Light of Divine Guidance*, vol. 1, pp. 53 et seq., in which Shoghi Effendi gives guidance to the German believers after Adolf Hitler seized power in Germany.

24   Compare Towfigh, *Die rechtliche Verfassung von Religionsgemeinschaften*, p. 153.

25   See the Court's 'Bahá'í' decision: Bundesverfassungsgericht, Beschluss v. 2. Februar 1991 – 2 BvR 263/86, BVerfGE 83, p. 341 et seq. (https://www.servat.unibe.ch/dfr/bv083341.html).

archy of laws within the religious legal order when attempting to decide whether a state prohibition or decree conflicts with an essential religious law to such an extent that it can be regarded as interference in his 'innermost being' and therefore justifies a form of civil disobedience.

Not all – in fact, probably only very few fundamental – religious norms really affect the individual's innermost being; in most cases of conflict, the individual will therefore decide to follow state law. Of course, this does not exclude the possibility of the individual seeking to defend himself by recourse to the means provided by state law, that is, by taking legal action. Only when the state has pronounced its final decision is the believer confronted with the question of how to deal with this conflict as an individual. In other words, only if a decision between obedience to a state law and compliance with a religious requirement is completely unavoidable does the Bahá'í law legitimate a decision to ignore either the state or the religious norm.

From a Bahá'í perspective religious communities do not have the same right to overrule the state's final decision, as only the individual can appeal to his conscience. This does not mean that Bahá'í communities or organizations such as the Bahá'í International Community would not make use of all legal means to gain the liberties necessary to let an individual and community live according to the standards of the Bahá'í teachings; but they do respect that the ultimate decision rests with the state authority. The Iranian Bahá'ís exemplified this view by following all state orders to dissolve their religious administrative bodies in Iran.[26]

Religion's Role in Identity Formation from a Bahá'í Perspective

Let us leave this question for the moment, and turn again to the issue of religion as a factor in identity formation and Bahá'í ideas on the subject, before drawing these two proposed solutions together and illustrating their application using the example of the Islamic headscarf. The initial question is whether, from a Bahá'í perspective, it is possible to find a compromise between the extreme positions of an exclusivist 'primary culture' on the one hand and laissez-faire multiculturalism on the other. Both of these approaches express, in their own ways, a lack of respect for differences. Our societies need a compromise solution – one that has the potential to regulate social conflicts, diminish prejudices, and effectively reduce the risk of a clash of civilizations.

The meaning and origin of the term 'identity' – '(essential) oneness'[27] – indicate the very Bahá'í principle whose realization forms the indispensable foundation for the peaceful coexistence of all human beings: the principle of unity.[28] Bahá'u'lláh admonishes humanity:

---

26   Universal House of Justice, 13 September 1983, in Universal House of Justice, *Messages from the Universal House of Justice 1963–1986*, p. 377.
27   See Guralnik et al. eds., *Webster's New World Dictionary*.
28   See Barnes, 'Rendering Service to the Oneness of Humanity and the Quest for Justice in the Global Legal Order'; Emmel, 'Equality and Security'.

The well-being of mankind, its peace and security, are unattainable unless and until its unity is firmly established. This unity can never be achieved so long as the counsels which the Pen of the Most High hath revealed are suffered to pass unheeded.[29]

But what is behind the concept of 'unity'? The principle of unity constitutes a 'meta-principle', the primal pivot of creation, which pervades all realms of life. Unity means that the aim – the unification of all contradictory and complementary elements – occurs not by forcing all aspects into line, but rather by bringing them together while preserving the identity of each individual aspect. This 'unity in diversity' preserves the individual elements in order to ensure the sustained coherence of the organism as a whole, while strongly emphasizing the importance of social diversity. 'Abdu'l-Bahá explains this principle in metaphorical terms:

Consider the flowers of a garden: though differing in kind, colour, form and shape, yet, inasmuch as they are refreshed by the waters of one spring, revived by the breath of one wind, invigorated by the rays of one sun, this diversity increaseth their charm, and addeth unto their beauty. Thus when that unifying force, the penetrating influence of the Word of God, taketh effect, the difference of customs, manners, habits, ideas, opinions and dispositions embellisheth the world of humanity. This diversity, this difference is like the naturally created dissimilarity and variety of the limbs and organs of the human body, for each one contributeth to the beauty, efficiency and perfection of the whole. When these different limbs and organs come under the influence of man's sovereign soul, and the soul's power pervadeth the limbs and members, veins and arteries of the body, then difference reinforceth harmony, diversity strengtheneth love, and multiplicity is the greatest factor for coordination.[30]

According to this quotation, that which unifies while preserving individual identity creates something entirely new. Although the original elements are still visible, their combination produces a harmonious reality that contains superior qualities.

This rejection of dualism and the striving for the unification of contrary elements is present throughout the revealed works of Bahá'u'lláh. Balance and unity always define the goal. These principles constitute a leitmotiv that runs through all the Bahá'í teachings. That may sound very abstract, but it can be illustrated by means of several concrete examples:

1. In the material world we are familiar with the principle of combining metals to create alloys. With alloys, the qualities of materials that may be unusable by themselves are completely changed and improved through combination with other materials. Iron, for instance, has many shortcomings when used alone: it rusts

---

29   Bahá'u'lláh, *Gleanings*, p. 286.
30   'Abdu'l-Bahá, *Selections*, p. 291.

quickly, is not very flexible, and so on. However, if it is improved by adding other elements and made into steel, it becomes a very valuable industrial product. When the structure of steel is analyzed, both the iron and the added substances remain recognizable, but combined together they assume completely different qualities.

2. When applied to social relations, the principle of unity reflects itself in marriage: here, too, husband and wife come together, each retaining their own personal identities on the one hand, but also contributing to something new, the marriage and the family, on the other.

3. Human dialogue or discourse also follows the same principle if conducted in a spirit of honesty, integrity, and openness. In the words of 'Abdu'l-Bahá: 'The shining spark of truth cometh forth only after the clash of differing opinions.'[31]

4. A completely new quality of understanding could be reached if humankind were to implement Bahá'u'lláh's principle that truth should be investigated using both religion and science – each applying its own criteria, without either regarding itself as superior to the other, and without the antagonism that frequently exists between them.

5. Finally, we each seek the highest state of unification – the unity of humanity with our Creator. Bahá'u'lláh has revealed in *The Hidden Words*: 'O Son of Man! If thou lovest Me, turn away from thyself; and if thou seekest My pleasure, regard not thine own; that thou mayest die in Me and I may eternally live in thee.'[32]

That may initially sound paradoxical: unification with God means complete abandonment of self, yet the life of God in man – eternal life – means that individuality is not lost. Shoghi Effendi's statement, when he says that the soul is the immortal identity of the individual, can be understood in this light.[33]

Of course, that is all easier said in theory than done in practice. Anyone who has tried to produce an alloy with certain qualities in his or her school chemistry lessons will know what difficulties can be encountered. Where social relationships are concerned, things are even more complicated because – unlike in chemistry – the elements react differently every time! This concept of unity requires a high degree of human maturity, an understanding of reality that focuses on self-responsibility, a consensus on basic human values, and a growing realization that humanity constitutes a single interdependent community. This culture of unity, something humankind still needs to develop, does not already exist – despite the views of some adherents of the exclusivist concept of a 'primary culture'.

---

31 ibid. p. 87.
32 Bahá'u'lláh, *Hidden Words*, Arabic, no. 7.
33 Shoghi Effendi, *Arohanui: Letters of Shoghi Effendi to New Zealand*, p. 90. See also the letters of Shoghi Effendi reproduced in Hornby, *Lights of Guidance*, no. 386 and no. 1820.

Mahatma Gandhi's pointed remark in response to a question posed by a journalist illustrates the point. Asked what he thought of Western culture, he is said to have replied: 'I think it would be a good idea!'[34]

The Bahá'í Faith's response to the question of cultural identity, then, dwells in the concept of diversity – in the sense of Rosa Luxemburg's idea of the freedom to think differently (*'die Freiheit der Andersdenkenden'*). This freedom and diversity are limited by the goal of social order – which creates, at the same time, the secure framework that preserves freedom. From a Bahá'í point of view, the framework of the social order must ultimately be drawn up in accordance with the divine law so that 'true liberty'[35] can be attained. As noted above, Bahá'u'lláh admonishes humankind that true unity cannot be achieved 'so long as the counsels which the Pen of the Most High hath revealed are suffered to pass unheeded'.

A Synthesis of the Approaches

After this brief excursion into the realm of the abstract and theoretical, let us return to the original question: How can the principles of the Bahá'í Faith, with its recognition of the secular nature and decision-making authority of the state and the principle of unity, inform the way in which law negotiates minority group rights?

In the first place, it explains in theological terms why neither an exclusivist 'primary culture' nor rampant multiculturalism – the two concepts discussed in recent European legal literature – are suitable principles on which to build a society. A 'primary culture' that considers other cultures to be subordinate – and demands complete convergence – neglects the importance of social diversity, leads to a monoculture, and therefore cannot ensure stable social cohesion. On the other hand, multiculturalism – the unlimited endorsement of divergence – loses sight of the overriding goal of social unity and risks the creation of parallel and potentially divisive sub-societies. Both of these approaches show a lack of respect for difference and an unwillingness to collaborate for the achievement of social cohesion. In the final analysis, the supporters of both approaches shy away from serious engagement with the unfamiliar; they create obstacles to the discovery of a shared identity, hiding instead behind a questionable concept of identity defined solely by dissociation and separation from others.

On the other hand, the Bahá'í concept of unity ultimately legitimates state intervention when social unity is endangered. If the goal is to preserve the diversity of the different elements in order to create a sustainable state of unity in the organism as a whole, then obviously that diversity cannot be allowed to go so far as to endanger unity. To put it briefly: the preservation of diversity outlines the fundamental principle, while the securing of unity delineates its limits or corrective elements.

From the perspective developed here, the state is authorized to protect the unity

---

34 Utley, 'A Definition of Folklore', p. 4.
35 Bahá'u'lláh, *Gleanings*, p. 336.

of society and to permit or to restrict diversity to the extent that is necessary to achieve that purpose. State and religious law and the striving for unity go hand in hand in this regard.

But when is social unity endangered? It is necessary to recognize that the ultimate authority to make decisions on this matter rests with the state. Owing to the prohibition on the investigation of motives and because unity is a matter of attitude,[36] however, the state must not take as its starting point the alleged convictions or ideals of the individual or any religious doctrine – however determined and perhaps interpreted by the state. Rather, it must base its judgment solely on the actual actions of the individual. If these actions pose a danger to social unity, the state can limit or prohibit them, at least from the point of view of legal theology. The question as to whether the unity of society is endangered must not be left solely to interpretation by other legal experts – for that would lead to the dictatorship of the majority – but should be determined by the shared values of a social framework that respects individual and minority liberty.

The Headscarf Issue

Do these considerations have any bearing on specific cases, such as the matter of the headscarf worn by a state-employed schoolteacher (as in Germany) or by a schoolgirl (as in France) or student (as in Turkey)? Yes, they do.

In principle, the headscarf worn by a Muslim teacher ought to be regarded as a sign of religious diversity. If the teacher wears it because she believes her religion requires her to do so, and if she holds the opinion that the headscarf does not signify an inferior social status for women, the state ought generally to accept this practice. It is the teacher herself who decides about the symbolic significance of her headscarf – not the state. In case the statement made by the teacher is plausible, the state has no right to investigate her motives above and beyond this; instead it must acknowledge her understanding of Islamic doctrine. Thus, it is not up to the state's authority to determine whether certain practices are authentically religious. Otherwise the state would actually be interpreting Islam – and interfering in the individual's conscience. From this viewpoint, as long as the wearing of headscarves does not lead to social friction and does not endanger social unity, the state has no right to intervene. On the other hand, when social unity is at risk, it can impose limits or – if there is no milder and equally effective means – it can prohibit the wearing of headscarves.[37]

Does the teacher who wears a headscarf threaten the unity of society? I would argue she does not – because compliance with this religious requirement is (as yet) compatible with the upholding of social order and social values. It does not in itself

---

36   See Holley, 'Introduction'.
37   In the recent European social and political discussions concerning the headscarf, the issue under consideration has been a limitation on the wearing of a headscarf, not its complete prohibition. Only the state-employed teacher in the one case, or the schoolgirl or student in the other, are to be forbidden to wear the headscarf during lessons.

constitute a threat to the framework of the social order, provided, on the basis of the wearer's statement, that wearing the headscarf is a matter of completely voluntary compliance with a religious requirement. Wearing a headscarf is not *in itself* evidence of a hostile attitude towards the identity of the society, nor does wearing it in any way disrupt social cohesion. A different situation arises, however, if the teacher engages in any form of indoctrination. In that case, *that particular teacher* could be declared unsuitable for public service employment and the state could take measures against her. This, of course, is unrelated to the fact of her wearing a headscarf; she could indoctrinate students and *not* be wearing one. In other words, according to the solution proposed here, the wearing of a headscarf itself is not a problem; only certain prohibited behavior would constitute a problem.

If, contrary to the views expressed here, the state were to consider wearing a headscarf to present a threat to unity and were to forbid teachers to wear it, this decision would fall within the authority of the state to make final decisions. However, before making such a far-reaching decision, the state should consult with the stakeholders – those members of the religious communities wishing to wear a headscarf, and those societal groups that oppose such a practice. If such a decision were taken after careful consideration, for the individual teacher affected this could mean a conflict between the two legal orders, which can only be avoided by choosing a different career or a different employer. Were the state to forbid all women to wear the headscarf, those affected would have to consider whether this prohibition is something that affects their inner spiritual life – in which case they would be justified in wearing the headscarf against the legal command – or not, in which case they would have to remove it. Of course, many Muslim women wearing the headscarf have given serious thought to the *spiritual necessity* of wearing it even *before* such an edict would come down from the state; but in the light of such a new situation, they would need to reconsider this decision.

Summary

In this chapter I have tried to make a humble first step towards developing solutions for one of the most eminent societal challenges modern Western societies face today: the conflict of 'worldly' law with religious ordinances, a conflict that gets more difficult to solve the larger religious plurality becomes. Accordingly, while states and their legal orders should strive to cultivate and allow for societal diversity, they are in principle entitled to rule against religious laws and ordinances when and if the unity of society is at stake. Such state law limiting an individual in living his or her life in accordance with religious standards may, however, never infringe upon any individual's conscience, or religious laws that pertain to one's innermost being. In case a state does indeed transgress this boundary, those individuals adversely affected by such a legal norm are free to disregard it and live according to their religious standard.

Bibliography

'Abdu'l-Bahá. *The Promulgation of Universal Peace: Talks Delivered by 'Abdu'l-Bahá During His Visit to the United States and Canada in 1912.* Wilmette, IL: Bahá'í Publishing Trust, 1982.

— *Selections from the Writings of 'Abdu'l-Bahá.* Compiled by the Research Department of the Universal House of Justice. Translated by a Committee at the Bahá'í World Centre and by Marzieh Gail. Wilmette, IL: Bahá'í Publishing Trust, 1996.

— *A Traveler's Narrative: Written to Illustrate the Episode of the Báb.* Translated by Edward G. Browne. Wilmette, IL: Bahá'í Publishing Trust, 1980.

Arani, Aliye Yegane. 'Religion als Medium der Integration: die Bahá'í in Deutschland', in Gerdien Jonker (ed.). *Kern und Rand: Religiöse Minderheiten aus der Türkei in Deutschland*, pp. 91–114. Berlin: Das Arabische Buch, 1999.

Armstrong, Karen. *The Battle for God.* New York: Random House, 2000.

Bahá'u'lláh. *Gleanings from the Writings of Bahá'u'lláh.* Translated by Shoghi Effendi. Wilmette, IL: Bahá'í Publishing Trust, 1976.

— *The Hidden Words.* Translated by Shoghi Effendi. Wilmette, IL: Bahá'í Publishing, 2002.

— *The Kitáb-i-Aqdas: The Most Holy Book.* Wilmette, IL: Bahá'í Publishing Trust, 1993.

— *The Summons of the Lord of Hosts: Tablets of Bahá'u'lláh.* Haifa: Bahá'í World Centre, 2002.

Barnes, Kiser. 'Rendering Service to the Oneness of Humanity and the Quest for Justice in the Global Legal Order', in Lepard, Brian D. (ed.). *Seeking Global Justice: Bahá'í Visions for Legal Reform.*

Bogner, Daniel. 'Säkularisierung als Programmierungswechsel: Der frühneuzeitliche Rollentausch von Religion und Politik', in Hildebrandt, Mathias; Manfred Brocker, and Hartmut Behr (eds.). *Säkularisierung und Resakralisierung in westlichen Gesellschaften: Ideengeschichtliche und theoretische Perspektiven*, pp. 52 et seq. Wiesbaden, Verlag für Sozialwissenschaften, 2001.

Czermak, Gerhard. 'Das Religionsverfassungsrecht im Spiegel der Tatsachen: Kritische Hinweise zum Verhältnis von Verfassungsrecht und Verfassungswirklichkeit'. *Zeitschrift für Rechtspolitik* 34. Jahrg., H. 12 (December 2001), pp. 565–70.

Emmel, Aaron. 'Equality and Security', in Lepard, Brian D. (ed.). *Seeking Global Justice: Bahá'í Visions for Legal Reform.*

Guralnik, David B. et al. (eds.). *Webster's New World Dictionary of the American Language.* Grand Central Pub. 1987.

Hildebrandt, Mathias; Manfred Brocker, and Hartmut Behr. 'Säkularisierung und Resakralisierung', in Hildebrandt, Mathias; Manfred Brocker, and Hartmut Behr (eds.). *Säkularisierung und Resakralisierung in westlichen Gesellschaften*, pp. 9–28. Wiesbaden, Verlag für Sozialwissenschaften, 2001.

Holley, Horace. 'Introduction', in 'Abdu'l-Bahá, *The Secret of Divine Civilization*, pp. v–xi. Translated from the original Persian text by Marzieh Gail. 2nd ed. Wilmette, IL: Bahá'í Publishing Trust, 1970.

Hornby, Helen Bassett, *Lights of Guidance: A Bahá'í Reference File.* 6th ed. New Delhi: Bahá'í Publishing Trust, 1999.

Langenfeld, Christine. 'Die Diskussion um das Kopftuch verkürzt das Problem der Integration'. *Recht der Jugend und des Bildungswesens*, vol. 52 (2004), pp. 4–10.

Leisner, Walter. 'Das kirchliche Krankenhaus im Staatskirchenrecht der Bundesrepublik Deutschland', in Marré, Heiner, and Johannes Stüting (eds.). *Essener Gespräche zum Thema Staat und Kirche*, pp. 9–61. vol. 17. Münster: Aschendorff, 1983.

Lepard, Brian D. 'Deficiencies in the Global Legal Order and the Reformative Potential of Bahá'í Principles', in Lepard, Brian D. (ed.). *Seeking Global Justice: Bahá'í Visions for Legal Reform.*

Loschelder, Wolfgang. 'Der Islam und die religionsrechtliche Ordnung des Grundgesetzes', in Marré, Heiner and Johannes Stüting (eds.). *Essener Gespräche zum Thema Staat und Kirche*, pp. 149–73, vol. 20. Münster: Aschendorff, 1986.

Magen, Stefan. 'Staatskirchenrecht als symbolisches Recht', in Lehmann, Harmut (ed.). *Koexistenz und Konflikt von Religionen im vereinten Europa*, pp. 30–53. Göttingen: Wallstein Verlag, 2004.

Mahmoudi, Hoda. 'Obligation and Responsibility in Constructing a World Civilization', in *Bahá'í World 2002–2003: An International Record*, pp. 147–77. Haifa: Bahá'í World Centre, 2004.

Mühlschlegel, Ursula and Günter Nicke. *'Und alle Wege werden frei': Das Leben der Hand der Sache Gottes Dr Adelbert Mühlschlegel*. Hofheim: Bahá'í Publishing, 1999.

Oebbecke, Janbernd. 'Das "islamische Kopftuch" als Symbol', in Muckel, Stefan (ed.). *Kirche und Religion im sozialen Rechtsstaat: Festschrift für Wolfgang Rüfner zum 70. Geburtstag*, pp. 593–5. Berlin: Duncker & Humblot, 2003.

— 'Tua res agitur – Die Rechte der Minderheitsreligionen und die Stellung der christlichen Kirchen: Warum die Diskussion über den Islam für die Kirchen wichtig ist', in Geerlings, Wilhelm; and Thomas Sternberg (eds.). *Kirchen in der Minderheit: Sozialgeschichtliche Untersuchungen – pastorale Aspekte*, pp. 105–35. Münster: Dialog-Medien und Emmaus-Reisen, 2004.

Sacks, Jonathan. *The Dignity of Difference: How to Avoid the Clash of Civilizations.* Rev. ed. Continuum, 2002.

Schaefer, Udo. 'Ficicchia's Presentation of Bahá'í Doctrine', in Schaefer, Udo; Nicola Towfigh, and Ulrich Gollmer. *Making the Crooked Straight: A Contribution to Bahá'í Apologetics*, pp. 260–316. Oxford: George Ronald, 2000.

Schavan, Annette. 'Das Kopftuch ist ein politisches Symbol'. *ZAR: Zeitschrift für Ausländerrecht und Ausländerpolitik*, 24 (1) (2004), p. 5.

Shoghi Effendi. *Arohanui: Letters of Shoghi Effendi to New Zealand.* Suva: Bahá'í Publishing Trust of Suva, Fiji Islands, 1982.

— *Light of Divine Guidance*, vol. 1. Hofheim: Bahai-Verlag Deutschland, 1982.

Towfigh, Emanuel. *Die rechtliche Verfassung von Religionsgemeinschaften: Eine Untersuchung am Beispiel der Bahai.* Tübingen: Mohr Siebeck, 2006.

Universal House of Justice. *Messages from the Universal House of Justice, 1963–1986.* Wilmette, IL: Bahá'í Publishing Trust, 1996.

Utley, Francis Lee. 'A Definition of Folklore', in Coffin, Tristram Potter (ed.). *Our Living Traditions: An Introduction to American Folklore*, pp. 3–14. New York: Basic Books, 1968.

Waldhoff, Christian. 'Kirchliche Selbstbestimmung und Europarecht', *JuristenZeitung* 58. Jahrg., no. 20 (17 October 2003), pp. 978–86.

Walter, Christian. 'Religiöse Toleranz im Verfassungsstaat: Islam und Grundgesetz', in Lehmann, Harmut (ed.). *Koexistenz und Konflikt von Religionen im vereinten Europa*, pp. 77–99. Göttingen: Wallstein Verlag, 2004.

Weiler, Joseph H. H. *Ein christliches Europa: Erkundungsgänge*. Salzburg–München: Pustet Anton, 2004.

4

Exploring the Unique Character of Ḥuqúqu'lláh: Insights from a Comparison with U.S. Tax Laws

Kathryn L. Moore

Say: O people, the first duty is to recognize the one true God – magnified be His glory – the second is to show forth constancy in His Cause and, after these, one's duty is to purify one's riches and earthly possessions according to that which is prescribed by God.[1]

One of the primary Bahá'í principles – the abolition of the extremes of wealth and poverty – calls for a spiritual solution to the world's economic problems. The Kitáb-i-Aqdas, the Bahá'í book of laws, establishes a unique and significant socio-economic and spiritual law to address these problems. Ḥuqúqu'lláh – also known as the 'right of God' – asks Bahá'ís to return a portion of their material wealth to God. In setting forth this law in the Kitáb-i-Aqdas, Bahá'u'lláh states, 'By this means He hath desired to purify what ye possess and to enable you to draw nigh unto such stations as none can comprehend save those whom God hath willed.'[2]

Bahá'u'lláh describes Ḥuqúqu'lláh, a spiritual obligation fundamental to each Bahá'í's life, as 'the source of grace, abundance, and of all good. It is a bounty which shall remain with every soul in every world of the worlds of God, the All-Possessing, the All-Bountiful.'[3] 'Abdu'l-Bahá said that Ḥuqúqu'lláh 'will be expended for the relief of the poor, the disabled, the needy, and the orphans and for other vital needs of the Cause of God'.[4] Dr Firaydoun Javaheri, a former long-time member of the Universal House of Justice, has explained that Ḥuqúqu'lláh constitutes a recognition that our material life and its bounties come, in the first instance, from God – and creates a bond between the spiritual world of God and the material world of man.[5]

---

1   *Compilation of Compilations*, vol. 1, p. 499 (no. 1129).
2   Bahá'u'lláh, *Kitáb-i-Aqdas*, p. 55, para. 97.
3   *Compilation of Compilations*, vol. 1, p. 490 (no. 1105).
4   ibid. p. 513 (no. 1173).
5   Waters, *A Workbook*, p. 231 (extract from presentation by Dr Firaydoun Javaheri, on 'The Social Dimensions of the Law of Ḥuqúqu'lláh').

Because Ḥuqúqu'lláh applies to material resources, it is perhaps not surprising that, at least superficially, Ḥuqúqu'lláh resembles a well-known material law in North America, the U.S. federal income tax.[6] On the other hand, because it is a spiritual law, it is likewise not surprising that Ḥuqúqu'lláh is profoundly different from the U.S. federal income tax. Indeed, because Ḥuqúqu'lláh is a spiritual law, it has the potential to transform society in a way that no human law could.

This chapter seeks to understand the unique character of Ḥuqúqu'lláh, as well as how it is determined, by comparing it with several tax laws. It begins by explaining how Ḥuqúqu'lláh is computed. It then briefly compares and contrasts Ḥuqúqu'lláh with a wealth tax and an estate tax. Next, it engages in a more in-depth comparison of Ḥuqúqu'lláh and the U.S. federal income tax. In so doing, it focuses on (1) the detail and complexity of the laws; (2) the differences in computation of Ḥuqúqu'lláh and the federal income tax; (3) the enforcement of the two laws; and (4) the goals or purposes of each law. It concludes by explaining how and why Ḥuqúqu'lláh has the ability to transform the social order in a way that a purely material tax like the U.S. federal income tax cannot.

Computation of Ḥuqúqu'lláh

Regarding the computation of Ḥuqúqu'lláh, the Kitáb-i-Aqdas provides: 'Should anyone acquire one hundred mithqáls of gold, nineteen mithqáls thereof are God's and to be rendered unto Him, the Fashioner of earth and heaven.'[7] In a tablet, Bahá'u'lláh explains that 'the minimum sum liable to Ḥuqúq is based on the number Nineteen, in accordance with the text of the blessed, the Most Holy Book. Therein reference is made to the amount of Ḥuqúq payable and not to the minimum sum on which Ḥuqúq falls due.'[8] The notes to the Kitáb-i-Aqdas make clear that this provision sets forth the rate at which Ḥuqúqu'lláh applies – 19 percent. Ḥuqúqu'lláh becomes due when an individual acquires possessions equal to at least 19 mithqáls of gold.[9]

The glossary to the Kitáb-i-Aqdas defines a mithqál as a unit of weight that is equivalent to about 3.5 grams, and 19 mithqáls of gold are equivalent to 69.192 grams or 2.22456 troy ounces.[10] Thus, if a Bahá'í acquires 'excess wealth' of 19 mithqáls of gold, which at the time of this writing is worth about $5,000,[11] Ḥuqúqu'lláh of $950 (that is, 19 percent of $5,000) is due.

Ḥuqúqu'lláh does not apply to all income or wealth that an individual acquires.

---

6 It also resembles the tax laws of other countries as well. However, in this chapter I focus on a comparison with the U.S. federal income tax law.
7 Bahá'u'lláh, *Kitáb-i-Aqdas*, p. 55, para. 97.
8 *Compilation of Compilations*, vol. 1, p. 498 (no. 1128).
9 Bahá'u'lláh, *Kitáb-i-Aqdas*, p. 218, note 125. See also *Compilation of Compilations*, vol. 1, p. 493 (no. 1116).
10 Bahá'u'lláh, *Kitáb-i-Aqdas*, p. 254.
11 According to the *Wall Street Journal*, a troy ounce of gold was worth $2,300 on 5 July 2024. See https://www.wsj.com/finance/commodities-futures/gold-edges-higher-fed-path-stays-in-focus-4ecc9f5f. Thus, as of 5 July 2024, 2.22456 troy ounces of gold were worth $5,116.49. (2.22456 x $2,300 = $5,116.48).

First, Ḥuqúqu'lláh does not apply to income or wealth used to pay necessary expenses. The question and answer section in the Kitáb-i-Aqdas clarifies that Ḥuqúqu'lláh does not apply to an individual's residence and necessary house-hold furnishings[12] as well as to 'appointments of a place of business, which are needed for carrying on one's work or profession'.[13] Similarly, 'Abdu'l-Bahá has explained that Ḥuqúqu'lláh does not apply to 'agricultural tools and equipment, and . . . animals used in ploughing the land, to the extent that these are necessary'.[14] 'Abdu'l-Bahá summarizes this principle by stating that Ḥuqúqu'lláh is 'payable on whatever is left over after deducting one's yearly expenses'.[15]

Beyond the examples above, only limited guidance is provided in the Bahá'í writings as to what constitute needful expenses exempt from Ḥuqúqu'lláh. Instead, it is left to the individual believers to determine their needful expenses. In the words of one of the original members of the International Board of Trustees of Ḥuqúqu'lláh, Dr Ramin Khadem, this determination 'depend[s] on the personal circumstances and the levels of understanding and spiritual maturity of the individual'.[16]

Second, the question and answer section in the Kitáb-i-Aqdas makes clear that Ḥuqúqu'lláh is only payable once.[17] Thus, wealth on which a Bahá'í has already paid Ḥuqúqu'lláh is exempt from Ḥuqúqu'lláh. Only earnings on that wealth are subject to Ḥuqúqu'lláh.[18] When the wealth changes hands, Ḥuqúqu'lláh may be due once again from the new recipient of that wealth.[19]

In a letter written to an individual in March 1988, the Universal House of Justice offered a simplified approach for calculating Ḥuqúqu'lláh.[20] Under this approach, property is divided into two parts: one part consists of all assets which are exempt from Ḥuqúqu'lláh as well as those which are dealt with on a current basis. The second part consists of accumulated savings which the individual wishes to bring into account for Ḥuqúqu'lláh plus annual additions to that amount. Each year, the savings from the first part are transferred to the second part.

The Universal House of Justice offered the following example to illustrate this approach:

---

12   Bahá'u'lláh, *Kitáb-i-Aqdas*, p. 108 (Question and Answer no. 8).
13   ibid. pp. 132–3 (Question and Answer no. 95).
14   *Compilation of Compilations*, vol. 1, p. 512 (no. 1166).
15   ibid. p. 512 (no. 1165).
16   Waters, *A Workbook*, p. 228 (extract from presentation by Dr Ramin Khadem on 'Ḥuqúqu'lláh and Prosperity').
17   See Bahá'u'lláh, *Kitáb-i-Aqdas*, p. 108 (Question and Answer no. 8).
18   ibid. pp. 108–9.
19   ibid. p. 109.
20   Waters, *A Workbook*, pp. 265–6 (enclosure from a letter on behalf of the Universal House of Justice to an individual).

	Gross Savings	Ḥuqúq Paid	Items spent after Ḥuqúq is Paid	Net Savings	Savings Cleared
1st Year	$1,000	$190		$810	$1,000
2nd Year	$1,000	$190		$810	$1,000
3rd Year	$1,000	$190	$500 (contribution)	$310	$1,000
4th Year	$1,000	$190	$800 (luxuries)	$10	$1,000
	$4,000	$760	$1,300	$1,940	$4,000

The final result:

The individual has accumulated gross savings of	$4,000
On which he has paid 19% as Ḥuqúqu'lláh	-$ 760
Leaving cleared savings amounting to	$3,240
From this he has used after paying Ḥuqúqu'lláh	-$1,300
Leaving him with a final net savings of	$1,940

At this point, all savings have been cleared for Ḥuqúqu'lláh purposes.

Comparison with a Wealth Tax

Because Ḥuqúqu'lláh applies when an individual acquires a certain level of wealth, that is, 19 mithqáls of gold, Ḥuqúqu'lláh is similar to a wealth tax. In theory, a wealth tax is simply a tax based on a taxpayer's wealth.[21] Like Ḥuqúqu'lláh, the tax may be an excise-type levy that is imposed once and only once on an individual's wealth, or it may be an accretion-type levy that is levied on a periodic basis on an individual's wealth. A wealth tax may be imposed at a flat rate, like the flat 19 percent rate imposed under Ḥuqúqu'lláh, or the rate may vary. In any event, according to one scholar, 'the tax simply withdraws for government use a portion of the taxpayer's resources based on the taxpayer's total resources'.[22]

The United States does not currently have a wealth tax. Indeed, wealth taxes are relatively and increasingly rare throughout the world. As of 2024, only four Organization for Economic Cooperation and Development (OECD) countries – Colombia, Switzerland, Norway, and Spain – had net wealth taxes,[23] compared to ten of the 26 OECD countries 15 years earlier.[24] Moreover, 13 countries have abolished net wealth taxes in the last 30 years.[25]

Commentators have debated the advantages and disadvantages of a wealth tax.[26] One of the principal justifications offered for a wealth tax is that it reduces

---

21 See Hasen, 'Accretion-Based Progressive Wealth Taxation', p. 281.
22 ibid.
23 Cristina Enache, *The High Cost of Wealth Taxes* (26 June 2024), available at https://taxfoundation.org/wp-content/uploads/2024/06/FF841_English.pdf
24 See Drometer, et al. 'Wealth and Inheritance Taxation', p. 47.
25 ibid. p. 48.
26 See, e.g. Schenck, 'Foreword', p. 257 (introducing the *Tax Law Review*'s invitational symposium to explore the desirability and feasibility of introducing a federal wealth tax).

inequality in the distribution of wealth.[27] In the same vein, Dr Javaheri has said:

> Ḥuqúqu'lláh may be regarded as a major instrument Bahá'u'lláh has given us for the achievement of economic justice and a more equitable distribution of wealth in this world. It provides the basis for the 'spiritual solution' to the economic problems of the world and forms the foundation of the 'Divine Economy' described by the Guardian in his *World Order of Bahá'u'lláh*. The solution is spiritual and the economy divine because the desire for its implementation is in the heart of the individual believer and its observance is a fundamental component of Bahá'u'lláh's covenant.[28]

Comparison with an Estate Tax

Because Ḥuqúqu'lláh applies to an individual's wealth at death if the individual did not pay Ḥuqúqu'lláh on that wealth prior to death, Ḥuqúqu'lláh might appear to resemble an estate tax. Ḥuqúqu'lláh, however, is fundamentally different from an estate tax because an estate tax is a tax on the right to transfer property at death,[29] while Ḥuqúqu'lláh is payable on the acquisition of wealth during life.

Furthermore, while some Ḥuqúqu'lláh may be due and payable at death, Ḥuqúqu'lláh is not a tax on the transfer of wealth at death, and to the extent possible, Bahá'ís are encouraged to pay Ḥuqúqu'lláh during their lifetimes. In this connection, the Universal House of Justice has said: 'Essentially, the Ḥuqúqu'lláh should be paid by a believer during the course of his life whenever his surplus property reaches the assessable level . . . Ideally, when a Bahá'í dies, the only payment of Ḥuqúqu'lláh which should need to be provided for in his Will is such additional liability as may be found to exist when his affairs are reckoned up as at the date of his death.'[30]

Comparison with an Income Tax

Technically, Ḥuqúqu'lláh resembles a wealth tax rather than an income tax because Ḥuqúqu'lláh is imposed on wealth and accretions to wealth rather than on income per se. Nevertheless, because Ḥuqúqu'lláh is only imposed on wealth once, and wealth is generally income less needful expenses,[31] Ḥuqúqu'lláh may also be said

---

27 See, e.g. Piketty, *Capital in the 21st Century*, pp. 515–34 (proposing a global wealth tax to reduce inequality).

28 Waters, *A Workbook*, p. 230 (extract from presentation by Dr Firaydoun Javaheri on 'The Social Dimensions of the Law of Ḥuqúqu'lláh').

29 See, e.g. 26 U.S.C. § 2001 (imposing a tax 'on the transfer of the taxable estate of every decedent who is a citizen or resident of the United States').

30 Letter written on 1 October 1989 to a Board of Trustees of Ḥuqúqu'lláh, quoted in Waters, *A Workbook*, p. 44 (no. 65).

31 For example, in a tablet 'Abdu'l-Bahá explained: 'As to the way the Ḥuqúq must be paid: Having deducted the expenses incurred during the year, any excess of income derived from one's property, profession or business is subject to the payment of Ḥuqúq.' *Compilation of Compilations*, vol. 1, p. 512 (no. 1167). Shoghi Effendi has also described Ḥuqúqu'lláh as essentially 19% of one's income. ibid.

to resemble an income tax. Accordingly, the balance of this chapter compares and contrasts Ḥuqúqu'lláh with a widely known income tax, the U.S. federal income tax, to obtain more insights into the nature and rules of Ḥuqúqu'lláh.

Computation of the U.S. Federal Income Tax

As its name suggests, the U.S. federal income tax is a tax imposed on income. The starting point for calculating the U.S. federal income tax is gross income. Generally, the Internal Revenue Code defines gross income quite broadly to encompass 'all income from whatever source derived',[32] and the U.S. Supreme Court has referred to gross income as 'undeniable accessions to wealth'.[33] Nevertheless, not all accessions to wealth are included in gross income. Congress has expressly excluded certain receipts, such as gifts and inheritances,[34] from the definition of gross income.

Once gross income is determined, 'above the line' deductions are taken in determining 'adjusted gross income'. The Internal Revenue Code expressly identifies 17 'above the line' deductions that are subtracted from gross income to determine adjusted gross income.[35] Above the line deductions include a deduction for ordinary and necessary expenses incurred in earning business income.[36]

After adjusted gross income is determined, taxpayers may either subtract from their adjusted gross income a 'standard deduction' or their 'itemized deductions' to determine their 'taxable income'.[37] In 2024, the standard deduction for a single taxpayer was $14,600 while the standard deduction for a married couple filing jointly was $29,200.[38] If a taxpayer's itemized deductions exceed his standard deduction, the taxpayer may elect to deduct his itemized deductions rather than take the standard deduction. The Internal Revenue Code authorizes a host of specific itemized deductions. These include a deduction for charitable contributions.[39]

Once the taxpayer's taxable income is calculated by subtracting the standard deduction or itemized deductions from the taxpayer's adjusted gross income, a graduated income tax rate schedule is applied to the taxpayer's taxable income to determine the taxpayer's tax liability.[40] The graduated income tax schedule

p. 516 (no. 1181).

32   26 U.S.C. § 61 (defining gross income as 'all income from whatever source derived, including but not limited to' a list of 16 different items).

33   Commissioner v. Glenshaw Glass Co., 348 U.S. 426, 431 (1955) (holding receipts were gross income where they were 'instances of undeniable accessions to wealth, clearly realized, and over which the taxpayers have complete dominion').

34   26 U.S.C. § 102.

35   26 U.S.C. § 62(a).

36   26 U.S.C. §§ 62(a)(1); 162(a).

37   Eligible taxpayers may also deduct the IRC § 199A qualified business income deduction in addition to deducting either the standard deduction or their itemized deductions. 26 U.S.C. § 63(b)(3).

38   Rev. Proc. 2023–34, Bull. 2023–48, at p. 1292.

39   26 U.S.C. § 170.

40   Special rules apply to capital gains. Generally, the rates are lower and depend on the taxpayer's total taxable income as well as the character of the capital gain. See 26 U.S.C. § 1(h).

increases the marginal rate at which a taxpayer's income is taxed as the taxpayer's income increases. For example, in 2024, there were seven different rates, ranging from 10 percent to 37 percent.[41]

Separate and apart from exclusions and deductions, the Internal Revenue Code provides tax credits that may be applied to reduce a taxpayer's income tax liability. For example, workers in low-income and moderate-income families may be eligible for an earned income tax credit.[42]

Comparison of Ḥuqúqu'lláh and the U.S. Federal Income Tax

Let us now compare and contrast four different facets of Ḥuqúqu'lláh and the U.S. federal income tax: (1) the detail and complexity of the laws; (2) the computation of Ḥuqúqu'lláh and the federal income tax; (3) the enforcement of the laws; and (4) the goals or purposes of the laws.

Detail and Complexity

As the preceding descriptions illustrate, calculating the U.S. federal income tax is much more complex than calculating Ḥuqúqu'lláh. Calculating the U.S. federal income tax involves a multi-step process that requires, among other things, distinguishing among exclusions from gross income, above-the-line deductions, and itemized deductions and distinguishing between refundable tax credits and non-refundable tax credits. Ḥuqúqu'lláh, in contrast, is simply, in the words of 'Abdu'l-Bahá, 'payable on whatever is left over after deducting one's yearly expenses'.[43]

That is not to suggest, however, that there is no complexity at all in calculating Ḥuqúqu'lláh. First, calculating Ḥuqúqu'lláh requires identifying which expenses and assets are necessary and thus deductible and which are not. Second, because Ḥuqúqu'lláh is only payable on wealth once, records must be kept to identify which savings have been cleared of the Ḥuqúqu'lláh obligation.

As discussed above, the Bahá'í writings provide some guidance to individuals in identifying which assets and needful expenses are exempt from Ḥuqúqu'lláh. For example, as already noted, the Bahá'í writings indicate that the value of one's residence, necessary household furnishings, business assets, and needed agricultural tools and equipment are exempt.

Nevertheless, at this point in time, the Universal House of Justice has declined to provide specific guidance for identifying needful expenses and left many decisions to the conscience of the individual believer. For example, the Universal House of Justice has written:

---

41 Rev. Proc. 2023–34, Bull. 2023–48, at pp. 1289–90.
42 26 U.S.C. § 32. For an overview of the earned income tax credit, see, for example, Book et al. 'Insights from Behavioral Economics', pp. 186–91.
43 *Compilation of Compilations*, vol. 1, p. 512 (no. 1165).

You ask about the applicability of the law of Ḥuqúqu'lláh to the money that a believer spends 'travelling for the Faith, living a little more generously', and so forth. Our impression from answers given to other questions is that this is a matter for the conscience of the individual. There is, in fact, a vast range of expenditures which could, or could not, be included under the heading of normal annual expenses which are to be set against income before arriving at the sum assessable to Ḥuqúqu'lláh.[44]

The U.S. federal income tax laws, in contrast, are highly detailed and regulated. Unlike Ḥuqúqu'lláh, which is codified in a single paragraph (paragraph 97) of the Kitáb-i-Aqdas, a paragraph consisting of less than 120 words, the U.S. federal income tax law begins with a very lengthy and detailed statute enacted by Congress and codified in title 26 of the United States Code.

In addition to the lengthy statute, the U.S. Department of the Treasury has issued a multitude of regulations that provide its official interpretation of the Internal Revenue Code. These regulations, codified in Title 26 of the Code of Federal Regulations, are even longer and more detailed than the Internal Revenue Code. According to the Tax Foundation, the Internal Revenue Code currently consists of about 2.4 million words, while there are about 7.7 million words in the tax regulations.

At present, the Universal House of Justice takes a completely different approach to regulating Ḥuqúqu'lláh. It has expressly discouraged Representatives of Ḥuqúqu'lláh from giving specific answers to questions regarding the method of computing Ḥuqúqu'lláh because the House of Justice 'wish[es] to avoid the proliferation of detailed instructions issuing from authoritative bodies. [The House of Justice's] preference is for Representatives to draw the individual believers' attention to the Compilation and Codification . . . and to encourage them to draw their own conclusions in light of the spirit of the law.'[45] The House of Justice has explained that 'the most important features of the law should be presented in as simple a form as possible, to avoid the dear friends obligated to pay Ḥuqúqu'lláh from becoming inhibited about doing so by an unwarranted fear of its complexity of application'.[46]

It is possible that, at some point in the future, the Universal House of Justice will provide more detailed guidance on how to calculate Ḥuqúqu'lláh. The House of Justice hinted at such an eventuality in a letter to a believer in March 1984:

As regards your question concerning the principal residence and subsidiary rulings relevant to it, we wish to let you know that *in these days* it is not deemed advisable to enact detailed rulings for Ḥuqúqu'lláh. Thus the friends are left free,

---

44   Universal House of Justice, Memorandum to the Office of Ḥuqúqu'lláh in the Holy Land, 14 February 1993, quoted in Waters, *A Workbook*, p. 46 (no. 70).

45   Universal House of Justice, Memorandum to an office in the Holy Land, 23 September 1997, quoted in Waters, *A Workbook*, p. 264.

46   ibid. p. 264 (quoting no. 100).

and whenever no definite rulings exist they may fulfil in each case that which they understand from the texts, and may honour their Ḥuqúqu'lláh obligations according to their own judgement and the prompting of their own conscience.[47]

It seems unlikely, however, that the House of Justice will ever provide rules and regulations as detailed as those governing the U.S. federal income tax. Much of the complexity of the U.S. federal income tax law is due to the need to control against the desire to evade, avoid, or simply minimize the payment of tax. Ḥuqúqu'lláh, in contrast, is a voluntary spiritual obligation, which benefits the individual who pays it. The Universal House of Justice has pointed out that 'the devoted believer who is privileged to pay 'the Right of God', far from seeking excuses for evading this spiritual obligation, will do his utmost to meet it'.[48]

Computation of Ḥuqúqu'lláh and the Federal Income Tax

This section compares some of the deductions and exclusions and items otherwise afforded favorable income tax treatment under the U.S. federal income tax to the rules of Ḥuqúqu'lláh. As will be seen, some of the provisions, such as the IRC §162 deduction for ordinary and necessary business expenses, are consistent with Ḥuqúqu'lláh's deduction of needful expenses. Others, such as the IRC §102 exclusion of gifts and inheritances, find no parallel in Ḥuqúqu'lláh.

PERSONAL EXEMPTIONS

Section 151 of the Internal Revenue Code allows each taxpayer a personal exemption.[49] Historically, the statute set the exemption at $2,000[50] and indexed that amount annually for inflation.[51] The statute also allows taxpayers an exemption for each dependent[52] and defines the term dependent to include a qualifying child or qualifying relative.[53] Exemptions are phased out for taxpayers with income above certain levels.[54]

Two theories support the personal exemption. Under one view, the personal exemption sets the amount of income that should be taxed at a zero rate. Under the second view, the personal exemption is a government subsidy for those with a subsistence level of income, especially those with children. The phase-out of exemptions is consistent with the second theory of personal exemptions, but not the first.[55]

---

47   *Compilation of Compilations*, vol. 1, p. 526 (no. 1210) (emphasis added).
48   ibid. p. 523 (no. 1202).
49   26 U.S.C. § 151.
50   26 U.S.C. § 151(d)(1).
51   26 U.S.C. § 151(d)(4).
52   26 U.S.C. § 151(c).
53   26 U.S.C. § 152.
54   26 U.S.C. § 151(d)(3).
55   Graetz and Schenk, *Federal Income Taxation*, pp. 400–1.

The personal exemptions are similar to some of Ḥuqúqu'lláh's exemptions. By exempting needful expenses and individuals with wealth of less than 19 mithqáls of gold, Ḥuqúqu'lláh ensures that some level of wealth or income is not subject to Ḥuqúqu'lláh. Moreover, just as the personal exemptions increase with the number of dependents a taxpayer supports, an individual's needful expenses necessarily increase as the number of dependents the individual supports increases and thus the amount exempt from Ḥuqúqu'lláh increases. Ḥuqúqu'lláh, however, is quite different in that Ḥuqúqu'lláh permits each individual to determine his or her needful expenses rather than identifying a specific dollar amount of income that is necessary for needful expenses.

In 2017, the United States Congress amended the Internal Revenue Code to set the personal exemption amount at zero for tax years 2018 through 2025.[56] At the same time, Congress increased the standard deduction for tax years 2018 through 2025.[57] As discussed below, the policy goals underlying the standard deduction are similar to those underlying the personal exemption.

STANDARD DEDUCTION

As noted above, taxpayers may subtract a standard deduction from their adjusted gross income to determine their taxable income. In 2017, the standard deduction for a single taxpayer was $6,350 while the standard deduction for a married couple filing jointly was $12,700.[58] When Congress in 2017 reduced the personal exemption to zero for tax years 2018 through 2025, it also dramatically increased the standard deduction.[59] Specifically, it increased the standard deduction for a single taxpayer to $12,000 and the standard deduction for a married couple filing jointly to $24,000.

Similar to Ḥuqúqu'lláh's exemption of individuals with wealth of less than 19 mithqáls of gold and its deduction of needful expenses, the standard deduction ensures that individuals with income below a certain level (the standard deduction) pay no income tax.[60] The standard deduction also serves another purpose. Because the standard deduction in essence replaces itemized deductions, it relieves taxpayers with modest incomes from the nuisance of keeping track of their itemized deductions.[61]

Again, like the personal exemption, the standard deduction differs from Ḥuqúqu'lláh in that Ḥuqúqu'lláh permits an individual to determine his necessary expenses rather than identifying a specific dollar amount that is deductible.

---

56   Pub. L. no. 115–97, Title I § 11041(a), 131 Stat. 2054, 2082 (22 December 2017).
57   Pub. L. no. 115–97, Title I § 11021(a), 131 Stat. 2054, 2072 (22 December 2017).
58   Rev. Proc. 2016–55, § 14.
59   Pub. L. no. 115–97, Title I § 11021(a), 131 Stat. 2054, 2072 (22 December 2017).
60   Klein, et al. *Federal Income Taxation*, p. 34.
61   ibid.

BUSINESS EXPENSES

Section 162 of the Internal Revenue Code allows taxpayers an above-the-line deduction[62] for all the ordinary and necessary business expenses paid or incurred during the taxable year in carrying on any trade or business.[63] Generally, expenses that are deductible under IRC § 162 should also be deductible under Ḥuqúqu'lláh because Ḥuqúqu'lláh allows individuals to deduct their needful expenses in calculating their Ḥuqúqu'lláh amount.

Because the U.S. federal income tax is an income tax while Ḥuqúqu'lláh is based on wealth, a significant, and often very challenging, issue arises under IRC § 162 that does not arise under Ḥuqúqu'lláh. Specifically, section 162 distinguishes between expenses, which are currently deductible, and capital expenditures, which are denied a current deduction under IRC § 263.[64] Although it can, at times, be extremely difficult to distinguish between an expense and a capital expenditure,[65] in essence, the difference between an expense and a capital expenditure is that an expense is current while a capital expenditure gives rise to an asset or a benefit that has a useful life that extends beyond a year. To illustrate, for an individual operating a restaurant, the cost of dishwashing detergent is normally an expense, because dishwashing detergent is typically used in the year purchased, while the cost of an oven is a capital expenditure, because an oven lasts many years. An immediate deduction for the cost of the dishwashing detergent is allowed because the cost is properly reflected in calculating income for the year in which it is used. On the other hand, an immediate deduction for the cost of the oven is not allowed because its cost is attributable to income earned over the years in which it is used.

Recognizing that most capital assets wear out over time, section 167 of the Internal Revenue Code allows a 'depreciation' deduction for capital assets subject to wear and tear and obsolescence.[66] In theory, the deprecation deduction allows taxpayers to spread the cost of the capital asset over the asset's useful life so that income is accurately reflected.[67]

Because Ḥuqúqu'lláh is imposed on wealth, not income, Ḥuqúqu'lláh does not distinguish between current expenses and capital expenditures. 'Abdu'l-Bahá has clarified that Ḥuqúqu'lláh does not apply to 'agricultural tools and equipment, and [to] animals used in ploughing the land, to the extent that these are necessary'.[68] Thus, necessary expenses, whether they take the form of current expenses or capital expenditures, are immediately and fully deductible when calculating Ḥuqúqu'lláh, and there is no need for depreciation deductions in calculating Ḥuqúqu'lláh.

---

62 See 26 U.S.C. § 62(a)(1).
63 26 U.S.C. § 162.
64 26 U.S.C. § 263.
65 See Freeland, et al. *Fundamentals of Federal Income Taxation*, p. 314.
66 26 U.S.C. § 167. Because land does not depreciate, no deprecation deduction is allowed for land.
67 See Freeland et al. *Fundamentals of Federal Income Taxation*, pp. 394–5.
68 *Compilation of Compilations*, vol. 1, p. 512 (no. 1166).

STATE AND LOCAL TAXES

Section 164 of the Internal Revenue Code allows taxpayers a deduction for the payment of certain state, local, and foreign taxes.[69] Taxes that are paid for business purposes are above-the-line deductions.[70] Personal taxes, in contrast, are itemized deductions that are only allowable for taxpayers who do not take the standard deduction.[71] Moreover, for tax years 2018 through 2025, the deduction is generally capped at $10,000 for personal taxes.[72]

Because taxes, whether they be federal, state, local, or foreign, are mandated by law, they fall within the category of needful expenses that should be considered exempt from Ḥuqúqu'lláh. Indeed, the *Codification of the Law of Ḥuqúqu'lláh*, prepared by the Research Department of the Bahá'í World Centre, expressly states that 'sums which are paid to the state, such as taxes and duties', are deductible in calculating the amount of Ḥuqúqu'lláh due.[73]

PERSONAL RESIDENCE

Generally, section 262 of the Internal Revenue Code prohibits a deduction for personal expenses.[74] The Code, however, does provide some exceptions to this general rule with respect to personal residences. First, section 163(h) of the Internal Revenue Code permits taxpayers who itemize their deductions[75] to deduct interest paid on mortgages on their principal place of residence.[76] Specifically, it permits taxpayers to deduct 'qualified residence interest' – interest paid for the purchase or renovation of a principal residence worth up to $750,000.[77] The home mortgage interest deduction is intended to encourage home ownership and stimulate residential construction. It is, however, subject to considerable criticism because it tends to favor higher-income individuals. To illustrate, it was estimated that in 2023 over 90 percent of the benefit accrued to taxpayers with income exceeding $100,000.[78]

In addition to the deductions for interest and taxes on personal residences, section 121 of the Internal Revenue Code permits taxpayers to exclude from their gross income gain of up to $250,000 ($500,000 for a married couple) from the sale of their principal residence.[79] Taxpayers may only take advantage of the

---

69   See 26 U.S.C. § 164(a).
70   See 26 U.S.C. § 62(a)(1).
71   See 26 U.S.C. § 67(b)(2).
72   See 26 U.S.C. § 164(b)(6).
73   Waters, *A Workbook*, p. 81 (quoting *Codification of the Law of Ḥuqúqu'lláh*, B.2.c).
74   26 U.S.C. § 262.
75   Specifically, the home interest deduction is a non-miscellaneous itemized deduction under 26 U.S.C. § 67(b)(1).
76   26 U.S.C. § 163(h).
77   26 U.S.C. §§ 163(h)(3)(B) and 163(h)(3)(F)(i)(II).
78   Joint Committee on Taxation, 'Estimates of Federal Tax Expenditures for Fiscal Years 2023–2027', JCX-59-23 (7 December 2023), p. 46, Table 3 (estimating that about $23.5 billion of the $25 billion deducted for mortgage interest is attributable to individuals with income exceeding $100,000).
79   26 U.S.C. § 121(a) and (b).

exclusion once every two years.[80]

Unlike the federal income tax, Ḥuqúqu'lláh does not differentiate between personal and business expenses. Instead, it differentiates between expenses that are needful and those that are not. The question and answer section of the Kitáb-i-Aqdas makes clear that an individual's residence and furnishings are exempt from Ḥuqúqu'lláh.[81] Although the size and cost of the residence and furnishings are left to the individual's discretion, the Universal House of Justice has counseled that 'it is obvious that the friends should not spend lavishly on residences and furnishings and rationalize those expenditures in their desire to avoid payment of Ḥuqúqu'lláh'.[82]

Interest on loans used to finance, and taxes paid with respect to, a needful residence would clearly seem to fall within the deduction for needful expenses. On the other hand, whether an individual's savings toward a residence are exempt is within the discretion of the individual. A letter written on behalf of the Universal House of Justice explains:

> Funds being saved up for the purchase of a residence are not *in themselves* exempt from Ḥuqúqu'lláh. Thus, if the person were to die before purchasing a residence, these savings would be assessable to Ḥuqúq. However . . . it is left to the individual who is saving to buy a residence, to decide whether to pay Ḥuqúqu'lláh on the money as he saves it, and then count the exemption when the residence is actually purchased, or to postpone the inclusion of the savings in his calculation of Ḥuqúqu'lláh until after the residence is purchased, at which time, of course, the value of the residence becomes exempt.[83]

When an individual dies, no Ḥuqúqu'lláh is due on the individual's residence. As the Universal House of Justice explained in a letter written on its behalf to an individual believer: 'The basic principle is that when a believer passes away, his principal residence, as well as items such as necessary furnishings and tools of the trade, remain exempt when computing how much, if any, Ḥuqúqu'lláh remains to be paid on his estate.'[84]

Whether Ḥuqúqu'lláh is due upon the transfer of the residence depends on how the residence is used. If the individual who inherits the residence continues to use the property as a residence, then no Ḥuqúqu'lláh is due upon the transfer of the residence. On the other hand, if the residence is sold, then the recipient of those proceeds may be subject to Ḥuqúqu'lláh on the receipt of the proceeds.[85]

---

80   26 U.S.C. § 121(b)(3).
81   Bahá'u'lláh, *Kitáb-i-Aqdas*, p. 119 (Question and Answer no. 42).
82   *Compilation of Compilations*, vol. 1, p. 524 (no. 1204).
83   Universal House of Justice, letter to an individual, 8 October 1993, reproduced in Waters, *A Workbook*, p. 47 (no. 72).
84   Universal House of Justice, letter, 21 May 2006, quoted in ibid. p. 51 (no. 79).
85   Waters, *A Workbook*, p. 51 (no. 79).

RETIREMENT SAVINGS[86]

The Internal Revenue Code has long provided favorable income tax treatment to retirement savings. The traditional form of favorable tax treatment is deferral of taxation. Specifically, the employer may deduct contributions to an employer-sponsored retirement plan at the time they are made, regardless of when the participants include the benefits in their income.[87] In addition, even though the employer is permitted an immediate deduction, plan participants are not required to include contributions in income until the benefits are distributed to them.[88] Finally, the trust that holds the plan assets is not required to pay income tax on the earnings from the investment of the contributions.[89] Assuming no change in tax rates, the economic effect of this tax deferral is the same as never taxing the earnings on the contributions.[90] More recently, an alternative form of favorable tax treatment has become available for the most common employer-sponsored pension, the 401(k) plan. Under this so-called Roth treatment, contributions to the plan are taxed when made,[91] but distributions from the plan, including earnings on contributions, are not taxed.[92] Assuming constant tax rates, this Roth treatment is essentially economically identical to the favorable treatment accorded traditional retirement plans.[93]

The orthodox justification for the favorable tax treatment accorded employer-sponsored pension plans is that it promotes retirement income security by encouraging retirement savings by individuals who would not otherwise save for retirement, including, or perhaps especially, lower-income and middle-income workers.[94] At first blush, using tax incentives to encourage lower-income and middle-income workers to save for retirement might seem irrational in light of the progressive tax rate structure in the United States.[95] The value of the tax deferral to an individual depends on the worker's marginal tax rate: the higher an individual's income, the higher the individual's marginal tax rate, and thus the greater the tax benefit. Accordingly, the system provides a greater tax benefit to a higher-income worker, who is in a better position to save for retirement, than a lower-income worker, who is less able to save for retirement. Despite the extraordinary complexity of the rules governing retirement savings and the enormous loss

---

86   This section draws liberally from Moore, 'An Overview of the U.S. Retirement Income Security System and the Principles and Values It Reflects', pp. 22–4 and Moore, *Understanding Employee Benefits Law*, pp. 41–4.
87   26 U.S.C. § 404(a).
88   26 U.S.C. § 402(a).
89   26 U.S.C. § 501(a).
90   Moore, *Understanding Employee Benefits Law*, Appendix B (illustrating the economic effect of the favorable tax treatment accorded to traditional qualified plans).
91   26 U.S.C. § 402A(a)(1).
92   26 U.S.C. § 402A(d)(1).
93   Moore, *Understanding Employee Benefits Law*, Appendix B (illustrating the economic equivalence of favorable tax treatment accorded to traditional qualified plans and Roth contributions to qualified plans).
94   See Halperin, 'Special Tax Treatment for Employer-Based Retirement Programs', p. 7.
95   Stein and Dilley, 'Leverage, Linkage, and Leakage', p. 1374.

in tax revenue attributable to the rules, inadequate retirement savings, particularly among lower-income workers, remains a serious problem in the United States.[96]

Unlike the U.S. federal income tax, Ḥuqúqu'lláh does not have lengthy and complex rules regarding retirement savings. Rather, like saving for a residence, the treatment of retirement savings is left to the discretion of the individual. In this connection, a letter written by the Office of Ḥuqúqu'lláh to an individual believer advised that the guidance with respect to savings for education and acquiring a residence applies equally to a private retirement fund.[97]

Thus, retirement savings are not in themselves exempt from Ḥuqúqu'lláh. Nevertheless, an individual may, in his or her discretion, elect to defer paying Ḥuqúqu'lláh on savings for retirement purposes. If, upon reaching retirement age, the savings are used to pay for needful expenses, then the savings will not be subject to Ḥuqúqu'lláh. On the other hand, if the retirement savings are not used for needful expenses, then Ḥuqúqu'lláh will be due on the savings. Moreover, if the individual dies leaving retirement savings, the retirement savings are subject to Ḥuqúqu'lláh, unless the individual has already paid Ḥuqúqu'lláh upon those savings.

It seems that whether an individual should pay Ḥuqúqu'lláh on his retirement savings depends in part on whether the individual expects his retirement savings to exceed his needful expenses in retirement. If the individual expects his retirement savings to exceed his needful expenses in retirement, it may be appropriate for the individual to pay Ḥuqúqu'lláh on the excess portion of his retirement savings as the savings accumulate. To the extent that Ḥuqúqu'lláh has been paid on the retirement savings, no Ḥuqúqu'lláh is due if the savings are later spent for non-exempt purposes. Similarly, to the extent that the individual has paid Ḥuqúqu'lláh on the retirement savings during life, no Ḥuqúqu'lláh should be due on the savings upon the individual's death.

CHARITABLE CONTRIBUTIONS

Section 170 of the Internal Revenue Code allows taxpayers an itemized deduction[98] for charitable contributions.[99] Charitable contributions are defined as 'contribution[s] or gift[s] to or for the use of' certain enumerated eligible donees.[100] These donees include governmental entities[101] and organizations that are 'organized and operated exclusively for religious, charitable, scientific, literary, or educational purposes'.[102] Thus, contributions to Bahá'í funds, including Ḥuqúqu'lláh, are deductible under the U.S. federal income tax law.

---

96 U.S. Government Accountability Office, GAO-15–419, 'Retirement Security: Most Households Approaching Retirement Have Low Savings', p. 7 (2015).
97 Office of Ḥuqúqu'lláh, letter to an individual, 3 February 1997 (on file with the author).
98 Specifically, the charitable contribution deduction is a non-miscellaneous itemized deduction under IRC § 67(b)(4).
99 26 U.S.C. § 170(a)(1).
100 26 U.S.C. § 170(c).
101 26 U.S.C. § 170(c)(1).
102 26 U.S.C. § 170(c)(2).

Section 170 of the Internal Revenue Code limits deductions for contributions to organizations 'organized and operated exclusively for religious, charitable, scientific, literary, or educational purposes' to 50 percent of the taxpayer's 'contribution base',[103] which is generally defined as the taxpayer's adjusted gross income.[104] The charitable contribution deduction is intended to encourage contributions to charitable organizations[105] that 'aid in the accomplishment of many social goals which our federal and local governments cannot or will not accomplish'.[106]

While U.S. federal tax law clearly provides that charitable contributions are deductible (for individuals who itemize their deductions) in calculating their taxable income, whether charitable contributions, including contributions to Bahá'í funds other than Ḥuqúqu'lláh, are deductible in calculating Ḥuqúqu'lláh is left to the conscience of the individual believer. Clearly, Ḥuqúqu'lláh takes priority over contributions to other funds. When asked whether 'contributions to the Mashriqu'l-Adhkár, teaching, and other activities of the Cause [are] considered a part of Ḥuqúq or should . . . be taken separately?' 'Abdu'l-Bahá is reported to have replied 'that Ḥuqúq was separate and independent of these and came first'.[107] The Universal House of Justice has also written:

> Contributions to the funds of the Faith cannot be considered as part of one's payment of Ḥuqúqu'lláh; moreover, if one owes Ḥuqúqu'lláh and cannot afford both to pay it and to make contributions to the Fund, the payment of Ḥuqúqu'lláh should take priority over making contributions. But as to whether contributions to the Fund may be treated as expenses in calculating the amount of one's assets on which Ḥuqúqu'lláh is payable; this is left to the judgement of each individual in the light of his own circumstances.[108]

EXCLUSION OF GIFTS, BEQUESTS, AND INHERITANCES

Section 102 of the Internal Revenue Code generally excludes gifts, bequests, and inheritances from the recipient's gross income.[109] Although this exclusion has existed since the inception of the U.S. federal income tax in 1913, there has been considerable disagreement about the propriety of this provision.[110] Some support the exclusion,[111] while others contend that gifts, bequests, and inheritances should be includible in gross income because they are economic accessions to wealth.[112]

---

103 26 U.S.C. § 170(b)(1)(A). The limit is increased to 60% for cash contributions for tax years between 2018 and 2025. 26 U.S.C. § 170(b)(1)(A).
104 26 U.S.C. § 170(b)(1)(H).
105 See Threlfall v. U.S., 302 F. Supp. 1114, 1118 (W.D. Wisc. 1969).
106 Brinley v. Comm'r, 782 F.2d 1326, 1336 (5th Cir. 1986) (Hill, J., dissenting).
107 *Compilation of Compilations*, vol. 1, p. 515 (no. 1176).
108 Universal House of Justice, letter 16 September 1979, *Compilation of Compilations*, vol. 1, pp. 523–4 (no. 1203).
109 26 U.S.C. § 102(a).
110 For a discussion of the debate, see Kahn and Kahn, 'Gifts, Gafts, and Gefts', pp. 452–76.
111 See, e.g. ibid. p. 483.
112 See, e.g. Schmalbeck, 'Gifts and the Income Tax'.

Although the recipient escapes income taxation on the transfer of gifts, bequests, and inheritances, in theory, the U.S. estate[113] and gift[114] tax regime imposes a tax on the transferor on such transfers. In fact, however, under current law, very few transfers are actually subject to estate and gift taxation because the law provides for very high exemptions, including a lifetime unified exemption for gifts and bequests.[115] If gifts and bequests exceed the lifetime unified exemption, the transfer is taxed at the rate of 40 percent. Because the exemptions are so high, only an estimated 0.2 percent of estates were expected to pay estate tax in 2023.[116]

Ḥuqúqu'lláh treats gifts, bequests, and inheritances very differently from the U.S. federal income tax regime. Although a Bahá'í need only pay Ḥuqúqu'lláh once on any capital that the Bahá'í has acquired, if the Bahá'í then makes a gift of the capital to a donee, the donee may be subject to Ḥuqúqu'lláh on the gift as well.[117] A Bahá'í recipient whose income, including gifts, bequests, and inheritances, exceeds her needful expenses is subject to Ḥuqúqu'lláh on the excess regardless of whether the donor paid Ḥuqúqu'lláh on the money when the donor initially received the money. This differs markedly from the U.S. federal income tax system described above, which exempts the donee.

Contrary to our society's current view of material wealth and inheritances, Bahá'u'lláh has explained the role of Ḥuqúqu'lláh and inheritances as follows:

> This ordinance is binding upon everyone, and by observing it one will be raised to honour inasmuch as it will serve to purify one's possessions and will impart blessing, and added prosperity. However, the people are as yet ignorant of its significance. They continually endeavour to amass riches by lawful or unlawful means in order to transmit them to their heirs, and this to what advantage, no one can tell. Say: In this day the true Heir is the Word of God, since the underlying purpose of inheritance is the preservation of the name and traces of men. It is indubitably clear that the passing of centuries and ages will obliterate these signs, while every word that hath streamed from the Pen of Glory in honour of a certain individual will last as long as the dominions of earth and heaven will endure.[118]

Moreover, Bahá'u'lláh has described the trouble that awaits those who fail to pay their share:

---

113 26 U.S.C. § 2001(a) (imposing a tax 'on the transfer of the taxable estate of every decedent who is a citizen or resident of the United States').

114 26 U.S.C. § 2501(a) (imposing a tax 'for each calendar year on the transfer of property by gift during such calendar year by any individual resident or nonresident'.).

115 See, e.g. 26 U.S.C. § 2503(b)(1), Rev. Proc. 2019–44, p. 20 (providing an annual gift-tax exemption equal to $15,000 in 2020) and 26 U.S.C. § 2010(a), Rev. Proc. 2019–44, p. 19 (providing a lifetime unified exemption for estate and gift taxes equal to $11.58 million per person or $23.16 million per couple in 2020).

116 Tax Policy Center, Briefing Book Table 1, available at https://www.taxpolicycenter.org/briefing-book/how-many-people-pay-estate-tax

117 See Bahá'u'lláh, *Kitáb-i-Aqdas*, p. 109 (Question and Answer no. 8) (stating that 'only when the principal changeth hands is it once more subject to payment of Ḥuqúq, as it was the first time').

118 *Compilation of Compilations*, vol. 1, p. 503 (no. 1140).

How many are the souls who with the utmost endeavour and effort, collect a handful of worldly goods and greatly rejoice in this act and yet in reality the Pen of the Most High hath decreed this wealth for others; that is, it is not meant to be their lot or it may even fall into the hands of their enemies! We seek shelter in God from such an evident loss. One's life is wasted; by day and by night, troubles are endured, and wealth becometh a source of affliction. Most of the wealth of men is not pure. Should they follow what is revealed by God, they would, in all circumstances, be protected under His bounty and blessed by His mercy.[119]

RATE STRUCTURE

Ḥuqúqu'lláh and the U.S. federal income tax also differ in their rate structure. Ḥuqúqu'lláh is calculated based on a single, flat rate of 19 percent on wealth exceeding the exempt amount. The U.S. federal income tax, in contrast, imposes a host of different rates on income. For example, in 2024, individuals' ordinary income was subject to seven different rates, ranging from 10 percent to 37 percent, depending on total taxable income.[120] Capital gains are subject to more favorable tax rates, ranging from 0 percent to 20 percent, depending on the taxpayer's total taxable income as well as the type of capital from which the gain was derived.[121] The complexity of the federal income tax is due, in part, to this graduated income tax rate structure.

In theory, the U.S. federal income tax could have a single tax rate. In fact, in five years of the 100-plus-year history of the U.S. federal income tax, all prior to 1913, when the Sixteenth Amendment explicitly authorized the federal income tax, a single tax rate, ranging from 2 percent to 5 percent, was imposed.[122] Moreover, the system's progressive rate structure has been criticized,[123] and a host of flat rate tax proposals have been introduced over the years. Nevertheless, political pressures have pushed the U.S. federal income tax system toward a progressive (multiple) tax rate structure (with rates increasing as income increases) rather than a rate structure like Ḥuqúqu'lláh's single rate of 19 percent.[124]

The fact that Ḥuqúqu'lláh has a single, flat rate seems to be due to the fact that it is calculated based on wealth and represents the share of our wealth that belongs to God. As the Kitáb-i-Aqdas provides, 'Should a person acquire one hundred mithqáls of gold, nineteen mithqáls thereof belong unto God.'[125] Thus, 19 percent of our excess wealth belongs to God, regardless of the size of that excess.

---

119 ibid. p. 505 (no. 1145).
120 26 U.S.C. § 1.
121 26 U.S.C. § 1(h).
122 See Federal Individual Income Tax Rates History, available at https://files.taxfoundation.org/legacy/docs/fed_individual_rate_history_nominal.pdf
123 For the classic critique of progressive taxation, see Blum and Kalven, 'The Uneasy Case for Progressive Taxation'. For a more recent discussion of the arguments in favor of and against the progressive rate structure, see Conway, 'Money, It's a Crime'.
124 For a history of the role of progressivity in the U.S. tax system, see Bank, 'Origins of a Flat Tax'.
125 Bahá'u'lláh, Kitáb-i-Aqdas, p. 55, para. 97.

With respect to income taxes, in contrast, the Bahá'í writings do support a progressive income tax rate structure. For example, in an address given in Montreal, Canada in 1912, on 'economic happiness for the human race', 'Abdu'l-Bahá asserted that the solution to the world's economic problems includes a progressive income tax.[126] Under such a system, no tax would be imposed on individuals whose income is equal to their expenditures, but the greater an individual's surplus, the higher the rate of tax that would be imposed. 'Abdu'l-Bahá offered the following example:

> A farmer with expenses of $1,000 and income of $2,000 would be subject to a 10 percent tax on the surplus. A farmer with expenses of $1,000 and income of $10,000 or $20,000 would be required to pay one-fourth of his surplus, while a farmer with income of $100,000 and expenses of $5,000 would be required to pay one-third. A farmer with income of $200,000 and expenses of $10,000 would be required to pay one-half of his surplus.[127]

'Abdu'l-Bahá explained that this graduated income tax is part of the solution to the world's economic problems because man 'is in need of cooperation and reciprocity . . . [I]f one member of the members [of humanity] be in distress or be afflicted with some disease all the other members must necessarily suffer.'[128] Members with a surplus must necessarily share their surplus with others to ensure that all have enough.

ENFORCEMENT

As we have already noted, the Kitáb-i-Aqdas, Bahá'u'lláh's book of laws, sets forth the law of Ḥuqúqu'lláh. Payment of Ḥuqúqu'lláh is one of the binding spiritual obligations imposed upon Bahá'ís.[129] As Bahá'u'lláh declared, 'It is incumbent on everyone to discharge the obligation of Ḥuqúqu'lláh.'[130]

At the same time, the calculation and payment of Ḥuqúqu'lláh remains a purely voluntary act, which depends entirely on the will of individual believers. According to Bahá'u'lláh, 'Let him who wisheth observe it, and let him who wisheth ignore it.'[131] In this respect it is very different from a tax.

Because Ḥuqúqu'lláh is a spiritual obligation that depends solely on the love of believers for Bahá'u'lláh,[132] Bahá'í institutions are prohibited from demanding the payment of Ḥuqúqu'lláh. Pressure and intimidation may play no role in the collection of Ḥuqúqu'lláh. The Universal House of Justice has cautioned, 'under

---

126 'Abdu'l-Bahá, 'Economic Happiness for the Human Race', p. 227.
127 See ibid. pp. 228–9.
128 ibid. p. 227.
129 *Compilation of Compilations*, vol. 1, p. 518 (no. 1194).
130 ibid. p. 490 (no. 1105).
131 Quoted in Waters, *A Workbook*, p. 53 (no. 81).
132 ibid. p. 167 (talk on the Elements of Ḥuqúqu'lláh by Dr 'Alí Muḥammad Varqá).

no circumstances may contributions to any of these funds, even the Ḥuqúqu'lláh, be demanded or solicited from individual believers'.[133]

Although Bahá'í institutions may not demand the payment of Ḥuqúqu'lláh, they may educate believers about their obligation to pay Ḥuqúqu'lláh. The Universal House of Justice has explained that the goal of such education is to attract the hearts of believers so that they obey the law 'as part of their yearning to pursue the path of spiritual development prescribed by Bahá'u'lláh'.[134] Bahá'í institutions may gently remind Bahá'ís of their obligation to pay Ḥuqúqu'lláh, but such reminders must be general in nature.

The payment of Ḥuqúqu'lláh is thus a spiritually binding obligation of Bahá'ís under Bahá'í law – but it is not an enforceable one. In this sense payment of Ḥuqúqu'lláh is voluntary. This is very different from the payment of U.S. federal income tax. U.S. federal law requires U.S. citizens (and certain other individuals) to pay federal income tax and imposes serious penalties if they fail to do so.

Some may argue that the payment of federal income tax, like the payment of Ḥuqúqu'lláh, is voluntary because the system relies on what the U.S. government refers to as 'voluntary compliance'[135] for collection of the tax. The payment of U.S. federal income tax, however, is only voluntary in the sense that individual taxpayers file their returns and pay their taxes without the IRS first calculating the amount of tax the taxpayers owe and then forcing taxpayers to pay the amount due.[136] The U.S. tax system may be better described as a system of 'voluntary compulsion'[137] or 'cooperative compliance'[138] than one of 'voluntary compliance'.

The U.S. tax system is structured so as to encourage – and ultimately compel – the payment of income tax in a number of ways. First, federal tax law encourages the payment of taxes by imposing reporting obligations. The Internal Revenue Code requires individuals and entities that pay wages, dividends, interest, and other items to file information returns reporting the amounts to the IRS[139] so that the IRS can determine whether the recipients of these items properly reported the items on their income tax returns. A study by the IRS shows that taxpayers are much more likely to report and thus pay tax on income that is reported to the IRS than on income that is not reported to the IRS.[140]

The information reporting requirements are bolstered by withholding requirements. For example, the Internal Revenue Code requires employers to withhold

---

133 *Compilation of Compilations*, vol. 1, p. 524 (no. 1205).
134 Quoted in Waters, *A Workbook*, p. 60 (no. 100).
135 See Manhire, 'What Does Voluntary Tax Compliance Mean?', p. 11.
136 U.S. v. Schiff, 876 U.S. 272 (2nd Cir. 1989), p. 275.
137 Lederman, 'The Interplay Between Norms and Enforcement in Tax Compliance', p. 1455 n. 6 (citing George Guttman, 'The Interplay of Enforcement and Voluntary Compliance', 83 *Tax Notes* 1683 (1999), p. 1685 (quoting former Commissioner of Internal Revenue Jerome Kurtz)).
138 Manhire, 'What Does Voluntary Tax Compliance Mean?' (arguing that it would be clearer for the IRS to use the term 'cooperative compliance' rather than 'voluntary compliance').
139 See 26 U.S.C. § 6401(a).
140 See Lederman, 'Reducing Information Gaps to Reduce the Tax Gap', p. 1738, quoting Charles P. Rettig, 'Nonfilers Beware: Who's That Knocking at Your Door?', *Journal of Tax Practice and Procedure* 19 (October–November 2006), pp. 19–20.

taxes from employees' wages.[141] According to one commentator, withholding 'has probably done more to increase the tax-collecting power of central governments than any other one tax measure at any time in history'.[142]

The Internal Revenue Service may further ensure that individuals pay their income tax by examining their income tax returns. IRS examinations, commonly referred to as audits, are intended to verify that taxpayers report their tax liability correctly.[143] If, after examination, the IRS finds that a taxpayer has underreported his or her income tax liability, the taxpayer must either pay the additional amount or appeal the IRS's determination to a court. If the court finds that the taxpayer owes additional tax, the taxpayer is required to pay the additional tax due as well as interest on the underpayment.[144] In addition, the taxpayer may be subject to civil penalties[145] and even, in certain circumstances, criminal sanctions[146] for failure to pay his or her income tax. If a taxpayer does not pay the amount owed to the IRS, the IRS may levy (lawfully seize) the taxpayer's property to pay the debt.[147]

It is possible that in the future, in accordance with relevant guidance of the Universal House of Justice, Bahá'ís may have the option to voluntarily have a portion of their income withheld and sent directly to the Ḥuqúqu'lláh trust fund in order to facilitate the payment of Ḥuqúqu'lláh. Similarly, it is at least conceivable that in the future Bahá'ís may be able to voluntarily disclose information about their income, wealth, and expenses to Ḥuqúqu'lláh representatives in order to obtain detailed guidance on how to calculate their Ḥuqúqu'lláh obligation.

On the other hand, it is inconceivable that mandatory withholding, reporting, and audits would ever be used to enforce Ḥuqúqu'lláh. Those methods of compliance would be contrary to Bahá'u'lláh's instruction:

> No one should demand the Ḥuqúqu'lláh. Its payment should depend on the volition of the individuals themselves, namely such souls that are devout, faithful, and well disposed, who would make their offerings of Ḥuqúqu'lláh in a spirit of willing submission and contentment.[148]

The mandatory enforcement mechanisms used to ensure compliance with U.S. federal income tax law would debase and thus violate the sacred law of Ḥuqúqu'lláh, contrary to Bahá'u'lláh's counsel that 'at all times one must have the utmost regard for the dignity and honour of the Cause of God'.[149]

This is not to suggest that there is no penalty whatsoever for failure to

---

141 26 U.S.C § 3402. Virtually all countries with an income tax impose a withholding requirement. See Soos, 'Self-Employed Evasion and Tax Withholding', pp. 126–7.
142 Soos, 'Self-Employed Evasion and Tax Withholding', p. 126, quoting MacGregor, 'Further Thoughts on Tax Levels and Prospective Welfare Expenditures', 4 *Canadian Tax Journal* 171 (1956), p. 173.
143 IRS News Release, *The Examination (Audit) Process*, FS-97–5, 1997 WL 81273 (February 1997).
144 26 U.S.C. § 6601.
145 26 U.S.C. § 6662.
146 26 U.S.C. § 7201.
147 26 U.S.C. § 6331.
148 *Compilation of Compilations*, vol. 1, p. 506 (no. 1149).
149 ibid. p. 506 (no. 1148).

voluntarily pay Ḥuqúqu'lláh. In setting forth the law in the Kitáb-i-Aqdas, Bahá'u'lláh warned, 'O people! Deal not faithlessly with the Right of God . . . He who dealeth faithlessly with God shall in justice meet with faithlessness himself.'[150]

GOALS OR PURPOSES

Undoubtedly, Ḥuqúqu'lláh and the U.S. federal income tax share at least one common goal or purpose: raising revenue. Raising revenue, however, is not the sole goal or purpose of either Ḥuqúqu'lláh or the U.S. federal income tax.[151] The U.S. federal income tax, with all of its complexity, may be said to further two additional goals: (1) promoting economic and social justice, and (2) regulating behavior.[152] Ḥuqúqu'lláh, which is fundamentally a spiritual law, also promotes economic and social justice and regulates behavior.

Raising Revenue

The quintessential purpose of taxation is to raise revenue.[153] As U.S. Supreme Court Justice Oliver Wendell Holmes famously said, 'Taxes are what we pay for civilized society.'[154] Federal taxes provide the federal government with the revenue necessary to run the government and provide services such as building roads, protecting the environment, enforcing safe workplaces, and protecting American citizens.[155]

Since its inception, the U.S. federal income tax has been used to raise revenue,[156] and the Internal Revenue Service's culture, practices, and procedures are directed toward its mission of raising revenue.[157] Indeed, Nina Olson, the National Taxpayer Advocate, has described the Internal Revenue Service as 'the federal government's accounts receivable department'.[158]

Similarly, Bahá'u'lláh has explicitly stated that 'the purpose underlying this law [Ḥuqúqu'lláh] is to ensure that the General Treasury is strengthened in the future'.[159] Bahá'u'lláh has explained that Ḥuqúqu'lláh 'was revealed in the Book of God for various necessary matters ordained by God to be dependent on material means'.[160] Bahá'u'lláh has further elaborated, 'inasmuch as God hath made the

---

150 Bahá'u'lláh, *Kitáb-i-Aqdas*, p. 56, para. 97.
151 Commentators have long argued that the U.S. federal income tax is used to achieve social and economic goals beyond raising revenue. See, e.g. Cush, 'Social and Economic Goals Through Federal Taxation'.
152 Avi-Yonah, 'The Three Goals of Taxation', pp. 3–4.
153 Duruigbo, 'Tackling Shareholder Short-Termism and Managerial Myopia', p. 547 (stating that the central purpose of taxation is to raise revenue).
154 Compañia General de Tabacos de Filipinas v. Collector of Internal Revenue, 275 U.S. 87 (1927), p. 100 (Holmes, J., dissenting).
155 Hickman, 'Administering the Tax System We Have', pp. 1723–4.
156 For an early history of the U.S. federal income and its role in raising revenue, see McMahon, 'A Law with a Life of its Own'.
157 Hickman, 'Administering the Tax System We Have', pp. 1723–4.
158 ibid.
159 *Compilation of Compilations*, vol. 1, pp. 493–4 (no. 1117).
160 ibid. p. 491 (no. 1107).

achievement of everything conditional upon material means, therefore the injunction prescribing payment of the Ḥuqúq hath been revealed from the heaven of His Will'.[161]

The Universal House of Justice has said that Ḥuqúqu'lláh 'will provide the material resources necessary for great collective enterprises designed to improve all aspects of life, and will be a powerful element in the growth of a world civilization'.[162] Similarly, the Universal House of Justice has also affirmed that the institution of Ḥuqúqu'lláh 'will expand and flourish in the centuries to come, and will provide material resources essential for the advancement of the human race'.[163] It is clear, then, that a central function of the material side of Ḥuqúqu'lláh is the raising of revenue to support the development of a new global civilization.

Promoting Economic and Social Justice

As discussed above, for the vast majority of its 100-plus-year history, the U.S. federal income tax has had a progressive rate structure; that is, as a taxpayer's income increases so does the rate at which she or he is taxed. Progressive income taxation, founded on the equitable principle of 'ability to pay', is, according to one scholar, 'guided by concerns for equity and economic and social justice'.[164]

Prior to the adoption of the progressive income tax, most revenue in the United States was collected through indirect taxes, principally tariffs and regressive taxes on alcohol and tobacco.[165] The progressive income tax, introduced in the early 20th century, attempted to shift the burden of financing the country to those with the greatest ability to pay.[166]

Although subject to considerable criticism over the years,[167] the progressive rate structure is intended to redistribute income or wealth from higher-income individuals to lower-income individuals by imposing a higher tax burden on individuals with higher incomes. According to Professor Avi-Yonah, the U.S. federal income tax has been quite successful in redistributing income because the vast majority of federal income tax comes from the taxpayers with the highest income.[168] As discussed above, the Bahá'í writings support a progressive income tax and the shifting of the burden of taxation on those most able to pay.

Although Ḥuqúqu'lláh is calculated based on a flat 19 percent rate, Ḥuqúqu'lláh, like the progressive U.S. federal income tax, promotes equity and economic and social justice. First, individuals with higher levels of income typically have higher levels of excess wealth and thus may be subject to Ḥuqúqu'lláh on a higher

---

161 ibid. p. 500 (no. 1132).
162 Waters, *A Workbook*, p. 31 (no. 30).
163 ibid. p. 58 (no. 96).
164 Mehrota, 'Envisioning the Modern American Fiscal State', p. 1795.
165 ibid. p. 1794.
166 ibid. p. 1798.
167 For discussions on the propriety of progressive taxation, see, for example, Byrne, 'Progressive Taxation Revisited'; Bankman and Griffith, 'Social Welfare and the Rate Structure'.
168 See Avi-Yonah, 'The Three Goals of Taxation', pp. 19–20.

percentage of their income than individuals with lower levels of income. Second, and more importantly, Ḥuqúqu'lláh can be seen as an integral part of the spiritual solution to the world's economic problems. By requiring that we voluntarily return a share of our wealth in a 'spirit of joy and radiance', Ḥuqúqu'lláh teaches us to approach our material wealth in a spiritual fashion. As Dr Ramin Khadem explained in his discussion of 'Ḥuqúqu'lláh and Prosperity',[169] a spiritual approach to wealth should lead us away from the excesses of our current society and toward a more equitable distribution of wealth as we learn to shift our focus from self and material thoughts and desires toward God and the happiness of humanity as a whole.

Regulating Behavior

The third overarching goal of the U.S. federal income tax is to regulate behavior.[170] Much of the complexity of the Internal Revenue Code is due to its attempt to regulate taxpayer behavior through 'tax expenditures'.[171] Tax expenditures are departures from standard income tax norms that are designed to encourage certain kinds of behavior by taxpayers or to aid taxpayers in special circumstances. Tax expenditures may take the form of income tax exclusions, deductions, credits, deferrals, or preferential tax rates.

The Internal Revenue Code is replete with more than one hundred tax expenditures,[172] although most of the revenue loss is attributable to a handful of expenditures. To illustrate, the Joint Committee on Taxation estimated that total tax expenditures (including both individual and corporate income tax expenditures) would cost almost $2.5 trillion in lost income tax revenue in 2023.[173] One of the largest individual tax expenditures was the exclusion for employer-sponsored health insurance: the cost of health insurance provided by employers is excluded from employees' gross income[174] and thus is not subject to federal income tax. This tax expenditure was estimated to represent about $202 billion in lost income tax revenue in 2023.[175] Other significant tax expenditures included the exclusion of contributions to and earnings on defined contribution retirement plans (about $224.5 billion)[176] and the mortgage interest deduction (about $25 billion).[177]

Unlike the U.S. federal income tax, Ḥuqúqu'lláh does not seek to regulate

169 In Waters, *A Workbook*, pp. 221–8.
170 For a brief overview of the arguments in favor of and against the use of taxes to regulate behavior, see Garbarino and Allevato, 'The Global Architecture of Financial Regulatory Taxes', pp. 610–13.
171 Stanley Surrey coined this term in the 1960's. Hickman, 'Administering the Tax System We Have', pp. 1728–9 and note 58, citing Stanley S. Surrey, *Pathways to Tax Reform* (1973), p. vii.
172 See U.S. Government Accountability Office, 'Tax Expenditures', p. 1 (stating that there were 169 tax expenditures in fiscal year 2015).
173 Joint Committee on Taxation, 'Estimates of Federal Tax Expenditures for Fiscal Years 2023–2027', p. 41.
174 26 U.S.C. § 106.
175 Joint Committee on Taxation, 'Estimates of Federal Tax Expenditures for Fiscal Years 2023–2027', p. 36.
176 ibid. p. 38.
177 ibid. p. 32.

behavior through tax expenditures. Ḥuqúqu'lláh does not have a host of deductions, credits, exclusions, and preferential rates that are intended to influence individuals' choices about how to spend or save money. Instead, a single rate of 19 percent and a single deduction for needful expenses apply. As discussed above, guidance from the Universal House of Justice indicates that individuals may, in their discretion, choose to deduct some expenses that qualify as tax expenditures under the federal income tax, such as retirement savings and home mortgage interest. Bahá'ís, however, are not encouraged to incur such expenses in order to avoid Ḥuqúqu'lláh. Quite to the contrary, as the Universal of House of Justice has written, 'the devoted believer who is privileged to pay "the Right of God", far from seeking excuses for evading this spiritual obligation, will do his utmost to meet it'. [178]

Although Ḥuqúqu'lláh does not encourage behavior through tax expenditures, it is intended to influence behavior. Indeed, 'Abdu'l-Bahá has assured Bahá'ís that paying Ḥuqúqu'lláh will have a great influence on their hearts and souls. [179]

Material wealth is a challenge for human beings. Dr Ali-Muhammad Varqá, Hand of the Cause of God and Chief Trustee of Ḥuqúqu'lláh, noted, 'In moderation [material wealth] is the source of prosperity, felicity, and good life; however, if it transgresses the boundary of moderation, it pulls man downward and becomes a source of selfishness and ego.'[180] By requiring individuals to voluntarily, with the utmost joy and pleasure, return a portion of their wealth to God, Ḥuqúqu'lláh uses this material test to help Bahá'ís develop spiritual qualities. As Dr Javaheri has said:

> The law of Ḥuqúqu'lláh is an opportunity – a laboratory in which everyone can, in the privacy of his or her conscience, develop [spiritual] qualities. It provides an evolutionary process for our spiritual growth. Its observance provides us with the unique opportunity to develop such qualities and virtues that are lamentably scarce in today's world and are the bedrock of a just and peaceful society.[181]

'Abdu'l-Bahá identified two of the spiritual qualities paying Ḥuqúqu'lláh promotes: firmness and steadfastness.[182] Ian Semple, long-time member of the Universal House of Justice, added trustworthiness, honesty, loyalty, and sincerity to the list of virtues.[183] Dr Javaheri added yet another virtue to the list: detachment. Paying Ḥuqúqu'lláh teaches Bahá'ís to distinguish their needs from their wants as they follow their conscience in determining which of their expenditures are exempt as needful expenses and which are subject to the payment of Ḥuqúqu'lláh.[184]

As individuals develop these virtues and see their worldly possessions play a

---

178 *Compilation of Compilations*, vol. 1, p. 523 (no. 1202).
179 ibid. p. 511 (no. 1160).
180 Quoted in Waters, *A Workbook*, p. 177.
181 Quoted in ibid. p. 235 (extract from presentation by Dr Firaydoun Javaheri on 'The Social Dimensions of the Law of Ḥuqúqu'lláh').
182 *Compilation of Compilations*, vol. 1, p. 511 (nos. 1160 and 1161).
183 Waters, *A Workbook*, p. 211.
184 ibid. p. 232.

role in their spiritual growth, a fundamental change in human behavior is expected to emerge. First, as Dr Ramin Khadem has pointed out, individuals should become more moderate in their spending habits and move away from the purely luxurious consumption so prevalent in the world today as they share their wealth with God and strive not to shortchange God by excessive consumption.[185]

Second, individuals should be motivated to work harder (and earn more) in their desire to pay Ḥuqúqu'lláh on their income. Indeed, in a talk on 'The Social Dimensions of the Law of Ḥuqúqu'lláh', Dr Javaheri shared two stories in which Bahá'ís explained how the desire to pay Ḥuqúqu'lláh transformed their lives as they changed their work and spending habits in order to receive the bounty of paying Ḥuqúqu'lláh.[186]

The desire to pay Ḥuqúqu'lláh, combined with Bahá'u'lláh's elevation of 'work to the rank of worship',[187] should lead to a healthy work ethic. Shoghi Effendi has explained that work 'has not only a utilitarian purpose, but has a value in itself, because it draws us nearer to God, and enables us to better grasp His purpose for us in this world'.[188]

Ḥuqúqu'lláh should also lead to a more equitable distribution of wealth throughout the world. First, the payment of Ḥuqúqu'lláh by individuals with excess wealth will necessarily reduce their wealth and thus reduce some of the disparity of wealth between individuals. Second, the Universal House of Justice may redistribute wealth through Ḥuqúqu'lláh spending policies. In this connection, according to 'Abdu'l-Bahá, Ḥuqúqu'lláh 'will be expended for the relief of the poor, the disabled, the needy, and the orphans and for other vital needs of the Cause of God'.[189] According to the Universal House of Justice, 'the vast majority of the world's Bahá'ís are poor and cannot adequately support their national funds'.[190] It has indicated that it is currently using Ḥuqúqu'lláh to redistribute wealth by subsidizing Bahá'í national funds in those countries in which needs cannot be met by the local Bahá'í population.[191] Finally, paying Ḥuqúqu'lláh should help teach individuals detachment from their wealth, and encourage them to voluntarily share their wealth to promote the well-being of all humanity.

Transformation of Society

In setting forth the law of Ḥuqúqu'lláh, Bahá'u'lláh declared, 'in it there are benefits and wisdoms beyond the ken of anyone but God'.[192] Although it is not

---

185 ibid. p. 228.
186 See ibid. p. 234.
187 Bahá'u'lláh, *Kitáb-i-Aqdas*, p. 31, para. 33.
188 'Redistribution of Wealth', by Bahá'u'lláh, 'Abdu'l-Bahá, Shoghi Effendi, and Universal House of Justice, compiled by Research Department of the Universal House of Justice, available at https://bahai-library.com/compilation_redistribution_wealth (no. 18 from a letter written on behalf of Shoghi Effendi to a National Spiritual Assembly on 22 March 1937).
189 *Compilation of Compilations*, vol. 1, p. 513 (no. 1173).
190 Waters, *A Workbook*, p. 65 (no. 110).
191 See ibid.
192 Bahá'u'lláh, *Kitáb-i-Aqdas*, p. 55, para. 97.

possible to fully understand or explain Ḥuqúqu'lláh, it is possible to glean from the Bahá'í writings some of the spiritual benefits of Ḥuqúqu'lláh and its potential to transform society.

Assuredly, the benefits of Ḥuqúqu'lláh fall to the individual who pays it. According to Bahá'u'lláh, it is 'a bounty which shall remain with every soul in every world in the worlds of God, the All-Possessing, the All-Bountiful'.[193] The Universal House of Justice explains that Ḥuqúqu'lláh 'purifies one's possessions, averts loss and disaster, and conduces to prosperity and honour and imparts divine increase and blessings'.[194] Dr Varqá has described Ḥuqúqu'lláh as 'a magnet which attracts divine blessings and confirmation . . . Bahá'u'lláh . . . showers His limitless benediction upon those who observe the law'.[195]

The benefits of Ḥuqúqu'lláh, however, are not limited to the individuals who pay it. In *The Secret of Divine Civilization*, 'Abdu'l-Bahá wrote:

> The primary purpose, the basic objective, in laying down powerful laws and setting up great principles and institutions dealing with every aspect of civilization, is human happiness; and human happiness consists only in drawing closer to the Threshold of Almighty God, and in securing the peace and well-being of every individual member, high and low alike, of the human race.[196]

Paying Ḥuqúqu'lláh draws us closer to God as we joyfully return His share of our wealth to Him, and it helps secure the well-being of every member of the human race by reducing the extremes of poverty and wealth.

In *Some Answered Questions*, 'Abdu'l-Bahá asked:

> Gracious God! How can one see one's fellow men hungry, destitute, and deprived, and yet live in peace and comfort in one's splendid mansion? How can one see others in the greatest need and yet take delight in one's fortune? That is why it has been decreed in the divine religions that the wealthy should offer up each year a portion of their wealth for the sustenance of the poor and the assistance of the needy. This is one of the foundations of the religion of God and is an injunction binding upon all. And since in this regard one is not outwardly compelled or obliged by the government, but rather aids the poor at the prompting of one's own heart and in a spirit of joy and radiance, such a deed is most commendable, approved, and pleasing.[197]

The Universal House of Justice has assured us that, in time, Ḥuqúqu'lláh will 'give rise to a transformation of society far beyond our present capacity to

---

193 *Compilation of Compilations*, vol. 1, p. 490 (no. 1105).
194 ibid. p. 521 (no. 1198).
195 Waters, *A Workbook*, p. 168.
196 'Abdu'l-Bahá, *Secret of Divine Civilization*, p. 60.
197 'Abdu'l-Bahá, *Some Answered Questions*, pp. 319–20.

comprehend'.[198] A lengthy tablet by 'Abdu'l-Bahá provides some insights into this transformation. In the tablet, 'Abdu'l-Bahá explains that the world is like the human body. Just as the human body, which outwardly appears to be composed of different limbs and organs, is an organic whole inseparably linked together, so too is the world of being. 'Abdu'l-Bahá writes:

> . . . co-operation, mutual aid and reciprocity are essential characteristics in the unified body of the world of being, inasmuch as all created things are closely related together . . . acts of co-operation, mutual assistance and reciprocity are not confined to the body and to things that pertain to the material world, but for all conditions, whether physical or spiritual, such as those related to minds, thoughts, opinions, manners, customs, attitudes, understandings, feelings, or other human susceptibilities. In all these thou shouldst find these binding relationships securely established. The more this interrelationship is strengthened and expanded, the more will human society advance in progress and prosperity . . . This is the basic principle on which the institution of Ḥuqúqu'lláh is established.[199]

Simply put, the fundamental idea is that all of humanity is inexorably linked together. What one person does or thinks has an impact on the rest of humanity. This concept is illustrated by the psychological phenomenon known as 'emotional contagion'. Emotional contagion is 'the tendency to automatically mimic and synchronize expressions, vocalizations, postures, and movements with those of another person and, consequently, to converge emotionally'.[200] Studies from a wide variety of disciplines, ranging from animal researchers to clinical researchers, social psychologists, and sociologists, show that people often catch emotions from one another.[201] Studies further show that emotional contagion may ripple through a group of individuals so as to influence the behavior of the entire group.[202]

In *The Hidden Words*, Bahá'u'lláh suggests that emotional contagion extends to the spirit. Specifically, one Hidden Word provides: 'The company of the ungodly increaseth sorrow whilst fellowship with the righteous cleanseth the rust from off the heart.'[203] This suggests that the spiritual bounties that accrue to individuals who pay Ḥuqúqu'lláh may also spread to those who accompany them.

Dr Varqá asserts that future scientific progress is expected to shed more light on the hidden realities of Ḥuqúqu'lláh, especially 'in the fields of cause and effect, reciprocity, and mutual assistance, which bind together all the component parts of the world of creation and control their cooperation in harmony and balance'.[204]

---

198 Waters, *A Workbook*, p. 59 (no. 98).
199 Quoted in *Compilation of Compilations*, pp. 509–10 (no. 1159).
200 Hatfield, Cacioppo and Rapson, 'Emotional Contagion', p. 96.
201 ibid. p. 99.
202 See, e.g. Barsade, 'The Ripple Effect'.
203 Bahá'u'lláh, *Hidden Words*, Persian no. 56.
204 Quoted in Waters, *A Workbook*, p. 184.

Undoubtedly, the law of Ḥuqúqu'lláh helps strengthen the bonds of humanity and will lead to a more connected, healthier, and spiritual society beyond our current capacity to imagine.

Conclusion

Outwardly, Ḥuqúqu'lláh bears some resemblance to the U.S. federal income tax. It is a law that raises revenue utilized by the central governing body of the Bahá'í Faith to help the needy and promote the principles of the Faith. At its heart, however, Ḥuqúqu'lláh is a fundamentally different law with a spiritual purpose that has the potential to transform society. As Bahá'u'lláh has said:

> Were the people to know that which hath been concealed from their eyes and become fully aware of the ocean of grace which lieth hid within this divine command, all the people of the world would offer everything they possess in order to be mentioned by Him.[205]

Bibliography

'Abdu'l-Bahá. 'Economic Happiness for the Human Race'. *Star of the West*, vol. XIII, no. 9 (December 1922), pp. 227–32.

— *The Secret of Divine Civilization*. Translated from the Persian by Marzieh Gail in consultation with Ali-Kuli Khan. Wilmette, IL: Bahá'í Publishing Trust, 1990.

— *Some Answered Questions*. Collected and translated from the Persian by Laura Clifford Barney. Newly revised ed. Haifa: Bahá'í World Centre, 2014.

Avi-Yonah, Reuven S. 'The Three Goals of Taxation'. 60 *Tax Law Review* 1 (2006).

Bahá'u'lláh. *The Hidden Words*. Translated by Shoghi Effendi with the assistance of some English friends. Wilmette, IL: Bahá'í Publishing Trust, 1993.

— *The Kitáb-i-Aqdas: The Most Holy Book*. Wilmette, IL: Bahá'í Publishing Trust, 1994.

Bank, Steven A. 'Origins of a Flat Tax'. 73 *Denver University Law Review* 329 (1996).

Bankman, Joseph and Thomas Griffith. 'Social Welfare and the Rate Structure: A New Look at Progressive Taxation'. 75 *California Law Review* 1905 (1987).

Barsade, Sigal J. 'The Ripple Effect: Emotional Contagion and Its Influence on Group Behavior'. 47 *Administrative Science Quarterly* 644 (December 2002).

Blum, Walter J. and Harry Kalven, Jr. 'The Uneasy Case for Progressive Taxation'. 19 *University of Chicago Law Review* 417 (1950).

Book, Leslie; David Williams, and Krista Holub. 'Insights from Behavioral Economics Can Improve Administration of the EITC'. 37 *Virginia Tax Review* 177 (2018).

Byrne, Donna M. 'Progressive Taxation Revisited'. 37 *Arizona Law Review* 739 (1995).

Conway, Meredith R. 'Money, It's a Crime. Share It Fairly, But Don't Take a Slice of My Pie!' 39 *Journal of Legislation* 119 (2012–2013).

---

205 *Compilation of Compilations*, vol. 1, pp. 509–10 (no. 1142).

Cush, Robert. 'Social and Economic Goals Through Federal Taxation'. 18 *Minnesota Law Review* 759 (1934).

Drometer, Marcus; Marco Frank, Maria Hofbauer Pérez, Carla Rhode, Sebastian Schworm, and Tanja Stitteneder. 'Wealth and Inheritance Taxation: An Overview and Country Comparison'. 16 *ifo DICE Report* 2 (June 2018).

Duruigbo, Emeka. 'Tackling Shareholder Short-Termism and Managerial Myopia'. 100 *Kentucky Law Journal* 531 (2011–2012).

Freeland, James J.; Daniel J. Lathrope, Stephen A. Lind, and Richard B. Stephens. *Fundamentals of Federal Income Taxation.* 19th ed. MN: West Academic, 2018.

Garbarino, Carlo and Giulio Allevato. 'The Global Architecture of Financial Regulatory Taxes'. 36 *Michigan Journal of International Tax* 603 (2015).

Graetz, Michael J. and Deborah H. Schenk. *Federal Income Taxation: Principles and Policies.* 7th ed. MN: Foundation Press, 2013.

Halperin, Daniel I. 'Special Tax Treatment for Employer-Based Retirement Programs: Is It "Still" Viable as a Means of Increasing Retirement Income, Should It Continue?' 49 *Tax Law Review* 1 (1993).

Hasen, David. 'Accretion-Based Progressive Wealth Taxation'. 20 *Florida Tax Review* 277 (2017).

Hatfield, Elaine; John T. Cacioppo, and Richard L. Rapson. 'Emotional Contagion'. 2 *Current Directions in Psychological Science* 96 (1993).

Hickman, Kristin E. 'Administering the Tax System We Have'. 63 *Duke Law Journal* 1717 (2014).

Joint Committee on Taxation. 'Estimates of Federal Tax Expenditures for Fiscal Years 2023–2027'. JCX-59–23 (7 December 2023).

Kahn, Douglas A. and Jeffrey H. Kahn. 'Gifts, Gafts, and Gefts – The Income Tax Definition and Treatment of Private and Charitable "Gifts" and a Principled Policy Justification for the Exclusion of Gifts from Income'. 78 *Notre Dame Law Review* 441 (2003).

Klein, William A.; Joseph Bankman, Daniel N. Shaviro, and Kirk J. Stark. *Federal Income Taxation.* 15th ed. Frederick, MD.: Aspen, 2015.

Lederman, Leandra. 'The Interplay Between Norms and Enforcement in Tax Compliance'. 64 *Ohio State Law Journal* 1453 (2003).

— 'Reducing Information Gaps to Reduce the Tax Gap: When Is Information Reporting Warranted?' 78 *Fordham Law Review* 1733 (2010).

Manhire, J.T. 'What Does Voluntary Tax Compliance Mean? A Government Perspective'. 164 *University of Pennsylvania Law Review Online* 11 (2015).

McMahon, Stephanie Hunter. 'A Law with a Life of its Own: The Development of the Federal Income Tax Statutes Through World War I'. 7 *Pittsburgh Tax Review* 1 (2009).

Mehrota, Ajay K. 'Envisioning the Modern American Fiscal State: Progressive-Era Economists and the Intellectual Foundations of the U.S. Income Tax'. 52 *UCLA Law Review* 1793 (2005).

Moore, Kathryn L. 'An Overview of the U.S. Retirement Income Security System and the Principles and Values It Reflects'. 33 *Comparative Labor Law and Policy Journal* 5 (2011).

— *Understanding Employee Benefits Law.* 2nd ed. N.J.: Carolina Academic Press, 2020.

Phillips, Richard and Steve Wamhoff. 'The Federal Estate Tax: An Important Progressive

Revenue Source'. *Institute on Taxation and Economic Policy Report* (December 2018).

Piketty, Thomas. *Capital in the Twenty-First Century.* Translated by Arthur Goldhammer. U.S.: Harvard University Press, 2014.

Schenck, Deborah H. 'Foreword'. 53 *Tax Law Review* 257 (2000).

Richard Schmalbeck. 'Gifts and the Income Tax – An Enduring Puzzle'. 73–WTR *Law and Contemporary Problems* 63 (Winter 2010).

Soos, Piroska. 'Self-Employed Evasion and Tax Withholding: A Comparative Study and Analysis of the Issues'. 24 *University of California Davis Law Review* 107 (1990).

Stein, Norman P. and Patricia E. Dilley. 'Leverage, Linkage, and Leakage: Problems with the Private Pension System and How They Should Inform the Social Security Reform Debate'. 58 *Washington and Lee Law Review* 1369 (2001).

United States Government Accountability Office. 'Tax Expenditures: Opportunities Exist to Use Budgeting and Agency Performance Processes to Increase Oversight'. GAO-16–622 (July 2016).

Universal House of Justice. *The Compilation of Compilations*, vol. 1. Bahá'í Publications Australia, 1991.

Waters, Allan. *A Workbook for Understanding, Appreciating and Applying the Law of Ḥuqúqu'lláh: The Right of God.* 3rd ed. Bahá'í Publications Australia, 2012.

5

Equality and Security

Aaron Emmel

Equality before the law, supported by the recognition of the oneness of humanity, is necessary for stable and prosperous human societies. This point, articulated by Bahá'u'lláh and 'Abdu'l-Bahá more than a century ago, has since been continually reaffirmed by history.

In fact, the importance of acting on this relationship only becomes more urgent today. As technology brings us in ever closer proximity and interweaves our fates, artificial divisions between people make this a more dangerous world and pose a threat to security both within and between nations. Yet political leaders use the dangers created and exacerbated by disunity to justify the creation of new divisions to keep themselves in power.

Bahá'u'lláh explains that unity contributes to security. He writes: 'The well-being of mankind, its peace and security, are unattainable unless and until its unity is firmly established.'[1]

In the contemporary legal sphere, we can measure a political system's commitment to unity through its support for equality before the law. Equality before the law means that all people are treated the same by the legal system, whether they are rich or poor, and regardless of their connections, ethnicity, religion, gender, or any other factor. Equality before the law is a necessary component of the 'rule of law', which means that all individuals and institutions are equally accountable before the same law. The American Bar Association describes the rule of law as a system in which 'no one is above the law, everyone is treated equally under the law, everyone is held accountable to the same laws, there are clear and fair processes for enforcing laws, there is an independent judiciary, and human rights are guaranteed for all'.[2]

It is deeply ironic that security, national and international, is often used to justify attacking equality generally and undermining equal protection before the law specifically, when security depends on those protections. Even leaders who are

---

1   Bahá'u'lláh, *Gleanings*, p. 286.
2   American Bar Association, 'Rule of Law'.

inclined to act more cooperatively work within networks, institutions, and norma-tive environments that presuppose division and make it easy to overlook patterns of legal and social discrimination. Our collective ability to end violence and build prosperous societies depends on resolving that unjust discrepancy.

This chapter will provide a working definition of 'security', examine the concept of equality before the law in the Bahá'í writings, explore why equality contributes to stability, provide examples of how equality and security are linked, and propose some solutions to the problems of inequality and social divisions.

Defining 'Security'

People can mean many different things by the word 'security'.[3] At the simplest level, security can be understood in terms of a state's ability to defend itself and its people from both external and internal violence. The Uppsala/Human Security Centre database compiles information on three categories of political violence: (1) conflicts between states or between a state and a non-state actor, (2) conflicts in which none of the parties is a government, and (3) attacks on civilians by either a government or a non-state actor.[4]

This essay will define security as freedom from armed violence and its direct, destabilizing effects. Within states, this means that governments retain control over the organized use of force, and that force is not used against their own citi-zens outside of the due process of law. This is often referred to as a 'legitimate monopoly' on force or violence that prevents the emergence of private militias or paramilitary activity and deters public displays of violence, such as bombings. Internationally, it means freedom from cross-border attacks and the absence of violence that forces refugees to seek a safer life in new states.

The term 'security' can also be used more broadly, of course. During the 1990s, political scientists began to realize that food shortages, climate change, pandemic diseases, and economic dislocation could all trigger violence and, therefore, become security threats. In fact, not only could they lead to violence, but they were damaging to human well-being in and of themselves. These concerns have only grown since then; in 2019, a study commissioned by the U.S. Army War College warned about mass migration from climate change triggering new conflicts.[5]

In some studies, the definition of security has broadened to include those categories, under the new name of 'human security' or 'comprehensive security'.[6]

---

3   For example, security can be thought of broadly. The United States Institute of Peace and the United
    States Army Peacekeeping and Stability Operations Institute include five parameters of stable states
    in their book *Guiding Principles for Stabilization and Reconstruction*: Safe and Secure Environment,
    Rule of Law, Stable Governance, Sustainable Economy, and Social Well-Being. However, while all of
    these principles are important, they are too broad for this purpose.
4   Human Security Report Project at the Human Security Centre, *Human Security Report 2005*, p. 67.
    The report also uses a different categorization of conflict, which has four types: interstate conflict,
    intrastate conflict, extrastate conflict, and internationalized internal conflict. See ibid. p. 20.
5   United States Army War College, 'Implications of Climate Change for the U.S. Army'.
6   See, for example, the U.N. Trust Fund for Human Security, 'What Is Human Security'.

This approach had the salutary effect of raising the profile of these threats. However, many experts pointed out that to be useful, definitions should be specific, and 'comprehensive security' was broad enough to mean everything and nothing. Additionally, some observers worried that describing all of these factors as security problems implied that they had military solutions.[7] In any case, while the realization of equality does have a significant impact on economic and environmental outcomes, and poor economic and environment conditions can drive conflict, the limited scope of this essay will focus on armed conflicts themselves.

Equality Before the Law

The rule of law is necessary for any society that wishes to protect the rights and security of its people. It means that citizens are governed by publicly known laws rather than by the whims of individual rulers. Aristotle referred to this concept as 'a government of laws, not men'. The rule of law implies that all people are equal before the law and that leaders cannot bend the law to suit their own purposes.

The World Justice Project defines the rule of law as 'a system of laws, institutions, norms and community commitments'.[8] According to this definition, laws are just and fair, protect fundamental rights, and are publicized. Everyone is accountable to these laws, including the government. They are enforced in an accessible, fair, and efficient manner. They are administered by competent, ethical, and independent actors, who reflect the makeup of the communities they serve.

Equality before the law has social implications. At a talk in Paris in 1911, 'Abdu'l-Bahá identified equality before the law as a fundamental principle of Bahá'u'lláh, explaining: 'The Law must reign, and not the individual; thus will the world become a place of beauty and true brotherhood will be realized.'[9]

Bahá'í administrative institutions enshrine this concept by investing authority in elected bodies, whose members are as bound by their decisions as any other individuals. 'Abdu'l-Bahá, in *The Secret of Divine Civilization*, also highlights the importance of what the World Justice Project terms 'laws [that] are clear, publicized, stable and fair':[10]

> Up to now the religious law has not been given a decisive role in our courts, because each of the 'ulamá has been handing down decrees as he saw fit, based on his arbitrary interpretation and personal opinion. For example, two men will go to law, and one of the 'ulamá will find for the plaintiff and another for the defendant. It may even happen that in one and the same case two conflicting decisions will be handed down by the same mujtahid, on the grounds that he was inspired first in one direction and then in the other. There can be no doubt

---

7   On this point, and for a discussion of the application of Bahá'í principles to human security issues, see
     Emmel, *Taking Action in a Changing World*, chapters 1–2.
8   World Justice Project, 'What is the Rule of Law?'.
9   'Abdu'l-Bahá, *Paris Talks*, p. 132.
10   World Justice Project, 'What is the Rule of Law?'.

that this state of affairs has confused every important issue and must jeopardize the very foundations of society.

> . . . it is incumbent on those learned members of the great consultative assembly who are thoroughly versed in the Divine law to evolve a single, direct and definite procedure for the settlement of litigations. This instrument should then be published throughout the country by order of the king, and its provisions should be strictly adhered to.[11]

In the same text, 'Abdu'l-Bahá explains the importance of the justice system in upholding equal rights before the law:

> When, for example, the people are genuinely religious and are literate and well-schooled, and a difficulty presents itself, they can apply to the local authorities; if they do not meet with justice and secure their rights and if they see that the conduct of the local government is incompatible with the Divine good pleasure and the king's justice, they can then take their case to higher courts and describe the deviation of the local administration from the spiritual law.[12]

The Bahá'í promotion of equality before the law is rooted in the concept of spiritual equality, which recognizes every soul as being equal before God and capable of recognizing spiritual truth. Some Sufis believed that because religious law exists to lead people to the truth, once they had found the truth for themselves, they no longer needed to follow the law. Bahá'u'lláh replies to this view in 'The Seven Valleys' by stating that the law applies to all:

> In all these journeys the wayfarer must stray not a hair's breadth from the Law, for this is indeed the secret of the Path and the fruit of the Tree of Truth. And in all these stages he must cling to the robe of obedience to all that hath been enjoined, and hold fast to the cord of shunning all that is forbidden, that he may partake of the cup of the Law and be informed of the mysteries of Truth.[13]

Equality and Security in the Bahá'í Writings

Bahá'u'lláh declares that security depends on unity.[14] This principle rests on a spiritual truth, the equality of all people. In the words of 'Abdu'l-Bahá: 'In the estimation of God all men are equal; there is no distinction or preferment for any soul in the dominion of His justice and equity.'[15] 'Abdu'l-Bahá explains that equality is necessary for eliminating conflict:

---

11   'Abdu'l-Bahá, *Secret of Divine Civilization,* pp. 37–8.
12   ibid. p. 18.
13   Bahá'u'lláh, 'The Seven Valleys', in *Call of the Divine Beloved,* pp. 49–50.
14   Bahá'u'lláh, *Gleanings,* pp. 286–7.
15   'Abdu'l-Bahá, *Promulgation of Universal Peace,* p. 182.

> When all mankind shall receive the same opportunity of education and the equality of men and women be realized, the foundations of war will be utterly destroyed. Without equality this will be impossible because all differences and distinction are conducive to discord and strife.[16]

In its 1985 statement 'The Promise of World Peace', a message addressed 'to the Peoples of the World', the Universal House of Justice drew from the Bahá'í writings to provide six steps for building a more secure and stable world. These steps had 'immediate relevance to establishing world peace':

- an end to racism and racial prejudice;
- addressing the inordinate disparities between the rich and poor;
- a wider loyalty to humanity that is compatible with a 'sane and legitimate patriotism' but not 'unbridled nationalism';
- mutual religious forbearance in place of religious conflict and fanaticism;
- the emancipation of women; and
- universal education.[17]

Three decades later, in 2019, the Universal House of Justice wrote to the Bahá'ís of the world: 'Today, many of the dominant currents in societies everywhere are pushing people apart, not drawing them together.' It said that while 'the unification of humanity is unstoppable by any human force . . . the course humanity takes to achieve its destiny may very well be tortuous.' It affirmed that the challenge presents humanity with a crisis of identity: 'Rival conceptions about the primacy of a particular people are peddled to the exclusion of the truth that humanity is on a common journey in which all are protagonists.'[18] We can see this crisis in discriminatory institutions and practices around the world. The Bahá'í teachings on peace and security make a subtle and important point: we cannot resolve conflict by solely addressing conflict. The only way to achieve sustainable peace is by recognizing and acting on the innate equality of humankind. In the words of the Bahá'í International Community, the nongovernmental organization that represents the global Bahá'í community:

> Efforts to protect the rights of minorities which are inspired only by the desire to avoid or suppress conflict between minority groups or between minority groups and the dominant group in society are doomed to failure. The principle of the oneness of humanity provides not only a more constructive and far-reaching approach for ensuring minority rights, but also a creative basis for the resolution of long-standing tensions and the construction of a new world-embracing civilization.[19]

---

16   ibid. p. 175.
17   Universal House of Justice, *Promise of World Peace*, pp. 5–6.
18   Universal House of Justice, Letter to the Bahá'ís of the World, 18 January 2019.
19   Bahá'í International Community, Oral statement to the 42nd session of the United Nations Sub-

Inclusive political, economic, social, and legal systems and institutions – those that base themselves on the principle of the oneness of humanity – are necessary for building that civilization. Equality before the law and inclusive institutions are mutually reinforcing.

How Equality Contributes to Security

World War II taught the world's leaders the importance of equal rights for maintaining international security. Article 55 of the UN Charter identifies 'universal respect for, and observance of, human rights and fundamental freedoms for all without distinction as to race, sex, language, or religion' as being conducive 'to the creation of conditions of stability and well-being which are necessary for peaceful and friendly relations among nations'.[20] In 2007, Condoleezza Rice, then the U.S. Secretary of State, articulated a link between lasting 'peace and security' and 'the rule of law, limits on state power, free speech, religious liberty, equal justice, property rights, tolerance of difference, and respect for women'.[21] According to General Wesley Clark, former NATO Supreme Allied Commander, 'to think that we have to choose between emphasizing human rights and security is to misunderstand the system'.[22]

The relationship between rule of law and security is acknowledged in the United Nations' Sustainable Development Agenda, in which the 16th of 17 goals is to 'promote peaceful and inclusive societies for sustainable development, provide access to justice for all, and build effective, accountable and inclusive institutions at all levels'. In alignment with target 16.1, which is entitled 'Significantly reduce all forms of violence and related death rates everywhere', are 16.3, entitled 'promote the rule of law at the national and international levels and ensure equal access to justice for all', 16.6, entitled 'develop effective, accountable and transparent institutions at all levels', and 16.B, entitled 'promote and enforce non-discriminatory laws and policies for sustainable development'.[23]

The rise of militant groups, like the Taliban in Afghanistan, provides numerous examples of how an inability to provide equal protection under the law can lead to security failures. Rashid Rehman is a human rights lawyer in Pakistan who represented a 16-year-old girl, Najma, for the Human Rights Commission of Pakistan. Najma was raped at gunpoint in her home in front of her family by a member of a group of masked men led by a police constable who lived next door and wanted to intimidate the family in order to take over their land. The police inspector, Mr Khan, closed the case because, he said, he interviewed '60 or 90 people in the village mosque' who all stated that the constable was incapable of committing such a crime. Mr Khan claimed that Najma was lying to protect her father, an old man

Commission on Prevention of Discrimination and Protection of Minorities.
20   U.N. Charter, art. 55.
21   Rice, 'U.S. Policy in the Middle East'.
22   Clark, Wesley. Personal notes from Georgetown conference (on file with the author).
23   United Nations, 'Sustainable Development Goal 16'.

who could hardly walk, from a previous charge of having assaulted the constable. He also claimed that certain measurements revealed Najma to be a 'habitual fornicator'.[24] After being told that the case was closed, Rehman reflected in an interview with a *National Geographic* correspondent:

> When government fails them, people get angry. They lose faith in the government and look for alternatives. Think how easy it would be for the Islamists – or Taliban or al Qaeda – to go to the brothers of this girl now and say, 'What happened to your family is not justice. This man dishonored your sister, he dishonored your father and your family name. Join us and we will help you get justice. We will make him pay.' When citizens are denied their basic human rights, they become radicalized.[25]

Two years later, in 2009, exactly that happened in Pakistan's Swat Valley. The Taliban took it by organizing peasants who were frustrated with government corruption. The peasants formed armed gangs, which intimidated and pushed out the wealthy landowners.[26]

In Najma's case, it is easy to identify numerous factors that prevented a fair trial: she was a girl, she was young, and she lived in a place with visible extremes of wealth and poverty. As 'Abdu'l-Bahá indicated, ending conflict means recognizing and acting on our inherent equality.[27] Violent conflict often begins with human rights violations, and the risk of those violations rises whenever the general community excludes certain people – especially those less likely to be protected when they are made to appear fundamentally different and less than human.

The Importance of Inclusive Institutions

Equality before the law must be supported by inclusive political and legal institutions – institutions that are open to all and treat people equally.

In the book *Why Nations Fail: The Origins of Power, Prosperity, and Poverty*, authors Daron Acemoglu and James A. Robinson provide a wealth of evidence for the conclusion that 'inclusive economic institutions foster economic activity, productivity growth, and economic prosperity', and these institutions (or the lack thereof) explain better than any other theory why some societies prosper while others collapse.[28] Acemoglu and Robinson explain: 'Inclusive economic institutions . . . are those that allow and encourage participation by the great mass of people in economic activities that make best use of their talents and skills and that enable individuals to make the choices they wish.' These are institutions that feature equality before the law, as well as private property and a provision of

---

24   Belt, 'Struggle for the Soul of Pakistan'.
25   ibid. p. 55.
26   Perlez and Shah, 'Taliban Exploit Class Rifts to Gain Ground in Pakistan'.
27   See 'Abdu'l-Bahá, *Promulgation of Universal Peace*, pp. 181–2.
28   Acemoglu and Robinson, *Why Nations Fail*, p. 75.

public services 'that provides a level playing field'.[29]

The founders of the United States recognized that the rule of law could be threatened by self-interested groups, which they called 'factions'. James Madison hoped the new Constitution would:

> . . . break and control the violence of faction . . . By a faction I understand a number of citizens, whether amounting to a majority or minority of the whole, who are united and actuated by some common impulse of passion, or of interest, adverse to the rights of other citizens, or to the permanent and aggregate interests of the community.[30]

George Washington worried about the rise of political parties. He did so because, in his words:

> the alternate domination of one faction over another, sharpened by the spirit of revenge, natural to party dissension, which in different ages and countries has perpetrated the most horrid enormities, is itself a frightful despotism.[31]

The division of people into exclusionary groups is always potentially destabilizing, but it can lead to a battleground when it is also the demarcation of political and legal power. This is true whether the division is based on ethnicity, nationality, or religion. In Iraq, prior to elections in 2005, the Associated Press reported on the deaths of three political candidates with the explanation, 'Sunni Muslim militants, who make up the bulk of Iraq's insurgency, are increasingly homing in on Shiites in their effort to ruin the election that is widely expected to propel their religious rivals to a position of dominance.'[32]

This example illustrates that stable societies cannot be built on structures and norms that define people according to disparate groups and keep those groups separate. Whether in Iraq or the Reconstruction-era United States, elections are important for countries transitioning from authoritarianism to democracy, but so are legal and structural frameworks that can prevent power from being held by factions, which can then wield it over other minorities or majorities. Inclusive institutions are necessary to defend the rule of law, and the rule of law is what enables them to exist.

Diversity is Not Dangerous: How Inequality Contributes to Insecurity

In the long run, communities cannot sustain prosperity or security at the expense of their neighbors, and factions that perpetuate group identities over the common

---

29 ibid. pp. 74–5.
30 Publius (James Madison, Alexander Hamilton, and John Jay). For a fuller discussion of these principles, see Emmel, *Taking Action in a Changing World*.
31 Washington, 'Washington's Farewell Address to the People of the United States'.
32 Mroue, 'Gunmen Kill Three Iraqi Candidates'.

good are inherently destabilizing. The field of security studies explains why this is the case, and identifies specific risk factors that threaten security. These risk factors, by and large, are the same ones that the Universal House of Justice listed in its 1985 statement, 'The Promise of World Peace'.

One of the most important findings from the field of security studies is that diversity is not inherently destabilizing. This finding is consistent with the Bahá'í teachings, which refer to human diversity as a source of beauty and strength. In the words of 'Abdu'l-Bahá:

> . . . when divers shades of thought, temperament and character, are brought together under the power and influence of one central agency, the beauty and glory of human perfection will be revealed and made manifest.[33]

Harmonious societies are not based on uniformity; they are based on the broader identity that citizens hold in common.

Of the more than 190 nations in existence today, fewer than 20 are ethnically homogenous, defined as states in which ethnic minorities account for less than five percent of the population.[34] Studies demonstrate that ethnic and religious diversity has no statistically significant relationship with the outbreak of civil wars,[35] and that civil wars and insurgencies divide along ethnic lines only where leaders try to create divisions for their own political gain.[36] Ethnic conflict is most likely in the middle of the continuum from ethnic homogeneity to heterogeneity, when one ethnic group is of sufficient size to permanently exclude other groups from power.[37] Thus, security and economic stability may actually be increased by 'enhancing ethnic diversity while strengthening political institutions', according to Nicholas Sambanis of the Political Science Department at the University of Pennsylvania.[38] This is more effective than partitioning adversarial ethnic groups into different states. Partition does not prevent war, according to an empirical critique of the literature on ethnic war in 2000; it simply makes wars international.[39]

If diversity is not dangerous, what is? Conflict is more likely when groups must compete, or think they must compete, for scarce resources and legal protections because they perceive those to be lacking. 'The first reason for violent conflict is political exclusion,' write actor Don Cheadle and John Prendergast, a senior advisor to the International Crisis Group. 'For example,' they state, 'Darfurians and southern Sudanese certainly rebelled because of deep-seated grievances that drove thousands of people in both these places to pick up a gun and fight for their rights.'[40]

---

33 'Abdu'l-Bahá, quoted in Shoghi Effendi, *World Order*, p. 42.
34 Brown, 'The Causes of Internal Conflict', p. 7.
35 See e.g. Fearon and Laitin, 'Ethnicity, Insurgency, and Civil War'.
36 See Mueller, 'The Banality of "Ethnic War"'; Kaufman, *Modern Hatreds*.
37 Sambanis, 'Partition as a Solution to Ethnic War', p. 479.
38 ibid.
39 ibid.
40 Cheadle and Prendergast, *Not on Our Watch*, p. 210.

This is what happened in the former Yugoslavia, which broke apart along ethnic and religious lines in the 1990s. Over 100,000 people were killed and another million were driven from their homes. According to Elizabeth M. Cousens, a researcher of peace processes:

> . . . the rapid escalation of conflict had been due partly to the sheer factor of uncertainty about the boundaries of the political community within which basic rights would be guaranteed and the preemptive mobilization of ethnic groups that ensued.[41]

The 1995 peace agreement in Dayton, Ohio ended the Bosnian war, but it also institutionalized ethnic divisions. As *Atlantic* writer George Packer states, ethnic leaders:

> . . . denounce one another publicly and stoke mutual fears at election time, but behind the scenes they're cronies who collaborate to stay in power and fatten themselves off the same spoils system . . . Ethnic politics produces rampant corruption that chokes the economy and stunts social change.[42]

Clearly, violence increasingly grows more likely when political leaders stoke division to advance their own power. The Fund for Peace's Fragile States Index, which rates 178 national states according to 12 social, economic, and political indicators, shows that failed states are often associated with 'factionalized elites'.[43] This means that the political leaders and state institutions are divided along group lines. Leaders in these states frequently bolster their political influence by using 'nationalistic political rhetoric . . . often in terms of communal irredentism (e.g. a "greater Serbia") or of communal solidarity (e.g. "ethnic cleansing" or "defending the faith")'.[44] This rhetoric often also identifies victims, using a two-step process. First, the essential identity of the victims is chosen for them; and then that allegedly inferior identity is used as justification for a denial of legal rights. This kind of depersonalization almost always precedes oppression and armed conflict. Prior to the 1994 genocide in Rwanda, Tutsis were consistently called 'cockroaches' on Hutu-controlled radio. Anti-Arab pogroms in 1950s Algeria were called 'rat-hunts' by French settlers.[45]

Where factionalized elites are common, states have often lost physical control over their territory or their monopoly on the legitimate use of force.[46] In other words, they cannot or will not stop non-state actors in their territory from

---

41 Cousens, 'From Missed Opportunities to Overcompensation', p. 538.
42 Packer, 'The End of the American Century'.
43 Fund for Peace, 'Fragile States Index', 2019.
44 Fund for Peace, 'Failed States Index', 2007.
45 Discussed in Ter Haar, 'Rats, Cockroaches, and People Like Us', pp. 88–9.
46 Amburn, 'The Failed States Index 2007'.

committing acts of violence, which can lead to insurrectionary violence.[47]

These divisions become possible when people fear that they will not receive the same legal protections and access to resources as their neighbors. Daniel L. Byman, a former researcher at the RAND Corporation, has identified four causes of ethnic conflict that stand out 'for their frequency and for their virulence'. First, *security dilemmas* compel groups that do not trust their neighbors, and do not trust their government to protect them, to arm themselves in self-defense. That in turn can impel their neighbors to arm and mobilize themselves. *Status concerns* compel groups to fight when they feel their cultural survival is threatened by rival groups. In the other two causes of conflict Byman identifies, leaders stoke mistrust and exacerbate and amplify group distinctions because they believe that doing so can advance their own interests. *Hegemonic groups* try to dominate their neighbors, while *ethnic elites* may stoke fear of other ethnic groups in order to build or maintain their own personal power.[48]

Other researchers have found a causal link between discrimination and violence. By converting social science findings on conflict risk factors into human rights language, Oskar N. T. Thoms, an independent research consultant, and James Ron, a professor of public affairs, have found that violations of civil and political rights based on discrimination can trigger violent conflict.[49] Civil and political rights mentioned in the Universal Declaration of Human Rights include the rights to life, liberty, security of person, recognition as a person and equality before the law, access to courts, the presumption of innocence until proven guilty, privacy, movement, asylum, a nationality, marriage, property ownership, thought and religion, opinion and expression, assembly and political participation, as well as freedom from slavery, torture, degrading punishment, arbitrary arrest and detention or exile and attacks on one's reputation.[50]

The Bahá'í writings also make a connection between respect for civil and political rights, including freedom of belief and expression, and the peaceful development of countries. For example, 'Abdu'l-Bahá states:

> Under an autocratic government the opinions of men are not free, and development is stifled, whereas in democracy, because thought and speech are not restricted, the greatest progress is witnessed. It is likewise true in the world of religion. When freedom of conscience, liberty of thought and right of speech prevail – that is to say, when every man according to his own idealization may give expression to his beliefs – development and growth are inevitable.[51]

Although the causation is less direct, the violation of social and economic rights

---

47   See Collier, Hoeffler, and Rohner, 'Beyond Greed and Grievance'. See also Fearon and Laitin, 'Ethnicity, Insurgency, and Civil War'.
48   Byman, *Keeping the Peace*, p. 14.
49   Thoms and Ron, 'Do Human Rights Violations Cause Internal Conflict?', pp. 692, 704.
50   See Universal Declaration of Human Rights, arts. 1–21.
51   'Abdu'l-Bahá, *Promulgation of Universal Peace*, p. 197.

also appears to cause and exacerbate conflict, by 'creating the grievances and group identities that may, in some circumstances, contribute to violence,' according to Thoms and Ron.[52] The authors add that inequality, or relative poverty, is a different phenomenon than absolute poverty, and that inequality itself 'appears to present the greater conflict risk'.[53]

Economic, social, and cultural rights mentioned in the Universal Declaration include the rights to social security, work and equal pay, rest and leisure, an adequate standard of living with special care for mothers, education, participation in a community's cultural life, and intellectual property rights.[54] The Bahá'í writings support these insights, as well. They call for the realization of social and economic rights, including the elimination of extremes of wealth and poverty, not only as a necessary means of achieving justice, but to preserve social peace. In the words of 'Abdu'l-Bahá:

> Every human being has the right to live; they have a right to rest, and to a certain amount of well-being. As a rich man is able to live in his palace surrounded by luxury and the greatest comfort, so should a poor man be able to have the necessaries of life. Nobody should die of hunger; everybody should have sufficient clothing; one man should not live in excess while another has no possible means of existence . . . Let us try with all the strength we have to bring about happier conditions, so that no single soul may be destitute.[55]

Solutions

The best way to prevent violent conflict involves building legal and political systems that protect equal rights before the consequences of disunity become entrenched. Once divisions have led to violence, peacekeeping between the antagonists becomes much more difficult.[56] According to Gregory Stanton, the president of Genocide Watch, the way to arrest the march to genocide – the most extreme form of mass violence, the deliberate extermination of an entire population – is to develop 'universalistic institutions' that transcend divisions and promote tolerance.[57]

This means building and maintaining inclusive political and legal institutions that support the rule of law and are constructed around the recognition of human equality. Melissa Williams, founding Director of the Centre for Ethics at the University of Toronto, has discovered that minorities are best served when their parliamentary representatives cooperate for the common good, rather than pitting

---

52 Thoms and Ron, 'Do Human Rights Violations Cause Internal Conflict? ', p. 704.
53 ibid.
54 See Universal Declaration of Human Rights, arts. 22–7.
55 'Abdu'l-Bahá, *Paris Talks*, pp. 131–2.
56 See, for example, Muller, 'Us and Them', p. 34. Muller here is advocating partition of states that are host to intractable ethnic conflicts, which I would not endorse.
57 See Stanton, 'The 8 Stages of Genocide'.

their constituents' interests against each other.[58] In other words, an appreciation of shared interests across groups can help protect the rights of members of all groups – rights, as we have already seen, that people might otherwise be willing to take up arms to assert.

How can we measure the rule of law, including equality before the law? Several well-established metrics exist. Five are highlighted by the Fragile States Index. In particular, the rule of law must provide for a *legal system* that can be addressed when rights are not protected, all people accused of breaking the law receive *fair and timely trials*, the government does not resort to *arbitrary arrests* or *illegal detention*, and *prison conditions* meet international standards.[59]

As some of these indicators suggest, the rule of law extends to enforcement. The RAND Corporation's National Security Research Division has found that police forces trained to protect human rights can help create secure environments in countries torn apart by armed conflict. These police forces are most effective when they are part of a justice system that ensures due process and equality before the law.[60] Relevant human rights standards and processes identified by United Nations agencies include accountability, limitations on the use of force, and related principles.[61]

Ultimately, the most important guarantor of equality before the law, and thus security within and between nations, is a reorientation of our personal lives, and our political and legal institutions, around the recognition of the oneness of humankind.

'Bahá'u'lláh taught that an equal standard of human rights must be recognized and adopted,' 'Abdu'l-Bahá stated in 1912. 'In the estimation of God all men are equal; there is no distinction or preferment for any soul in the dominion of His justice and equity.'[62] Shoghi Effendi, the Guardian of the Bahá'í Faith, elaborated on this principle in a 1925 letter to the Bahá'ís of Iran, saying that Bahá'ís:

> . . . should have the most scrupulous regard to safeguarding the legitimate personal and civil rights of all individuals, whatever may be their chosen career or station in life, and irrespective of their racial, religious or ideological backgrounds. It is not permissible in matters relating to such rights to make distinctions and discriminations or show preferences. In all transactions and dealings that affect basic human rights, the standard required by the chosen supporters of Bahá'u'lláh – a standard that must claim their unhesitating and unreserved acceptance, and which they must meticulously and assiduously uphold – is that they should not make the slightest distinction between friend and stranger, believer and unbeliever, supporter and antagonist.[63]

---

58 Williams, *Voice, Trust, and Memory*, pp. 138, 221.
59 The Fund for Peace, 'P3: Human Rights and Rule of Law' (emphasis added).
60 Dobbins et al. *Beginner's Guide to Nation-Building*, pp. 58, 74.
61 Office of the United Nations High Commissioner for Human Rights, 'Human Rights Standards and Practice for the Police'.
62 'Abdu'l-Bahá, *Promulgation of Universal Peace*, p. 182.
63 Translation of a letter from Shoghi Effendi to the Bahá'ís of Iran, July 1925, courtesy of Research Department of the Universal House of Justice, quoted in Weinberg, 'The Human Rights Discourse', p. 260.

This is the central challenge of our time: to respond to conflicts and crises by bringing people together rather than pushing them apart. Equality before the law, as a crucial component of the rule of law, provides a minimum standard for societies wishing to avoid the pain and destruction of hatred, conflict, and war. Legal equality contributes to political security.

Bibliography

'Abdu'l-Bahá. *Paris Talks*. Oakham, Rutland: U.K. Bahá'í Publishing Trust, 1972.

— *The Promulgation of Universal Peace: Talks Delivered by 'Abdu'l-Bahá During His Visit to the United States and Canada in 1912*. Compiled by Howard MacNutt. 2nd ed. Wilmette, IL: Bahá'í Publishing Trust, 1982.

— *The Secret of Divine Civilization*. Translated from the Persian by Marzieh Gail in consultation with Ali-Kuli Khan. Wilmette, IL: Bahá'í Publishing Trust, 1990.

Acemoglu, Daron and James A. Robinson. *Why Nations Fail: The Origins of Power, Prosperity, and Poverty*. New York: Crown Business, 2012.

Amburn, Brad. 'The Failed States Index 2007'. *Foreign Policy,* 13 October 2009. https://foreignpolicy.com/2009/10/13/the-failed-states-index-2007/

American Bar Association. 'Rule of Law'. https://www.americanbar.org/groups/public_education/resources/rule-of-law/

Bahá'í International Community – United Nations Office. Protection of Minorities: Oral statement to the 42nd session of the United Nations Sub-Commission on Prevention of Discrimination and Protection of Minorities, Agenda Item 18: Protection of minorities, Geneva, Switzerland, 15 August 1990. BIC Document #90–0815.

Bahá'u'lláh. 'The Seven Valleys', in *The Call of the Divine Beloved.* Haifa: Bahá'í World Centre, 2018.

Belt, Don. 'Struggle for the Soul of Pakistan'. *National Geographic* (September 2007), p. 54.

Brown, Michael E. 'The Causes of Internal Conflict: An Overview', in Brown, Michael E. et al. (eds.). *Nationalism and Ethnic Conflict*, pp. 3–25. Rev. ed. Cambridge, MA: MIT Press, 2001.

Byman, Daniel L. *Keeping the Peace: Lasting Solutions to Ethnic Conflicts.* Baltimore and London: The Johns Hopkins University Press, 2002.

Cheadle, Don and John Prendergast. *Not on Our Watch: The Mission to End Genocide in Darfur and Beyond*. New York: Hyperion, 2007.

Collier, Paul; Anke Hoeffler, and Dominic Rohner. 'Beyond Greed and Grievance: Feasibility and Civil War'. *Oxford Economic Papers* 61, no. 1 (January 2009), pp. 1–27.

Cousens, Elizabeth M. 'From Missed Opportunities to Overcompensation: Implementing the Dayton Agreement on Bosnia', in Stedman, Stephen John; Donald Rothchild, and Elizabeth M. Cousens (eds.). *Ending Civil Wars: The Implementation of Peace Agreements*, pp. 531–66. Boulder: Lynne Rienner, 2002.

Dobbins, James, et al. *The Beginner's Guide to Nation-Building.* Santa Monica: RAND Corporation, 2007.

Emmel, Aaron. *Taking Action in a Changing World.* Oxford: George Ronald, 2006.

Fearon, James D. and David D. Laitin. 'Ethnicity, Insurgency, and Civil War'. *American Political Science Review* 97, no. 1 (February 2003), pp. 75–90.

Fund for Peace. 'Failed States Index', 2007.

— 'Fragile States Index', 2019. https://fundforpeace.org/2019/04/10/fragile-states-index-2019/

— 'P3: Human Rights and Rule of Law'. The Failed States Index. https://fragiles-tatesindex.org/indicators/p3/

Human Security Report Project at the Human Security Centre, Liu Institute for Global Issues, University of British Columbia. *Human Security Report 2005: War and Peace in the 21st Century*. Oxford: Oxford University Press, 2005.

Kaufman, Stuart J. *Modern Hatreds: The Symbolic Politics of Ethnic War*. Ithaca and London: Cornell University Press, 2001.

Mroue, Bassem. 'Gunmen Kill Three Iraqi Candidates'. *Associated Press*, 18 January 2005.

Mueller, John. 'The Banality of "Ethnic War."' *International Security* 25, no. 1 (Summer 2000), pp. 42–70.

Muller, Jerry Z. 'Us and Them: The Enduring Power of Ethnic Nationalism'. *Foreign Affairs* (March/April 2008), pp. 18–35.

Office of the United Nations High Commissioner for Human Rights. 'Human Rights Standards and Practice for the Police'. New York and Geneva: United Nations, 2004. https://www.ohchr.org/Documents/Publications/training5Add3en.pdf

Packer, George. 'The End of the American Century'. *The Atlantic*, May 2019.

Perlez, Jane and Pir Zubair Shah. 'Taliban Exploit Class Rifts to Gain Ground in Pakistan'. *The New York Times*, 16 April 2009. http://www.nytimes.com/2009/04/17/world/asia/17pstan.html?hp

Publius (James Madison, Alexander Hamilton, and John Jay). 'The Federalist Papers', in Cohen, Mitchell and Nicole Fermon (eds.). *Princeton Readings in Political Thought: Essential Texts Since Plato*, pp. 335–46. Princeton: Princeton University Press, 1996.

Rice, Condoleezza. 'U.S. Policy in the Middle East'. Opening remarks before the House Foreign Affairs Committee, 24 October 2007. https://2001-2009.state.gov/secretary/rm/2007/10/94058.htm

Sambanis, Nicholas. 'Partition as a Solution to Ethnic War: An Empirical Critique of the Theoretical Literature'. *World Politics* 52, no. 4 (July 2000), pp. 437–83.

Shoghi Effendi. *The World Order of Bahá'u'lláh: Selected Letters.* Wilmette, IL: Bahá'í Publishing Trust, 1991.

Stanton, Gregory H. 'The Eight Stages of Genocide'. https://www.keene.edu/academics/ah/cchgs/resources/educational-handouts/the-eight-stages-of-genocide/download/

Ter Haar, Gerrie. 'Rats, Cockroaches, and People Like Us: Views of Humanity and Human Rights', in Runzo, Joseph; Nancy M. Martin, and Arvind Sharma (eds.). *Human Rights and Responsibilities in the World Religions*, pp. 79–96. Oxford: Oneworld, 2003.

Thoms, Oscar N.T. and James Ron. 'Do Human Rights Violations Cause Internal Conflict?' *Human Rights Quarterly* 29, no. 3 (August 2007), pp. 674–705.

U.N. Charter. 1945. https://www.un.org/en/charter-united-nations/

U.N. Trust Fund for Human Security. 'What is Human Security'. https://www.un.org/humansecurity/what-is-human-security/

United Nations. 'Sustainable Development Goal 16'. Sustainable Development Goals Knowledge Platform. https://sustainabledevelopment.un.org/sdg16

United States Army War College. 'Implications of Climate Change for the U.S. Army'. https://climateandsecurity.files.wordpress.com/2019/07/implications-of-climate-change-for-us-army_army-war-college_2019.pdf

United States Institute of Peace and the United States Army Peacekeeping and Stability Operations Institute. *Guiding Principles for Stabilization and Reconstruction.* Washington, D.C.: United States Institute of Peace Press, 2009. https://www.usip.org/publications/2009/11/guiding-principles-stabilization-and-reconstruction

Universal Declaration of Human Rights. 1948. G.A. Res. 217A (III).

Universal House of Justice. Letter to the Bahá'ís of the World, 18 January 2019. https://www.bahai.org/library/authoritative-texts/the-universal-house-of-justice/messages/20190118_001/1#276724432

— *The Promise of World Peace.* https://www.bahai.org/documents/the-universal-house-of-justice/promise-world-peace

Washington, George. 'Washington's Farewell Address to the People of the United States'. United States Senate Historical Office. https://www.senate.gov/artandhistory/history/resources/pdf/Washingtons_Farewell_Address.pdf

Weinberg, Matthew. 'The Human Rights Discourse: A Bahá'í Perspective', in *The Bahá'í World: 1996–1997: An International Record*, pp. 247–73. Haifa: Bahá'í World Centre, 1998.

Williams, Melissa S. *Voice, Trust, and Memory: Marginalized Groups and the Failings of Liberal Representation.* Princeton: Princeton University Press, 1998.

World Justice Project. 'What is the Rule of Law?' https://worldjusticeproject.org/about-us/overview/what-rule-law

6

Implementing International Law on Combating Systemic Racism in the United States: Legal, Psychological, and Spiritual Insights from the Bahá'í Teachings

Brian D. Lepard

Chapter 1 highlighted the tenacious problem of racism in the U.S., a racism intensified by the U.S.'s sordid history of the enslavement of Black people and its often unsuccessful attempts to mitigate the entrenched effects of institutionalized slavery. These effects continue to be felt throughout American culture, including in the American legal system.

Of course, the disease of racism is not unique to the U.S.; it also afflicts many other countries and infects their legal systems as well. In the last 80 years the global community, acting through the United Nations and other international institutions, has adopted important norms of international law, both in treaties and customary international law, prohibiting racial discrimination and requiring states (meaning countries) to combat it – including through both legal and educational measures.

There have been some notable successes in implementing at least some of these norms. However, the protests against racial injustice that roiled the U.S. and other countries beginning in the second decade of the 21st century, and the just grievances that motivated them, testify to the failure of the U.S. and the global community successfully to eradicate racial discrimination and racism – and especially racism entrenched in legal and cultural institutions, so-called 'systemic racism'.

How can these international legal norms aimed at combating racism be better implemented in practice? The Bahá'í teachings, which focus on establishing the oneness of humanity, put the elimination of racial inequality and the building of interracial unity front and center, and suggest many approaches to closing the gap between international law and reality.

This chapter explores some of these approaches – legal, psychological, and spiritual – based on insights offered by the Bahá'í teachings. Those teachings call for a restructuring of society sufficient to uproot the systematic endorsement of racial preferences, often unconscious, that permeates the legal system and culture of the U.S. and other countries. The chapter also makes some specific suggestions regarding reforms that can be undertaken to restructure society in this way, in both the near-term and the long-term. These reforms relate to laws and legal institutions, on the one hand, and individual patterns of belief and action, on the other.

Recognition in the Bahá'í Writings of the Problem of Systemic Racism

The Bahá'í writings forthrightly declare that American culture has been racist, that racism has infected all societies, and that one of the primary purposes of Bahá'u'lláh's mission is to uproot this evil through widespread recognition and organic implementation of the overarching principle of the oneness of humanity. Bahá'u'lláh indirectly alluded to the horrors inflicted by racism and other forms of division, writing:

> The winds of despair are, alas, blowing from every direction, and the strife that divideth and afflicteth the human race is daily increasing. The signs of impending convulsions and chaos can now be discerned, inasmuch as the prevailing order appeareth to be lamentably defective.[1]

We are now witnessing such 'convulsions and chaos' wreaked by racial injustice, and we can readily see that the current order is 'lamentably defective' in safeguarding the rights of people.

'Abdu'l-Bahá directly addressed America's particularly egregious institutionalization of racism, which began with slavery and continued, in His lifetime, with Jim Crow laws and a practice, particularly in the U.S. South, of strict racial segregation. He gave numerous talks during His visit to the U.S. in 1912 calling upon Americans to combat this patent evil that had long tarnished the American nation.[2] For example, he said: "'If this matter [racial prejudice] remaineth without change . . . enmity will be increased day by day, and the final result will be hardship and may end in bloodshed.'"[3]

Shoghi Effendi, the grandson of 'Abdu'l-Bahá and the Guardian of the Bahá'í Faith, pointedly called racism America's 'most vital and challenging issue' when he wrote to the Bahá'í community in 1939.[4] In a series of letters to the believers in America, he urged them to arise to combat this brazen repudiation of human oneness, and to model instead a community of Black people and White people united in their eagerness to serve the whole of humanity. He reiterated the dire

---

1   Bahá'u'lláh, *Tablets of Bahá'u'lláh*, para. 11.26.
2   For a discussion of 'Abdu'l-Bahá's efforts to promote racial justice and unity during His visit to America in 1912, and the role of Hand of the Cause Louis Gregory and other Bahá'ís in supporting 'Abdu'l-Bahá's efforts, see Ruhe-Schoen, *Champions of Oneness*, pp. 99–115.
3   'Abdu'l-Bahá, quoted in Shoghi Effendi, *Advent of Divine Justice*, para. 56.
4   Shoghi Effendi, *Advent of Divine Justice*, para. 51.

predictions of Bahá'u'lláh and 'Abdu'l-Bahá should America fail to remove the cancer of racism and other forms of materialism. For example, Shoghi Effendi referred to that:

> . . . cancerous materialism . . . which Bahá'u'lláh in unequivocal and emphatic language denounced in His writings, comparing it to a devouring flame and regarding it as the chief factor in precipitating the dire ordeals and world-shaking crises that must necessarily involve the burning of cities and the spread of terror and consternation in the hearts of men.[5]

In the 1930s, Shoghi Effendi strongly emphasized the:

> . . . inescapable and urgent duty – so repeatedly and graphically represented and stressed by 'Abdu'l-Bahá in His arraignment of the basic weaknesses in the social fabric of the nation – of remedying, while there is yet time, through a revolutionary change in the concept and attitude of the average white American toward his Negro fellow citizen, a situation which, if allowed to drift, will, in the words of 'Abdu'l-Bahá, 'cause the streets of American cities to run with blood'.[6]

He warned that the 'American nation . . . stands . . . in grave peril', in part because of the 'accumulated dross' produced by 'ingrained racial prejudice' and other ills.[7] He repeatedly referred to the 'evils', including racism, that 'stain' the 'character' of the American nation.[8]

Shoghi Effendi also identified racism as a destructive global force, one that Bahá'ís and others must persistently combat. He wrote:

> The theories and policies, so unsound, so pernicious, which . . . seek to subordinate the sister races of the world to one single race, which discriminate between the black and the white, and which tolerate the dominance of one privileged class over all others – these are the dark, the false, and crooked doctrines for which any man or people who believes in them, or acts upon them, must, sooner or later, incur the wrath and chastisement of God.[9]

Shoghi Effendi further wrote of the global unrest unleashed by racism and the other evils of nationalism and materialism:

> As we view the world around us, we are compelled to observe the manifold evidences of that universal fermentation which, in every continent of the globe

---

5   Shoghi Effendi, *Citadel of Faith*, p. 125.
6   ibid. p. 126.
7   ibid. p. 127.
8   ibid.
9   Shoghi Effendi, *Promised Day is Come*, pp. 113–14.

and in every department of human life, be it religious, social, economic, or political, is purging and reshaping humanity in anticipation of the Day when the wholeness of the human race will have been recognized and its unity established.[10]

Bahá'í National Spiritual Assemblies, including that of the U.S., have also repeatedly addressed the need to tackle the problem of systemic racism head-on, and acknowledge its tenacious grip on society, while working tirelessly to eradicate it. For example, in a statement entitled *The Vision of Race Unity*, issued in 1991, the U.S. National Spiritual Assembly affirmed:

Notwithstanding the efforts already expended for its elimination, racism continues to work its evil upon this nation. Progress toward tolerance, mutual respect, and unity has been painfully slow and marked with repeated setbacks. The recent resurgence of divisive racial attitudes, the increased number of racial incidents, and the deepening despair of minorities and the poor make the need for solutions ever more pressing and urgent. To ignore the problem is to expose the country to physical, moral and spiritual danger.[11]

The Universal House of Justice has in recent decades provided a wealth of guidance to the worldwide Bahá'í community, including the American Bahá'ís, on the problem of racism and how Bahá'ís can arise to remedy it. For example, in a letter addressed to the Bahá'ís of the United States on 22 July 2020, it declared:

Racism is a profound deviation from the standard of true morality. It deprives a portion of humanity of the opportunity to cultivate and express the full range of their capability and to live a meaningful and flourishing life, while blighting the progress of the rest of humankind. It cannot be rooted out by contest and conflict. It must be supplanted by the establishment of just relationships among individuals, communities, and institutions of society that will uplift all and will not designate anyone as 'other'.[12]

How do we establish the 'just relationships among individuals, communities, and institutions of society' that will uplift everyone? First, the Bahá'í teachings indicate that law is an essential means for achieving justice. At the global level, in the last three-quarters of a century, nations have developed a variety of international legal norms and institutions aimed at achieving racial justice, all of them inspired in turn by the torturous and bloody struggle for racial equity within nations, including the American nation.

---

10   Shoghi Effendi, *World Order*, p. 170.
11   National Spiritual Assembly of the Bahá'ís of the United States, *Vision of Race Unity*, p. 1.
12   Universal House of Justice, Letter to the Bahá'ís of the United States, 22 July 2020.

The Evolution of International Legal Norms on Combating Systemic Racism

There is no need to recount here the sorrows and tribulations of the American Civil War, a war fomented in the last resort by the ideological battle over slavery. To even begin to rectify this most blatant of racial injustices a nation had to be torn apart and rebuilt. What emerged, on paper, was the abolition of slavery and a guarantee of equal rights without discrimination based on race. These were carried out by the Thirteenth to Fifteenth Amendments to the U.S. Constitution, which were adopted between 1865 and 1870.[13]

However, these legal promises rang hollow. From the moment the ink was dry on their lofty words, malevolent forces sought to undermine them through devious legal strategies, including spurious literacy requirements for voting, the incarceration and virtual enslavement of Black people for the most minor allegedly criminal offenses, and a whole series of other measures adopted in the so-called 'Jim Crow' era.[14] Meanwhile, Black people in the South were relegated to *de facto* second-class status through the legally mandated practice of racial segregation, while Black people in the North suffered from racial discrimination and isolation in Black 'ghettos'.[15] It was not until the milestone case of *Brown v. Board of Education*,[16] decided in 1954, that the U.S. Supreme Court declared this practice unconstitutional. However, it took decades of civil rights protests, many led by the Reverend Dr Martin Luther King, Jr., to produce basic national legislation guaranteeing equal rights to Black people in employment, voting, housing, access to credit, and the enjoyment of other fundamental human rights.[17]

Meanwhile, throughout Africa, the Black majority population demanded equal rights against White colonial settlers who had long occupied their lands

---

13   See U.S. Constitution, Amendment XIII (generally prohibiting slavery and involuntary servitude), Amendment XIV, sec. 1 (generally guaranteeing due process of law and equal protection of the law by states), and Amendment XV (providing that the right to vote shall not be denied or abridged on account of 'race, color, or previous condition of servitude'). Available at https://www.archives.gov/founding-docs/constitution

14   On the practice of *de facto* re-enslavement of Black people between the Civil War and the Second World War, see Blackmon, *Slavery by Another Name.*

15   For a discussion of these practices manifesting white racism in the 20th century in the U.S., see Thomas, *Racial Unity*, pp. 61–79.

16   See Brown v. Board of Education of Topeka, 347 U.S. 483 (1954), p. 495, where the Supreme Court stated: 'We conclude that, in the field of public education, the doctrine of "separate but equal" has no place. Separate educational facilities are inherently unequal. Therefore, we hold that the plaintiffs and others similarly situated for whom the actions have been brought are, by reason of the segregation complained of, deprived of the equal protection of the laws guaranteed by the Fourteenth Amendment.'

17   See, e.g. Title VII of the Civil Rights Act of 1964 (Title VII) (prohibiting racial discrimination in purpose or effect (referred to as 'disparate impact') in employment); the Voting Rights Act of 1964 (prohibiting voting practices and procedures that have a disparate impact on the basis of race or color); the Fair Housing Act (Title VIII of the Civil Rights Act of 1968) (prohibiting discrimination in the sale, rental, and financing of dwellings based on race or color); the Equal Credit Opportunity Act (prohibiting creditors from discriminating against credit applicants on the basis of race or color); Title VI of the 1964 Civil Rights Act (prohibiting practices having the effect of discrimination by state or local governments or private entities receiving federal financial assistance). On the challenges of ending racial segregation in practice, over 70 years after *Brown*, with 'all deliberate speed', a phrase used in the opinion, see Ogletree, Jr., *All Deliberate Speed.*

and established, in some countries, blatant systems of racial oppression, such as the policy of apartheid in South Africa. The 1960s witnessed the emergence of a powerful 'decolonization' movement led by leaders of the African Black majority, and many former colonies won their independence from colonial masters and became majority-ruled states. All these developments in the U.S. and throughout the world inspired the adoption of important new legal norms at the global level, particularly through the agency of the United Nations.

As we saw in Chapter 1, back in 1945, when racial segregation still ruled in the U.S. and colonialism continued to besmirch the continent of Africa, the framers of the U.N. Charter decided to declare their 'faith in fundamental human rights, in the dignity and worth of the human person, [and] in the equal rights of men and women'.[18] The Charter affirms that one of the U.N.'s purposes is to promote and encourage 'respect for human rights and for fundamental freedoms for all without distinction as to race', among other factors.[19] One of the specific functions of the U.N. General Assembly, in which all 193 current member states of the U.N. are represented, is to 'initiate studies and make recommendations for the purpose of . . . assisting in the realization of human rights and fundamental freedoms for all without distinction as to race'.[20] Article 55 proclaims that the U.N. as a whole shall promote 'universal respect for, and observance of, human rights and fundamental freedoms for all without distinction as to race', while under Article 56 every U.N. member state commits itself to 'undertake joint and separate action in co-operation with' the U.N. to achieve this purpose.[21]

Three years after the adoption of the U.N. Charter, the 1948 Universal Declaration of Human Rights ('UDHR'), which was drafted by the new U.N. Commission on Human Rights under the leadership of American First Lady Eleanor Roosevelt, provided a historic list of rights to which everyone is entitled.[22] It asserts that everyone is guaranteed these rights 'without distinction of any kind, such as race [or] color'.[23] It says that men and women of full age have a right to marry 'without any limitation due to race'.[24] It also affirms that education shall strengthen respect for human rights, and shall 'promote understanding, tolerance and friendship among all nations, racial or religious groups'.[25]

Then, in 1965, the General Assembly approved the text of the International Convention on the Elimination of All Forms of Racial Discrimination ('ICERD').[26] This far-reaching treaty, inspired in part by the civil rights movement in the U.S. and the decolonization movement overtaking the world, reaffirmed the norm of racial nondiscrimination in the UDHR. For example, under the treaty, states parties

---

18   U.N. Charter, Preamble.
19   ibid. art. 1, para. 3.
20   ibid. art. 13, para. 1(b).
21   ibid. art. 56.
22   See Universal Declaration of Human Rights.
23   ibid. art. 2.
24   ibid. art. 16, para. 1.
25   ibid. art. 26, para. 2.
26   ICERD.

'undertake to prohibit and to eliminate racial discrimination in all its forms and to guarantee the right of everyone, without distinction as to race, colour, or national or ethnic origin, to equality before the law', notably in the enjoyment of enumerated civil and political rights as well as economic, social, and cultural rights.[27]

This entails, of course, an obligation on the part of all public authorities not to discriminate on the basis of race. The ICERD obligates states parties 'to engage in no act or practice of racial discrimination against persons, groups of persons or institutions and to ensure that all public authorities and public institutions, national and local, shall act in conformity with this obligation'.[28] Furthermore, states parties must provide victims of prohibited racial discrimination with 'effective protection and remedies, through the competent national tribunals and other State institutions', and victims must have 'the right to seek from such tribunals just and adequate reparation or satisfaction for any damage suffered as a result of such discrimination'.[29]

At the same time, the ICERD broke new ground in a number of respects and went well beyond simply requiring governments to treat people of different races equally and provide them with legal remedies for state-sponsored discrimination. First, under the treaty, states committed themselves to 'pursue by all appropriate means and without delay a policy of eliminating racial discrimination in all its forms and promoting understanding among all races'.[30] Thus, the treaty requires parties to combat all forms of racial discrimination, not just by the state, and also to promote interracial understanding.

In particular, the treaty requires each state party 'not to sponsor, defend or support racial discrimination by any persons or organizations'.[31] Moreover, each party must 'prohibit and bring to an end, by all appropriate means, including legislation as required by circumstances, racial discrimination by any persons, group or organization'.[32]

In addition, each state party must change not only laws and policies that have a racially discriminatory purpose, but those that have a racially discriminatory *effect*. It provides in particular: 'Each State Party shall take effective measures to review governmental, national and local policies, and to amend, rescind or nullify any laws and regulations *which have the effect* of creating or perpetuating racial discrimination wherever it exists.'[33]

The treaty mandates, too, that parties 'encourage, where appropriate, integrationist multiracial organizations and movements and other means of eliminating barriers between races, and . . . discourage anything which tends to strengthen racial division'.[34] Going beyond this, it calls for states to take action to combat racist hate speech and activities by organizations promoting racism. Regarding the regulation of

---

27   ibid. art. 5.
28   ibid. art. 2, para. 1(a).
29   ibid. art. 6.
30   ibid. art. 2, para. 1.
31   ibid. art. 2, para. 1(b).
32   ibid. art. 2, para. 1(d).
33   ibid. art. 2, para. 1(c) (emphasis added).
34   ibid. art. 2, para. 1(e).

racist hate speech, states parties 'undertake to adopt immediate and positive measures designed to eradicate all incitement to, or acts of', racial discrimination.[35] They must:

> . . . declare an offence punishable by law all dissemination of ideas based on racial superiority or hatred, incitement to racial discrimination, as well as all acts of violence or incitement to such acts against any race or group of persons of another color or ethnic origin, and also the provision of any assistance to racist activities, including the financing thereof.[36]

They must also 'declare illegal and prohibit organizations, and also organized and all other propaganda activities, which promote and incite racial discrimination, and shall recognize participation in such organizations or activities as an offence punishable by law'.[37]

Furthermore, the treaty permits, and in some circumstances requires, actions to ensure equality in the enjoyment of human rights in fact through special measures, often referred to in the U.S. as 'affirmative action'. For example, it asserts that 'special measures taken for the sole purpose of securing adequate advancement of certain racial or ethnic groups or individuals requiring such protection as may be necessary in order to ensure such groups or individuals equal enjoyment or exercise of human rights and fundamental freedoms shall not be deemed racial discrimination'.[38] However, these affirmative action measures are allowed only if they 'do not, as a consequence, lead to the maintenance of separate rights for different racial groups' and if they are not 'continued after the objectives for which they were taken have been achieved'.[39] Thus, the treaty contemplates that these measures will be potentially time-limited.

At the same time, the treaty *requires* states parties, 'when the circumstances so warrant', to:

> . . . take, in the social, economic, cultural and other fields, special and concrete measures to ensure the adequate development and protection of certain racial groups or individuals belonging to them, for the purpose of guaranteeing them the full and equal enjoyment of human rights and fundamental freedoms.[40]

However, again it envisions these measures as being temporary, at least in the long run, providing that they 'shall in no case entail as a consequence the maintenance of unequal or separate rights for different racial groups after the objectives for which they were taken have been achieved'.[41]

---

35   ibid. art. 4.
36   ibid. art. 4, para. a.
37   ibid. art. 4, para. b.
38   ibid. art. 1, para. 4.
39   ibid.
40   ibid. art. 2, para. 2.
41   ibid.

Under the treaty, parties are obligated to take action to change racial prejudices, and, indeed, transform the entire culture of their countries to support racial equality. They must do so primarily through education. Thus, parties:

> . . . undertake to adopt immediate and effective measures, particularly in the fields of teaching, education, culture and information, with a view to combating prejudices which lead to racial discrimination and to promoting understanding, tolerance and friendship among nations and racial or ethnical groups.[42]

In 1966, the year following the adoption of ICERD, the U.N., after 18 years of arduous negotiations, agreed on the text of a treaty on civil and political rights, known as the International Covenant on Civil and Political Rights ('ICCPR').[43] This treaty reiterated, in legal form, the UDHR's guarantee of equal enjoyment of human rights without discrimination on the basis of race or color.[44] It also demanded that equal protection of the law be provided to everyone, without distinction based on race, asserting:

> All persons are equal before the law and are entitled without any discrimination to the equal protection of the law. In this respect, the law shall prohibit any discrimination and guarantee to all persons equal and effective protection against discrimination on any ground such as race, colour, sex, language, religion, political or other opinion, national or social origin, property, birth or other status.[45]

Importantly, like the ICERD, the ICCPR obligates states parties to make racist hate speech unlawful (although it does not specify whether they must necessarily criminalize this speech). It asserts: 'Any advocacy of national, racial or religious hatred that constitutes incitement to discrimination, hostility or violence shall be prohibited by law.'[46]

Since 1966, the U.N. has engaged in various activities related to the elimination of racial discrimination. It has adopted many other treaties and declarations, and has undertaken multiple studies, including on contemporary forms of racism.[47] A number of treaties, including the ICERD and the ICCPR, have established supervisory bodies of experts that receive state reports on the efforts states parties have made to implement their obligations, and the committees in turn offer their views and recommendations to the parties.[48]

---

42 ibid. art. 7.
43 See International Covenant on Civil and Political Rights.
44 See ibid. art. 2, para. 1.
45 ibid. art. 26.
46 ibid. art. 20, para. 2.
47 For example, the U.N. Human Rights Council has appointed a Special Rapporteur on Contemporary Forms of Racism, Racial Discrimination, Xenophobia and Related Intolerance. See generally 'Special Rapporteur on Contemporary Forms of Racism', https://www.ohchr.org/EN/Issues/Racism/SRRacism/Pages/IndexSRRacism.aspx
48 See generally 'Treaty Bodies', https://www.ohchr.org/en/treaty-bodies. The ICERD established the Committee on the Elimination of Racial Discrimination ('CERD'), while the ICCPR established the

Treaties, such as the U.N. Charter, the ICERD, and the ICCPR, just discussed, represent but one form of international law on combating racism. As noted in Chapter 1, those treaties are like contracts and obligate only states that have ratified them. However, as also indicated there, there are two other generally recognized sources of international law, as well, that potentially obligate all states to eliminate racism: customary international law and general principles of law.[49] Based in part on the widespread ratification of treaties proclaiming a norm of racial nondiscrimination, including the treaties mentioned above, this norm has been recognized by both international and national courts as a rule of customary international law binding all nations.[50] Moreover, it has frequently been acknowledged to be a special category of customary law known as *jus cogens*; this means that the norm of nondiscrimination on racial grounds can never be violated, including by a contrary treaty.[51] As such, it has been recognized as a 'super rule' of customary international law. Regarding general principles of law, which are those principles recognized in the principal legal systems of the world,[52] because so many of these systems formally prohibit racial discrimination (even if many condone it in practice), the norm of racial nondiscrimination is also considered to be a general principle of law binding all nations.[53]

Challenges in Implementing These Norms

Needless to say, the United States, and all countries, have faced tremendous challenges in implementing these global legal norms in treaties, customary international law, and general principles of law relevant to combating systemic racism. Importantly, the U.S. is bound to eradicate racial discrimination by various treaties its government has ratified, including the U.N. Charter, the ICERD, and the ICCPR.[54] In particular, the U.S. is a party to the ICERD, having ratified it in 1994, and thus is bound by its norms. However, the U.S. made a number of 'reservations, understandings, and declarations' with respect to it, including a declaration that its terms are 'non-self-executing'.[55] This means that an aggrieved individual cannot directly bring a cause of action in a U.S. court under the treaty. However, under U.S. constitutional principles, the treaty, and customary international law against

Human Rights Committee.

49   See Statute of the International Court of Justice, art. 38, para. 1.

50   See e.g. *Barcelona Traction Case*, 1970 I.C.J. Rep. 3, 32, para. 34.

51   See e.g. Lepard, *Customary International Law*, pp. 37–8.

52   See ibid. pp. 28, 164–5.

53   See e.g. *Barcelona Traction Case*, 1970 I.C.J. Rep. 3, 32, para. 34 (apparently recognizing the prohibition of racial discrimination as a general principle of international law by including it among human rights 'principles and rules' that have 'entered into the body of general international law').

54   This is a principle of customary international law reflected in the Vienna Convention on the Law of Treaties, which codified much customary law relating to treaties. See Vienna Convention on the Law of Treaties, art. 26 ('Every treaty in force is binding upon the parties to it and must be performed by them in good faith.').

55   See https://treaties.un.org/Pages/ViewDetails.aspx?src=TREATY&mtdsg_no=IV-2&chapter=4&clang=_en#EndDec

racism, may still be relevant in interpreting U.S. civil rights laws.[56]

In any event, while the U.S. has made some significant strides in implementing its obligations under international law to combat systemic racism, including through the adoption of the civil rights laws mentioned above, it is obvious that it has also fallen short – in large part because of the persistence of the ingrained racial prejudices mentioned in the ICERD. According to Jenina S. Lepard, a licensed clinical social worker:

> To be racially prejudiced . . . means to prejudge on the basis of race – primarily skin color – and to maintain such a prejudgment even in the face of evidence that all human beings are equal . . . In the USA and around the world, racial prejudice usually takes the form of showing preference toward people born with lighter skin.[57]

Obviously, too many Americans, including some holding positions of public trust, still subscribe to these negative prejudgments of those with darker skin, particularly Black people. Their widespread prejudgments, and the actions they result in, continue to threaten the ability of the U.S. to realize the international law-mandated guarantee of racial nondiscrimination.

The Universal House of Justice has commented on the U.S.'s shortcomings in achieving this goal. In its letter of 22 July 2020 to the Bahá'ís of the United States, it underscored that:

> Sadly . . . your nation's history reveals that any significant progress toward racial equality has invariably been met by countervailing processes, overt or covert, that served to undermine the advances achieved and to reconstitute the forces of oppression by other means.[58]

We can see those countervailing processes alive and well today. As already underscored in Chapter 1, Black Americans face a significantly higher rate of incarceration than White Americans. They are far more likely to be beaten or killed by police than White people. Black women suffer special stigma and face their own harsh repression in America's prisons.[59] The United States continues to see entrenched patterns of *de facto* segregation in housing, despite legislation such as the Fair Housing Act. Disparities in income and net worth continue to grow along racial lines. Racist hate speech has proliferated on the internet and in other media, often resulting in extreme violence against Black people, including mass shootings. Many of the participants in the unprecedented violent occupation of the

---

56 In Murray v. Schooner Charming Betsy, 6 U.S. (2 Cranch) 64 (1804), p. 118, the Supreme Court stated: 'It has also been observed that an act of Congress ought never to be construed to violate the law of nations if any other possible construction remains.'
57 Lepard, 'Obstacles to Interracial Unity: Some Psychological and Spiritual Insights', p. 64.
58 Universal House of Justice, Letter to the Bahá'ís of the United States, 22 July 2020.
59 See Richie, *Arrested Justice*, pp. 99–124.

U.S. Capitol in January 2021 were White supremacists proudly carrying symbols of racial hate.

Apparently, despite the undoubted progress made in formally guaranteeing equality in law in accordance with the U.S.'s international law obligations, the United States has not succeeded in rooting out *de facto* discrimination by public authorities (including the police, prosecutors, judges, and juries), and certainly not by private persons, including, for example, businesses, individual landlords, and hate groups. The country has failed to change a national culture permeated with racial bias, sometimes unconscious bias. All of these forces have led to the creation of what scholar Andrew Hacker has called 'two nations'. He writes:

> America may be seen as two separate nations. Of course, there are places where the races mingle. Yet in most significant respects, the separation is pervasive and penetrating. As a social and human division, it surpasses all others – even gender – in intensity and subordination.[60]

Many U.N. human rights bodies and experts have expressed their grave concern about the failure of the U.S. to make more progress in the fight against systemic racism. They spoke out with particular urgency following the death of George Floyd in the summer of 2020, and against other acts of police violence perpetrated against Black people that demonstrated, once again, the intransigence of racism within American society. Thus, for example, on 5 June 2020, the independent experts of the special procedures of the Human Rights Council issued an unprecedented joint statement, which began:

> The recent killing of George Floyd has shocked many in the world, but it is the lived reality of black people across the United States. The uprising nationally is a protest against systemic racism that produces state-sponsored racial violence, and licenses impunity for this violence. The uprising also reflects public frustration and protest against the many other glaring manifestations of systemic racism that have been impossible to ignore in the past months, including the racially disparate death rate and socioeconomic impact of the COVID-19 pandemic and the disparate and discriminatory enforcement of pandemic-related restrictions. This systemic racism is gendered. The protests the world is witnessing are a rejection of the fundamental racial inequality and discrimination that characterize life in the United States for black people, and other people of color.[61]

In June of 2020 the U.N. Human Rights Council adopted a resolution following the killing of George Floyd.[62] It strongly condemned:

---

60 Hacker, *Two Nations*, pp. 3–4.
61 United Nations Office of the High Commissioner for Human Rights, 'Statement on the Protests against Systemic Racism in the United States'.
62 See generally 'Human Rights Council Calls on Top U.N. Rights Official to Take Action on Racist Violence'.

> . . . the continuing racially discriminatory and violent practices perpetrated by law enforcement agencies against Africans and people of African descent, in particular which led to the death of George Floyd on 25 May 2020 in Minnesota . . . and the deaths of other people of African descent, and also . . . the structural racism in the criminal justice system.[63]

It deplored 'the recent incidents of excessive use of force and other human rights violations by law enforcement officers against peaceful demonstrators defending the rights of Africans and of people of African descent',[64] and it requested the U.N. High Commissioner for Human Rights:

> . . . to prepare a report on systemic racism, violations of international human rights law against Africans and people of African descent by law enforcement agencies, especially those incidents that resulted in the death of George Floyd and other Africans and people of African descent, to contribute to accountability and redress for victims.[65]

This resolution underscores the gravity of the problem facing the United States and other countries.

From a Bahá'í perspective, how can the systemic racism that continues to infect American culture be combatted? How can racial justice finally be achieved? What practical legal reforms do the Bahá'í teachings prescribe or imply? What changes in individual psychological perspectives do they indicate are necessary? These important questions make it essential first to identify Bahá'í principles relevant to systemic racism and racial justice.

Bahá'í Principles Relevant to Systemic Racism and Racial Justice

As we have seen, the Bahá'í writings are clear-eyed about the depth of the roots of systemic racism in American society and other countries. They also recognize – and have done so for more than a century – the imperative of uprooting this racism. They offer hope that this can be accomplished through a new awareness of our human oneness and a corresponding commitment to upending longstanding discriminatory attitudes and structures. The Universal House of Justice has pointed to the potentialities of this time in American history, including in the wake of the mass protests that began in the year 2020. It wrote to the Bahá'ís of the United States in its letter of 22 July 2020:

> A moment of historic portent has arrived for your nation as the conscience of its citizenry has stirred, creating possibilities for marked social change . . .

---

63 Human Rights Council Resolution 43/1 (2020), para. 1.
64 ibid. para. 2.
65 ibid. para. 3.

We ardently pray that the American people will grasp the possibilities of this moment to create a consequential reform of the social order that will free it from the pernicious effects of racial prejudice and will hasten the attainment of a just, diverse, and united society that can increasingly manifest the oneness of the human family.[66]

A number of Bahá'í principles combat systemic racism and work toward the achievement of racial justice – with the most important such principle being the oneness of the human family. In the words of Bahá'u'lláh, 'Ye are the fruits of one tree, and the leaves of one branch.'[67] He says again, in a passage from his mystical book *The Hidden Words*:

O Children of Men! Know ye not why We created you all from the same dust? That no one should exalt himself over the other. Ponder at all times in your hearts how ye were created. Since We have created you all from one same substance it is incumbent on you to be even as one soul, to walk with the same feet, eat with the same mouth and dwell in the same land, that from your inmost being, by your deeds and actions, the signs of oneness and the essence of detachment may be made manifest.[68]

At a spiritual level, then, the Bahá'í teachings assert that there is only one race – the human race – and we are all equal members of it. Furthermore, Bahá'u'lláh teaches that we should love everyone without regard to their skin color: 'Close your eyes to racial differences, and welcome all with the light of oneness.'[69]

'Abdu'l-Bahá explained that we are all children of God, regardless of color, and should love one another as family members:

Now Bahá'u'lláh has proclaimed the 'Unity of the World of Mankind'. All peoples and nations are of one family, the children of one Father, and should be to one another as brothers and sisters! I hope that you will endeavour in your lives to show forth and spread this teaching.[70]

'Abdu'l-Bahá therefore taught that:

God maketh no distinction between the white and the black. If the hearts are pure both are acceptable unto Him. God is no respecter of persons on account of either color or race . . . Inasmuch as all were created in the image of God, we must bring ourselves to realize that all embody divine possibilities.[71]

---

66   Universal House of Justice, Letter to the Bahá'ís of the United States, 22 July 2020.
67   Bahá'u'lláh, *Gleanings*, p. 218.
68   Bahá'u'lláh, *Hidden Words*, Arabic no. 68.
69   Quoted in Shoghi Effendi, *Advent of Divine Justice*, p. 37.
70   'Abdu'l-Bahá, *Paris Talks*, p. 140.
71   Quoted in Shoghi Effendi, *Advent of Divine Justice*, p. 37.

'Abdu'l-Bahá also likened humanity to a garden, in which the different skin complexions of human beings are akin to the marvelous variety of colors that render the garden so luscious and delightful to the eye:

> Consider the flowers of a garden: though differing in kind, color, form, and shape, yet, inasmuch as they are refreshed by the waters of one spring, revived by the breath of one wind, invigorated by the rays of one sun, this diversity increaseth their charm, and addeth unto their beauty . . . How unpleasing to the eye if all the flowers and plants, the leaves and blossoms, the fruits, the branches and the trees of that garden were all of the same shape and color! Diversity of hues, form and shape, enricheth and adorneth the garden, and heighteneth the effect thereof.[72]

Referring specifically to the need for Black people and White people to come together and appreciate the unity in their diversity, 'Abdu'l-Bahá also affirmed:

> In fact numerous points of partnership and agreement exist between the two races; whereas the one point of distinction is that of color. Shall this, the least of all distinctions, be allowed to separate you as races and individuals?[73]

Shoghi Effendi elaborated on this teaching of Bahá'u'lláh and 'Abdu'l-Bahá of unity in diversity. He emphasized, as They did, that we are all interconnected as members of a single human family, and thus (whether or not we are fully conscious of it) are injured whenever any part of that family, such as Black people, suffer from oppression. In this connection, Shoghi Effendi writes:

> We belong to an organic unit and when one part of the organism suffers all the rest of the body will feel its consequence. This is in fact the reason why Bahá'u'lláh calls our attention to the unity of mankind.[74]

Taken together, these passages from the Bahá'í writings underscore that one of the key reasons racism persists is ingrained racial prejudice, which in turn results from a failure to appreciate the wondrous diversity of the human race as a manifestation of its essential unity. Entrenched racial prejudice in the hearts and minds of individuals in turn sustains systemic racial discrimination.

At the same time, the principle of unity in diversity not only functions as an inner ethic to guide our relations with one another; it calls us to action to reform society, eradicate racial injustice, protect the fundamental human rights of everyone, especially of oppressed minorities, including racial minorities, and bring about local, national, and global peace. In short, *acting* on the oneness of humanity

---

72   'Abdu'l-Bahá, quoted in ibid. pp. 54–5.
73   'Abdu'l-Bahá, *Promulgation of Universal Peace*, p. 68.
74   Hornby, *Lights of Guidance*, no. 446.

constitutes an essential precondition for achieving interracial peace and justice.

Bahá'u'lláh Himself declared: 'The well-being of mankind, its peace and security, are unattainable unless and until its unity is firmly established.'[75] The establishment of unity also necessitates the recognition, and effective implementation, of universal human rights and the elimination of tyranny and oppression, including on racial grounds. For example, immediately after He declares that we are the 'fruits of one tree', in the same tablet Bahá'u'lláh mandates the realization of justice: 'We cherish the hope that the light of justice may shine upon the world and sanctify it from tyranny.'[76] Unquestionably, the oppression of Black people in the name of white supremacy fits the definition of 'tyranny' in the sense referred to by Bahá'u'lláh.

Bahá'u'lláh calls on each one of us to be 'an upholder and defender of the victim of oppression'[77] – which clearly includes Black people and other minorities. He also writes, in an unabashedly stern tone: 'If ye stay not the hand of the oppressor, if ye fail to safeguard the rights of the down-trodden, what right have ye then to vaunt yourselves among men?'[78]

In connection with these principles, the Bahá'í teachings advocated a global system of human rights protection long before the creation of the United Nations. Thus, 'Abdu'l-Bahá said:

> Bahá'u'lláh taught that an equal standard of human rights must be recognized and adopted. In the estimation of God all men are equal; there is no distinction or preferment for any soul in the dominion of His justice and equity.[79]

Clearly, Bahá'u'lláh's teachings on human rights imply the necessity of upholding global efforts, such as those at the United Nations, to eradicate discrimination based on race and to ensure that justice is achieved for victims of systemic racism.

'Abdu'l-Bahá also promoted the spread of literacy among the people, which would, He said, enable them to assert their human rights, including in legal proceedings before the authorities. He wrote in *The Secret of Divine Civilization*:

> Close investigation will show that the primary cause of oppression and injustice, of unrighteousness, irregularity and disorder, is the people's lack of religious faith and the fact that they are uneducated. When, for example, the people are genuinely religious and are literate and well-schooled, and a difficulty presents itself, they can apply to the local authorities; if they do not meet with justice and secure their rights and if they see that the conduct of the local government is incompatible with the divine good pleasure and the king's justice, they can then take their case to higher courts and describe the deviation of the local

---

75   Bahá'u'lláh, *Gleanings*, p. 286.
76   ibid. p. 218.
77   ibid. p. 285.
78   ibid. p. 252.
79   'Abdu'l-Bahá, *Promulgation of Universal Peace*, p. 181.

administration from the spiritual law. Those courts can then send for the local records of the case and in this way justice will be done. At present, however, because of their inadequate schooling, most of the population lack even the vocabulary to explain what they want.[80]

Certainly this passage could apply to Black people in the U.S. and members of racial minorities everywhere. It underscores, first, that everyone must be educated about their rights, and second, that it is appropriate for them to seek legal avenues to redress the injustices that have been committed against them – including systemic injustices.

In this regard, the Bahá'í writings explain that justice is not simply a matter of rectifying wrongs committed against particular individuals. It is a far more holistic and potent concept, ultimately defined by divinely-revealed principles such as the unity of humankind, whose full realization requires a wholesale reordering of society and its institutions, including legal institutions. In this connection, Shoghi Effendi writes:

> If long-cherished ideals and time-honored institutions, if certain social assumptions and religious formulae have ceased to promote the welfare of the generality of mankind, if they no longer minister to the needs of a continually evolving humanity, let them be swept away and relegated to the limbo of obsolescent and forgotten doctrines. Why should these, in a world subject to the immutable law of change and decay, be exempt from the deterioration that must needs overtake every human institution? *For legal standards, political and economic theories are solely designed to safeguard the interests of humanity as a whole, and not humanity to be crucified for the preservation of the integrity of any particular law or doctrine.*[81]

In 'The Promise of World Peace', issued in 1985, the Universal House of Justice not only identified racism as a forbidding obstacle to peace, but called for necessary 'legal measures' against it. It wrote:

> Racism, one of the most baneful and persistent evils, is a major barrier to peace. Its practice perpetrates too outrageous a violation of the dignity of human beings to be countenanced under any pretext. Racism retards the unfoldment of the boundless potentialities of its victims, corrupts its perpetrators, and blights human progress. Recognition of the oneness of mankind, *implemented by appropriate legal measures*, must be universally upheld if this problem is to be overcome.[82]

In short, the elimination of systemic racism, and the achievement of racial justice, both goals to which the U.S. is committed under its own law and under inter-

---

80   'Abdu'l-Bahá, *Secret of Divine Civilization*, p. 18.
81   Shoghi Effendi, *World Order*, p. 142 (emphasis added).
82   Universal House of Justice, *Promise of World Peace* (emphasis added).

national law, require in the Bahá'í view a panoply of legal measures. From a Bahá'í perspective, patchwork reforms will not be enough. Instead, it is critical to rethink legal norms and institutions 'from the ground up'. Possibly some may need, in the words of Shoghi Effendi, to 'be swept away and relegated to the limbo of obsolescent and forgotten doctrines'. Consequently, we will now turn to an examination of some needed reforms in the national and global legal orders, with a focus on the U.S. legal system.

Needed Reforms in the National and Global Legal Orders

The Bahá'í writings acknowledge that the path to making needed reforms in the national and global legal orders will not be an easy one. Shoghi Effendi called it a 'long and thorny road, beset with pitfalls'.[83] To begin, it is critical that United Nations treaties prohibiting racial discrimination, including the U.N. Charter, the ICERD, and the ICCPR, be faithfully upheld by member states, and of course the same is true for corresponding norms of customary international law and general principles of law. To take one example, the provisions of the ICERD relating to the elimination of racial discrimination and its underlying root cause of racial prejudice are in complete accordance with the Bahá'í teachings. Moreover, it is a fundamental Bahá'í principle that international agreements should be honored. The Bahá'í International Community, in its statement entitled 'A Governance Befitting', issued on the occasion of the 75th anniversary of the United Nations in 2020, made a similar point. It affirmed that:

> The moral framework already defined by the United Nations Charter must be applied with increasing fidelity. Respect for international law, upholding fundamental human rights, adherence to treaties and agreements – only to the extent that such commitments are honored in practice can the United Nations and its Member States demonstrate a standard of integrity and trustworthiness before the people of the world. Barring this, no amount of administrative reorganization will resolve the host of long-standing challenges before us. As Bahá'u'lláh declared, 'Words must be supported by deeds, for deeds are the true test of words.'[84]

In short, the international legal norms on racism, and the institutions that have been created to help supervise their implementation, must be constantly supported and strengthened. One minimal requirement for eliminating systemic racism through law, and implementing relevant obligations under treaties such as the ICERD, is that all states, including the U.S., ensure that their laws call for the full enjoyment of all human rights without discrimination based on race. On the importance of law in achieving unity and justice, 'Abdu'l-Bahá stated: 'The Law must reign, and not

---

83   Shoghi Effendi, *Advent of Divine Justice*, p. 34.
84   Bahá'í International Community, *A Governance Befitting*, pp. 7–8.

the individual; thus will the world become a place of beauty and true brotherhood will be realized.'[85]

We have already seen that equality and nondiscrimination based on race represents a divine law in the Dispensation of Bahá'u'lláh, a law that He emphasizes must be fully enforced by everyone: 'Nowhere doth your true and abiding glory reside except in your firm adherence unto the precepts of God, your wholehearted observance of His laws, your resolution to see that they do not remain unenforced, and to pursue steadfastly the right course.'[86]

Without guarantees of racial equality in law, individuals harboring racial prejudices would be free to discriminate and even perpetrate violence against Black people and members of other racial groups they view as inferior. The civil rights movement in the United States, which claimed the lives of so many noble souls laboring for racial justice, focused on the need for such minimal legal guarantees. We have already seen that those guarantees are demanded by international treaty law and customary international law as well. From a Bahá'í perspective they are a critical first step.

However, formal equality in law is not sufficient from the standpoint of international law, nor from a Bahá'í perspective. The Bahá'í teachings clearly affirm that the goal of the legal order in each country, and globally, should be to ensure that people of different races are treated without discrimination in *fact*, and not just according to formal law. They emphasize the role of every individual, organ of society, and government in looking upon others with the 'eye of oneness' and treating them as a member of the same human family.

Furthermore, as we have seen, the Bahá'í writings candidly acknowledge the history of race prejudice in shaping law and social institutions. This means that societies have a critical duty to re-examine every legal rule and every legal institution to uncover the possible role of race prejudice in its evolution and to rectify any resulting injustices – even if the rule or institution appears superficially to be race-neutral. Such an approach runs counter to some jurisprudential doctrines that permit institutions to create *de facto* disadvantages for people of color so long as they do not manifest a conscious discriminatory purpose. For example, the U.S. Supreme Court held, in a 1987 decision,[87] that in order to assert a violation under the Equal Protection Clause of the Fourteenth Amendment based on alleged racial discrimination in application of the death penalty, a criminal defendant 'must prove that the decisionmakers in *his* case acted with discriminatory purpose'.[88] It found that general statistical evidence showing that persons who murder White people are more likely to be sentenced to death than persons who murder Black people, and that Black murderers are more likely to be sentenced to death than White murderers, was not sufficient to make out a violation.[89] Legal scholar Michelle

---

85   'Abdu'l-Bahá, *Paris Talks*, p. 132.
86   Bahá'u'lláh, *Gleanings*, p. 253.
87   McCleskey v. Kemp, 481 U.S. 279 (1987).
88   ibid. p. 292 (emphasis in original).
89   See ibid. pp. 292–3.

Alexander has underscored that, following the Supreme Court's decision, 'lower courts consistently rejected claims of race discrimination in the criminal justice system, finding that gross racial disparities do not merit strict scrutiny in the absence of evidence of explicit race discrimination'.[90]

By contrast, it seems clear that from a Bahá'í perspective we need to strictly scrutinize laws and institutions that appear to be racially neutral but that either (1) were established with a racially discriminatory purpose, or (2) have in fact a racially disproportionate impact. Here are just a few examples of how this approach might apply to particular fields of law.

First, consider the problem of disproportionate police violence against Black people in the U.S. While most police officers apparently carry out their duties without at least conscious bias, it appears that a significant number manage to enter the ranks with extreme racial prejudices. Many more may harbor unconscious biases based on the socialization that all White people – and even Black people themselves – experience in the course of their lifetimes. Unfortunately, the mere fact that Black people are incarcerated at a much higher rate than White people, a situation itself that results from racial prejudice, may give unconscious 'justification' to some police officers to arrest proportionately more Black people.[91] The same bias may infect the application of the vast discretionary powers granted to prosecutors in the U.S. legal system. Understanding the pervasiveness of these biases may help police forces, and the legal system, appreciate the importance of 'implicit bias' training programs to help police officers and prosecutors be alert to their own preconceptions.[92]

Second, consider the problem of racial disparities in the prison population in the U.S. In part these are due to disparities in the application of seemingly neutral sentencing rules. Under these rules, possession of some illicit drugs is punished with longer prison terms than possession of other illicit drugs. A close examination of the history of these sentencing rules may well disclose that the drugs attracting longer prison sentences are those more popular with Black users, such as crack cocaine, and those entailing shorter sentences are those more popular with White users, such as powder cocaine.[93] While there might be non-race-based 'rational' explanations for these differences, a keen appreciation for the often subtle and deeply pervasive role of race prejudice in influencing laws may reveal problems such as these – and lead to reforms in drug sentencing laws aimed at eliminating the *de facto* racial disparities.

A third example of systemic racism fueled by the vestiges of historic racism

---

90   Alexander, *New Jim Crow*, p. 113.
91   See ibid. p. 134 (referring to comments by the former New Jersey attorney general that the 'disproportionate imprisonment of people of color [is], in part, a product of racial profiling – not a justification for it').
92   On these training programs, see, e.g. U.S. Department of Justice, 'FAQs on Implicit Bias', available at https://www.justice.gov/opa/file/871121/dl
93   See Alexander, *New Jim Crow*, p. 112 (describing discriminatory sentencing in the 'war on drugs', and noting that federal laws punish 'crack offenses one hundred times more severely than offenses involving powder cocaine').

involves the housing market. In the U.S., up until the 1960s, Black people were systematically excluded from living in certain 'White' areas through a host of legal doctrines and practices, including racially restrictive covenants in White housing developments, zoning laws that reserved particular areas for larger homes (less affordable to average Black people), the practice of 'redlining', and the foisting of much higher mortgage interest rates on Black borrowers, thus effectively excluding them from pricier housing areas.[94] Scholar Richard Rothstein has shown that far from being the product of decisions by private actors (such as homeowners' associations or mortgage lenders), federal, state and local governments in the U.S. conspired to define 'where whites and African Americans should live'.[95] He concludes that:

> Today's residential segregation in the North, South, Midwest, and West is not the unintended consequence of individual choices and of otherwise well-meaning law or regulation but of unhidden public policy that explicitly segregated every metropolitan area in the United States.[96]

A Bahá'í-inspired perspective on racial integration in housing would insist upon, yet again, a probing and skeptical examination of current legal rules and practices involving housing to uncover those that bear the scars of prejudice and ensure that the effect of these rules and practices is to encourage effective integration. It would of course fully support the creation of racially integrated communities and the destruction of systemic barriers to equal access to housing based on race. This might involve creating new laws setting aside houses in every development for low-income residents (thus encouraging diversity), and facilitating access to mortgage funds for those who might not qualify based on banks' typical underwriting criteria.

The systemic discrimination and violence experienced by Black women creates a fourth social phenomenon in the U.S. that deserves critical attention from a Bahá'í perspective. This is especially so because this discrimination and violence is an affront not only to the Bahá'í principle of racial equality, but to that of the full equality and dignity of women and men. Black women in the U.S. and other countries often suffer from a 'double stigma' based on race and gender,[97] which makes it vital to investigate how every legal norm or institution may intentionally or unintentionally perpetuate their subjugation.

Fifth, we need to resolve the extent to which, legally, countries must or should regulate racist hate speech. There is no doubt that the terrible and potentially dangerous impacts of racist hate speech must be candidly acknowledged. We

---

94   See e.g. Rothstein, *Color of Law*, p. vii.
95   ibid.
96   ibid. pp. vii–viii.
97   See e.g. Richie, *Arrested Justice*, p. 128. Richie writes: 'Black women are subject to a tangled web of concentrated structural disadvantages that are profoundly intense and forceful in their ability to stigmatize and create subordinate social status. Sexism, for example, is experienced differently by Black women than white women in part because it is not the only source of oppression that Black women face; it is complicated by institutional racism and the particular way that white patriarchy imparts racial hierarchy on Black bodies.'

cannot turn a 'blind eye' to the deleterious effects of hate speech and view it as benign merely because it has become so ubiquitous. The challenge from a legal and ethical perspective is determining how to respond to it.

We have seen that treaties such as the ICCPR and the ICERD require states parties to prohibit racist hate speech if it constitutes, in the words of article 20 of the ICCPR, 'incitement to discrimination, hostility or violence'.[98] Additionally, the ICERD requires parties to:

> . . . declare an offence punishable by law all dissemination of ideas based on racial superiority or hatred, incitement to racial discrimination, as well as all acts of violence or incitement to such acts against any race or group of persons of another color or ethnic origin.[99]

On the other hand, the Committee on the Elimination of Racial Discrimination, in a general recommendation on combatting racist hate speech issued in 2013, has said that not all racist hate speech should be criminalized. It wrote:

> The Committee recommends that the criminalization of forms of racist expression should be reserved for serious cases, to be proven beyond reasonable doubt, while less serious cases should be addressed by means other than criminal law, taking into account, inter alia, the nature and extent of the impact on targeted persons and groups.[100]

The Committee has also noted its concern 'that broad or vague restrictions on freedom of speech have been used to the detriment of groups protected by the Convention' and has said that 'measures to monitor and combat racist speech should not be used as a pretext to curtail expressions of protest at injustice, social discontent or opposition'.[101]

Furthermore, the Human Rights Committee established under the ICCPR has said that:

> For article 20 to become fully effective there ought to be a law making it clear that propaganda and advocacy as described therein are contrary to public policy and providing for an appropriate sanction in case of violation.[102]

However, it has not indicated that that 'appropriate sanction' needs to be criminal in character.[103] With respect to the parallel context of defamation laws, the Committee

---

98   ICCPR, art. 20, para. 2.
99   ICERD, art. 4, para. (a).
100 Committee on the Elimination of Racial Discrimination, General Recommendation no. 35, para. 12.
101 ibid. para. 20.
102 Human Rights Committee, General Comment no. 11, para. 2.
103 See ibid. See also Human Rights Committee, General Comment no. 34, para. 52 (stating that 'it is only with regard to the specific forms of expression indicated in article 20 that States parties are obliged to have legal prohibitions', but not specifying that the prohibitions need to be criminal in character).

has said that 'the application of the criminal law should only be countenanced in the most serious of cases and imprisonment is never an appropriate penalty'.[104]

Turning to the Bahá'í teachings, no clear Bahá'í perspective exists on the legal regulation of hate speech – but a number of Bahá'í principles are relevant. One set of principles might counsel in favor of restrictions on racist hate speech. Among these, a key principle is that of racial unity and equality, discussed at length earlier. Furthermore, the Bahá'í writings clearly condemn racist attitudes, and one of Bahá'u'lláh's most important teachings is to avoid backbiting and harmful or aggressive speech. He declares:

> For the tongue is a smouldering fire, and excess of speech a deadly poison. Material fire consumeth the body, whereas the fire of the tongue devoureth both heart and soul. The force of the former lasteth but for a time, whilst the effects of the latter endure a century.[105]

We can see an example of the deleterious impact of the 'fire of the tongue' that Bahá'u'lláh addresses in the persecution of Bahá'ís in the land of the Faith's birth. The Bahá'ís in Iran have endured the terrible effects of hate speech, as they have been subjected to a barrage of media propaganda sponsored or funded by the Iranian government seeking to besmirch their moral character and stir up hatred and acts of discrimination against them among the Iranian population.

On the other hand, the Bahá'í writings uphold freedom of expression, within the bounds of moderation, and generally counsel in favor of liberty of speech. For example, 'Abdu'l-Bahá praised the U.S.'s protection of free speech, affirming that:

> When freedom of conscience, liberty of thought and right of speech prevail – that is to say, when every man according to his own idealization may give expression to his beliefs – development and growth are inevitable.[106]

At a practical level, the global Bahá'í community is keenly aware of the potential for abuses by governments in the name of restraining 'immoral' speech, as exemplified by the Iranian government's oppression of Bahá'ís and their liberty of expression. A number of scholars have cited such examples of government overreach as a reason not to criminalize or punish hate speech, no matter how odious.[107]

The Universal House of Justice has emphasized therefore the importance of adopting a measured, moderate approach to freedom of speech. It has stated:

---

104 Human Rights Committee, General Comment no. 34, para. 47.
105 Bahá'u'lláh, *Kitáb-i-Íqán*, p. 193.
106 'Abdu'l-Bahá, *Promulgation of Universal Peace*, p. 198.
107 See, e.g. Strossen, *Hate*, p. 182 (affirming that 'even if constitutionally protected "hate speech" did notably contribute to the feared harms, and even if "hate speech" laws would meaningfully help to reduce them, we still should reject such laws because non-censorial measures can effectively counter the feared harms, and because "hate speech" laws would deeply damage freedom of speech, democracy, equality, and societal harmony').

Speech is a powerful phenomenon. Its freedom is both to be extolled and feared. It calls for an acute exercise of judgement, since both the limitation of speech and the excess of it can lead to dire consequences. Thus there exist in the system of Bahá'u'lláh checks and balances necessary to the beneficial uses of this freedom in the onward development of society. A careful examination of the principles of Bahá'í consultation and the formal and informal arrangements for employing them offer new insights into the dynamics of freedom of expression.[108]

Because of these more nuanced Bahá'í principles and competing policy consider-ations, it is not possible to draw firm conclusions about what legal reforms governments and international organizations such as the U.N. should undertake to combat racist hate speech, and whether or not criminal sanctions against hate speech are desirable. Nevertheless, the Bahá'í teachings imply at a minimum that racist hate speech ought to be countered by speech that upholds the unity of the human family and the right to equal rights and dignity for all human beings in the U.S. and everywhere.

Moreover, governments themselves can be viewed as having legal obligations, both under treaties such as the ICERD and the ICCPR, and under corresponding norms of customary international law, (1) to refrain from ever engaging in racist hate speech themselves; (2) to condemn racist hate speech generally as well as specific egregious instances of hate speech; (3) to educate the public about the genuine harms of racist hate speech, including its potential to incite discrimination and violence against Black people; (4) to criminalize hate speech that constitutes immediate incitement to violence (a point on which U.S. jurisprudence and that of virtually every other country agrees); and (5) actively to promote, through a variety of educational measures, appreciation for the fundamental unity of the human race and of the equality of Black people and White people.

The Bahá'í teachings also include specific principles relating to what is often called 'affirmative action' – efforts to help further equality of opportunity in fact by recognizing the historical impact of racial discrimination, and therefore to seek to achieve appropriate representation of racial minorities in particular milieu. We have already seen that the ICERD authorizes temporary 'special measures' to eradicate past discrimination.[109]

The Bahá'í writings would apparently support such measures strongly and enthusiastically.[110] For example, they call for a type of affirmative action in Bahá'í elections. Shoghi Effendi wrote that in the case of a tie in a Bahá'í election, 'priority should unhesitatingly be accorded [to the person] representing the minority'.[111] Shoghi Effendi explicitly says this includes a racial minority, and explains that the

---

108 Universal House of Justice, Letter to the Followers of Bahá'u'lláh in the United States of America, 29 December 1988.
109 See ICERD, art. 1, para. 4.
110 For a comprehensive discussion of a Bahá'í perspective on affirmative action, see Gonzales, 'Affirmative Action and the Jurisprudence of Equitable Inclusion'.
111 Shoghi Effendi, *Advent of Divine Justice*, p. 135.

reason for this policy is to 'stimulate and encourage [the minority], and afford it an opportunity to further the interests of the community'.[112]

Moreover, in any Bahá'í election, the voters are urged to take racial diversity into account in making their choices, so that every Bahá'í participating in an election ought to be mindful of the importance of giving opportunities to serve to Black people and other racial minorities. For example, in a letter to the Bahá'ís of the world of 25 March 2007, the Universal House of Justice stated: 'From among the pool of those whom the elector believes to be qualified to serve, selection should be made with due consideration given to such other factors as age distribution, *diversity*, and gender.'[113]

These Bahá'í principles clearly endorse efforts, implemented through law, to enhance representation of people of diverse races in various professions and institutions. These might take a variety of forms, including educational and recruitment outreach initiatives aimed at creating equal opportunities of access to these professions and institutions. These measures to enhance diversity must be undertaken in many milieu and fortified, rather than weakened in the name of preserving *de jure* equality. Nevertheless, the Bahá'í principles of democratic elections, and of giving a preference to minorities only in the case of a tie, imply that such measures must be aimed at achieving the broader concept of racial equity and justice foreseen in the Bahá'í writings, and must not be applied mechanically or become an end in themselves.

The Bahá'í principle of consultation also suggests a number of other reforms in law and legal institutions. With respect to this principle, Bahá'u'lláh teaches: 'Take ye counsel together in all matters, inasmuch as consultation is the lamp of guidance which leadeth the way, and is the bestower of understanding.'[114] 'Abdu'l-Bahá elaborated on this concept, affirming that in a process of consultation, everyone participating should seek to learn from the views of others and value their perspectives, being willing to modify their own in light of this learning, all with the goal of reaching a unified view. He said:

> Consultation must have for its object the investigation of truth. He who expresses an opinion should not voice it as correct and right but set it forth as a contribution to the consensus of opinion, for the light of reality becomes apparent when two opinions coincide . . . Before expressing his own views he should carefully consider the views already advanced by others. If he finds that a previously expressed opinion is more true and worthy, he should accept it immediately and not willfully hold to an opinion of his own. By this excellent method he endeavors to arrive at unity and truth.[115]

---

112 ibid.
113 Universal House of Justice, Letter to the Bahá'ís of the World, 25 March 2007 (emphasis added).
114 Bahá'u'lláh, *Tablets of Bahá'u'lláh*, p. 168.
115 'Abdu'l-Bahá, *Promulgation of Universal Peace*, pp. 72–3.

The Bahá'í principle of consultation points to the importance of including as many Black people as possible in decisions affecting them, as part of a broadly consultative process aimed at achieving equality in the enjoyment of human rights in fact as well as in law. To take a few examples, in the case of legislatures, it supports efforts to remove obstacles to Black people being fairly elected, including by eliminating gerrymandering that can effectively silence the Black community by making it impossible for Black candidates to be elected despite significant representation in the general population. It would also encourage measures to make voting accessible to everyone, and especially Black people and other racial minorities, by eliminating a variety of 'neutral' restrictions that can effectively impede them from exercising this right.

Beyond taking legal steps to ensure fair representation of Black people in legislatures and other deliberative bodies, the Bahá'í principle of consultation suggests that multiple opportunities for Black people's input be provided in actual decision-making that affects their well-being and the enjoyment of their rights. These opportunities should be integrated into decision-making processes at all levels. One example would be the establishment of local community councils, including significant Black representation, to meet regularly with local police officials about policing practices in neighborhoods.

However, none of these reforms of legal and governmental institutions will be effective, as experience has taught, without a profound change of outlook on the part of all participants in the legal system, and all individuals in every walk of life.

The Bahá'í writings are clear about this required change: it must be rooted in a sober recognition of the reality of racial prejudice and its far-ranging effects, supplemented by a keen awareness of the spiritual unity of humanity and of the imperative to build bonds of friendship with people of all races. Since this alteration of outlook on the part of people of all races can best be effected through education, we will now turn to a closer examination of needed reforms in education based on psychological and spiritual insights from the Bahá'í writings.

Needed Reforms in Education Based on Psychological and Spiritual Insights from the Bahá'í Writings

One critical precondition for eliminating systemic racism from American and global society involves extirpating the racial prejudice that sustains it. Changing legal norms and institutions that perpetuate racism will be a quixotic exercise, and doomed to ultimate failure, without addressing its root cause. In this connection, the Universal House of Justice has called on American Bahá'ís to contribute their 'decisive share to the eradication of racial prejudice from the fabric of [their] nation'.[116]

The Bahá'í writings assert that doing so will require a concerted effort on the part of both Black people and White people, an effort motivated by an overarching

---

116 Universal House of Justice, Letter to the Bahá'ís of the United States, 22 July 2020.

love for humanity. Thus, 'Abdu'l-Bahá taught: 'Each one should endeavor to develop and assist the other toward mutual advancement.'[117] He furthermore stated: 'Love and unity will be fostered between you, thereby bringing about the oneness of mankind.'[118] He counseled: 'If you meet those of a different race and color from yourself, do not mistrust them, and withdraw yourself into your shell of conventionality, but rather be glad and show them kindness.'[119] He emphasized that ultimately racial justice will come about through a change of heart, not through force – and by implication, legal reform alone either: 'The oppressed who have right on their side, must not take that right by force; the evil will continue. Hearts must be changed.'[120]

Shoghi Effendi addresses in some detail the particular kinds of changes that Black and White Bahá'ís in the U.S. need to make in their outlook, attitudes, and behaviors towards one another. In *The Advent of Divine Justice*, written in 1938, he counseled them:

> A tremendous effort is required by both races if their outlook, their manners, and conduct are to reflect, in this darkened age, the spirit and teachings of the Faith of Bahá'u'lláh . . . Let neither think that the solution of so vast a problem is a matter that exclusively concerns the other. Let neither think that such a problem can either easily or immediately be resolved.[121]

In fact, Shoghi Effendi directed specific counsels to members of both races:

> Let the white make a supreme effort in their resolve to contribute their share to the solution of this problem, to abandon once for all their usually inherent and at times subconscious sense of superiority, to correct their tendency towards revealing a patronizing attitude towards the members of the other race, to persuade them through their intimate, spontaneous and informal association with them of the genuineness of their friendship and the sincerity of their intentions, and to master their impatience of any lack of responsiveness on the part of a people who have received, for so long a period, such grievous and slow-healing wounds. Let the Negroes, through a corresponding effort on their part, show by every means in their power the warmth of their response, their readiness to forget the past, and their ability to wipe out every trace of suspicion that may still linger in their hearts and minds.[122]

Shoghi Effendi further wrote:

> Let neither [Black people nor White people] think that anything short of genuine love, extreme patience, true humility, consummate tact, sound initiative, mature

---

117 'Abdu'l-Bahá, quoted by Shoghi Effendi in *Advent of Divine Justice*, p. 39.
118 ibid.
119 'Abdu'l-Bahá, *Paris Talks*, p. 53.
120 'Abdu'l-Bahá, *'Abdu'l-Bahá in London*, p. 92.
121 Shoghi Effendi, *Advent of Divine Justice*, p. 40.
122 ibid.

wisdom, and deliberate, persistent, and prayerful effort, can succeed in blotting out the stain which this patent evil has left on the fair name of their common country.[123]

The Universal House of Justice has elaborated on these principles articulated by Bahá'u'lláh, 'Abdu'l-Bahá, and Shoghi Effendi, and underscored the imperative of fostering a moral transformation grounded in Bahá'u'lláh's teachings. Such a transformation is required if legal and societal reforms are to endure and not fall victim to renewed setbacks and failures. In this connection, the Universal House of Justice has counseled Bahá'ís to be wary of succumbing to the conflictual tendencies of present-day society, writing in its 22 July 2020 letter to the American Bahá'í community:

> The change required is not merely social and economic, but above all moral and spiritual . . . It is not possible for you to effect the transformation envisioned by Bahá'u'lláh merely by adopting the perspectives, practices, concepts, criticisms, and language of contemporary society. Your approach, instead, will be distinguished by maintaining a humble posture of learning, weighing alternatives in the light of His teachings, consulting to harmonize differing views and shape collective action, and marching forward with unbreakable unity in serried lines.[124]

In that same letter, the Universal House of Justice highlighted that this approach, and Bahá'u'lláh's teachings on race unity, must be anchored in the personal virtue of love:

> Ultimately, the power to transform the world is effected by love, love originating from the relationship with the divine, love ablaze among members of a community, love extended without restriction to every human being. This divine love, ignited by the Word of God, is disseminated by enkindled souls through intimate conversations that create new susceptibilities in human hearts, open minds to moral persuasion, and loosen the hold of biased norms and social systems so that they can gradually take on a new form in keeping with the requirements of humanity's age of maturity. You are channels for this divine love; let it flow through you to all who cross your path. Infuse it into every neighborhood and social space in which you move to build capacity to canalize the society-building power of Bahá'u'lláh's Revelation. There can be no rest until the destined outcome is achieved.[125]

The Universal House of Justice also urges us to follow the example of 'Abdu'l-Bahá in transforming our own hearts and cleansing them of the defilements of racism. It writes:

---

123 ibid.
124 Universal House of Justice, Letter to the Bahá'ís of the United States, 22 July 2020.
125 ibid.

Ahead of you lie times of trial and promise, of hardship and progress, of anguish and joy. Under all conditions, the Master ['Abdu'l-Bahá] is your solace and support. For those who aspire to lasting change, His example guides the way – tactful and wise in His approach, penetrating in utterance, indiscriminating in fellowship, unfailing in sympathy for the downtrodden, courageous in conduct, persevering in action, imperturbable in the face of tests, unwavering in His keen sense of justice. And to all who arise to emulate Him, He offers this unfailing assurance: 'that which is confirmed is the oneness of the world of humanity. Every soul who serveth this oneness will undoubtedly be assisted and confirmed.'[126]

These attributes of 'Abdu'l-Bahá, as described by the Universal House of Justice, suggest the qualities we each need to acquire to combat inner prejudices and systemic racism as we work to reform unequal legal and governance structures. The first of those qualities is to become 'penetrating in utterance'. We must, in whatever sphere of endeavor we work – including law or public service – be advocates for racial justice. Silence is not an option. We must speak up on behalf of Black people and other victims of injustice.

The second quality calls everyone to become 'indiscriminating in fellowship'. We must reach out to people of other races in a deliberate way, not just in a professional or work capacity, but in a sustained effort to build close bonds of fellowship and unity. Of course, we can do so in our workplaces as well. One way to root out systemic racism is to create these intense bonds of friendship, bonds that can also pave the way for frank and honest discussions with friends or co-workers who have experienced racial injustice about how to remedy these injustices in the spheres in which we live and work.

The third attribute of 'Abdu'l-Bahá asks us to be 'unfailing in sympathy for the downtrodden'. This kind of true sympathy can lead White people, especially, to probe the insidious ways racism has injected itself into well-accepted legal and social norms and systems. This expression of actual sympathy can motivate White people – and all people – to strive to comprehend the impacts of systemic racism on Black people and other racial minorities from a new perspective. This awareness brings about the first steps to reform. Moreover, showing sympathy also means listening, and listening attentively – meaning that we must purposefully seek out and include Black people in our consultations, and give empathic attention to their voices and views.

'Abdu'l-Bahá's example of being 'courageous in conduct' is also critical to winning the battle against systemic racism. The forces of racism are strong in the U.S. and other societies; racism is like a rushing river current. If we do nothing, we will inevitably be swept downriver by its power. To eliminate systemic racism, we must courageously swim against this fierce current with all our might – and we must not fear the labels that may be falsely attached to us when we do so, such as 'idealists' or 'advocates for racial preferences' and therefore a species of 'reverse

---

126 ibid.

discrimination'. We must remember that according to the Bahá'í teachings the goal of our efforts is to eliminate racial discrimination and prejudices based on an awareness of our fundamental unity as human beings.

Like 'Abdu'l-Bahá, we must also be 'persevering in action' for the same reasons. The battle against systemic racism has been, and will be, a long and difficult one. It will require consistent and persistent effort across decades. At each point in the process, it will be tempting to throw up our hands, feeling helpless and hopeless that real change can happen. However, the Bahá'í writings assure us that unification of the human race is not only possible, but inevitable. How soon we put it into practice is within our control, and the more we persevere the quicker we will achieve it.

Nevertheless, challenges and setbacks will come, one after another, and we must follow 'Abdu'l-Bahá's example in being 'imperturbable in the face of tests'. Uprooting systemic racism will require patient, persistent effort. This is especially true for efforts to reform longstanding legal and governance practices. Those reforms will typically meet with opposition, sometimes fierce, because so many individuals have so many vested interests in perpetuating systems that provide them with status, wealth, and power. We must be patient and resolute in the face of such opposition, while practicing those virtues of consultation and respectfulness of speech described by Bahá'u'lláh, 'Abdu'l-Bahá, Shoghi Effendi, and the Universal House of Justice.

Finally, we must draw inspiration from 'Abdu'l-Bahá in being 'unwavering in our sense of justice' when we fight systemic racism. It is far too easy to fall into accepting existing practices and legal norms without questioning whether they actually achieve just outcomes, especially for Black people. We must always put justice at the forefront of our motives, and not waver in seeking to advance it.

In short, when we cultivate these personal and spiritual qualities exhibited by 'Abdu'l-Bahá we create the prerequisites for success in undertaking more practical legal and institutional reforms. Yet how can more individuals at every level of society develop these qualities? Education is critical to the endeavor. According to the Universal Declaration of Human Rights, everyone has the right to education, and in particular, education that is 'directed to the full development of the human personality and to the strengthening of respect for human rights and fundamental freedoms'. Everyone has the right to education that will 'promote understanding, tolerance and friendship among all nations, racial or religious groups.'[127]

The Bahá'í teachings clearly support education aimed at promoting 'understanding, tolerance and friendship' among all 'racial . . . groups', among others. Yet, as a practical matter, how can this be accomplished? At the United Nations' Second World Conference to Combat Racism and Racial Discrimination, held in 1983, the Bahá'í International Community proposed the adoption 'in individual countries of a universal, yet culturally adaptable, curriculum on the organic oneness of mankind'.[128] According to the statement:

---

127 Universal Declaration of Human Rights, art. 26, paras. 1, 2.
128 Bahá'í International Community, 'Combating Racism: Statement submitted to the United Nations

This curriculum must be inspired by a recognition that racial prejudice will not be eliminated solely by studying the problem of racial discrimination; rather, the eradication of racial prejudice requires the development at an early age of a consciousness of the basic human and spiritual bonds uniting peoples of different races, colours and ethnic origins.[129]

That 1983 statement went on to propose various elements of such a curriculum, which would include:

1. Understanding how racial prejudice grows out of a failure to perceive the bonds uniting all peoples;
2. The importance of contact with people of other races as a means of breaking down prejudices and perceiving shared human bonds;
3. The different forms and manifestations of racial prejudice in our everyday lives; and
4. United Nations action in the field of human rights and the human rights standards already established by the United Nations.[130]

These concepts are more timely than ever. We can see, in the rise of racist movements and ideologies documented earlier, the imperative of developing, from the youngest age, a consciousness of our common humanity and an appreciation for the unity in diversity of all racial groups among the peoples of the world.

At the same time, another kind of education has also become essential: Education allowing us to perceive our own biases, especially if we are White and have benefitted from the social advantages that our racial background can bring. This does not mean White people should feel guilt or shame. Rather, an awareness of the prejudices they have inherited simply by being born and raised in a culture infused with racism can help them become more aware of the subtle ways in which they may be treating Black people as inferior – an often-unconscious view that has serious legal and social ramifications. White people can begin to make changes in their actions by becoming aware of these subtle biases.

Moreover, White people can become aware of another psychological tendency – to ascribe to Black people characteristics in themselves that they view as unacceptable, a tendency often called 'projection'.[131] For example, too often White people have derided Black people as lazy or hypersexualized – characteristics they actually fear in themselves.[132] The despicable history in the U.S. of White juries unjustly convicting Black men of sexual crimes against White women is but one example of the harsh legal consequences of such projection.

A related phenomenon is that of 'projective identification', in which some

Second World Conference to Combat Racism and Racial Discrimination', 1 August 1983.
129 ibid.
130 ibid.
131 On projection, see generally Lepard, 'Obstacles to Interracial Unity', p. 64.
132 On the projection of hypersexuality onto Black people, see ibid. pp. 64–5.

Black people internalize these White projections and come to believe they are real – and hate themselves as a consequence. As psychotherapist Jenina Lepard explains, 'Black self-hatred is an example of projective identification, in which the projected-upon person internalizes the projection as if it were his or her own.'[133] This can also be described as 'introjective identification'.[134]

Dr Joy DeGruy has identified the similar phenomenon of 'post-traumatic slave syndrome'. She argues that:

> Television, newspapers and magazines projecting negative images of black males as pitiable, ignorant, violent and criminal have contributed to the overall poor self-images of black boys . . . We rarely look at our history to understand how African Americans adapted their behavior over centuries in order to survive the stifling effects of chattel slavery, effects which are evident today . . . [T]he behaviors in the scenarios described above . . . are in large part related to trans-generational adaptations associated with the past traumas of slavery and on-going oppression. I have termed this condition 'Post Traumatic Slave Syndrome', or PTSS.[135]

Many elements of legal rules and institutions are the product of these injurious processes of projection, projective identification, and PTSS. I have already referred to the example of White juries spuriously convicting Black men of sexual crimes. The unjust mass incarceration of Black people may also be the product of White projection that leads White prosecutors, juries, and judges to label Black people 'criminals' and not give them the benefit of the doubt that White people enjoy. It may be in part the result of the negative self-image of Black people themselves engendered by projective identification and PTSS, which can lead them to behave in ways consistent with this false self-image. If White people in positions of responsibility in the legal system understand these insidious processes and the way they have shaped the American system, they may be better able to see racial justice issues through the eyes of Black people and identify needed reforms more readily.

Unfortunately, White people have too often rejected seeing these entrenched biases in Black-White relations and their impact on the legal order because of an inherent sense of superiority that may, as Lepard suggests, really be 'a defense against feelings of personal inferiority'.[136] This has led many White people to deny the existence of systemic racism in the legal system. So a critical first step to rooting out racism in the legal order involves overcoming this denial and seeing these often invisible processes at work – which means, according to Lepard, that 'Whites must be willing to reexamine their own attitudes with open minds.'[137] This includes becoming aware of the many ways in which the legal system privileges White people.

---

133 ibid. p. 65.
134 ibid.
135 DeGruy, *Post Traumatic Slave Syndrome*, p. 13.
136 Lepard, 'Obstacles to Interracial Unity', p. 66.
137 ibid. p. 68.

Indeed, another prerequisite for reforming the national and global legal orders to promote racial justice and unity is for White people to reach out to Black people with the aim of engaging in genuine, free, and open conversations.[138] Listening, just listening, is critical. White people too often are used to 'lecturing' Black people or telling them how they should think or feel. Both White people and Black people should approach these conversations with courage, and without fear of their own personal limitations. As Lepard writes:

> We do not need to wait to perfect our interactive skills before reaching out to members of other races and daring to expose ourselves to possible suspicion or rejection on the part of the 'other'. We need a safe haven – each other – for practicing our interactive skills until we get stronger. We must be forgiving of ourselves and others, as we strive for unity in diversity.[139]

These conversations can start at the grass roots, but they must also occur among members of the legal profession and in more structured settings aimed at reforming the many elements of the existing legal order, especially in the U.S., that are vestiges of systemic racism.

Conclusion

In this chapter, we have explored the challenge of combating systemic racism within the legal system of the United States – a challenge that the Bahá'í writings, and authoritative Bahá'í institutions, demand be pursued with vigor. International law must be an important part of this crucial endeavor. At the global level, international law has now crystallized around a foundational principle of racial equality, insisting that nations take a myriad of steps to eliminate racial discrimination in all its forms.

Nevertheless, nations in general, and the U.S. in particular, have fallen short in meeting their obligations under international law. As the Bahá'í writings underscore, the roots of systemic racism are too deep and knotted to allow any easy solutions, including ones that lack a foundation in the essential truth of the oneness of humanity. Yet this principle, and others articulated in the Bahá'í writings, offer hope for an eventual solution. Those aspirational principles suggest to us a number of potential reforms in the U.S. legal order and in the global legal order, as well.

However, even these legal reforms, no matter how well-intentioned or how far-reaching, will be short-lived and ineffectual without a fundamental change in individuals at the psychological and spiritual levels.

One avenue for bringing about this transformation involves the engagement of individuals of all faiths or no faith in the activities the Bahá'í community

---

138 On the importance of 'embracing a cross-racial dialogue', see Tatum, *'Why Are All the Black Kids Sitting Together in the Cafeteria?'*, pp. 193–206.
139 Lepard, 'Obstacles to Interracial Unity', p. 71.

undertakes to abolish prejudice and racism. Bahá'í communities everywhere invite all people of goodwill to work side by side with others to build racism-free communities, engage in meaningful action on racial justice, and participate in the discourses of society on this critical social issue. All of these simultaneous and mutually reinforcing actions must form part of that 'consequential reform of the social order' called for by the Universal House of Justice that will, in its words, free the American nation 'from the pernicious effects of racial prejudice and will hasten the attainment of a just, diverse, and united society that can increasingly manifest the oneness of the human family'.[140]

Bibliography

'Abdu'l-Bahá. *'Abdu'l-Bahá in London.* London: Bahá'í Publishing Trust, 1982.

— *Paris Talks.* Oakham, Rutland: U.K. Bahá'í Publishing Trust, 1972.

— *The Promulgation of Universal Peace: Talks Delivered by 'Abdu'l-Bahá During His Visit to the United States and Canada in 1912.* Compiled by Howard MacNutt. 2nd ed. Wilmette, IL: Bahá'í Publishing Trust, 1982.

— *The Secret of Divine Civilization.* Translated from the Persian by Marzieh Gail in consultation with Ali-Kuli Khan. Wilmette, IL: Bahá'í Publishing Trust, 1990.

Alexander, Michelle. *The New Jim Crow: Mass Incarceration in the Age of Colorblindness.* Rev. ed. New York: The New Press, 2012.

Bahá'í International Community. 'Combating Racism: Statement submitted to the United Nations Second World Conference to Combat Racism and Racial Discrimination'. Geneva, 1 August 1983. https://www.bic.org/statements/combating-racism-1

— *A Governance Befitting: Humanity and the Path Toward a Just Global Order.* New York, 21 September 2020. https://www.bic.org/news/governance-befitting-bic-statement-75th-anniversary-un-looks-future

Bahá'u'lláh. *Gleanings from the Writings of Bahá'u'lláh.* Wilmette, IL: Bahá'í Publishing Trust, 1983.

— *The Hidden Words.* Translated by Shoghi Effendi with the assistance of some English friends. Wilmette, IL: Bahá'í Publishing Trust, 1993.

— *The Kitáb-i-Íqán: The Book of Certitude.* Translated by Shoghi Effendi. Wilmette, IL: Bahá'í Publishing Trust, 1989. https://www.bahai.org/library/authoritative-texts/bahaullah/kitab-i-iqan/1#990539395

— *Tablets of Bahá'u'lláh Revealed after the Kitáb-i-Aqdas.* Translated by Habib Taherzadeh. Compiled by the Research Department of the Universal House of Justice at the Bahá'í World Centre. Wilmette, IL: Bahá'í Publishing Trust, 1998.

Blackmon, Douglas A. *Slavery by Another Name: The Re-Enslavement of Black Americans from the Civil War to World War II.* New York: Anchor Books, 2008.

Committee on the Elimination of Racial Discrimination. General Recommendation no. 35. 'Combating Racist Hate Speech'. U.N. Doc. CERD/C/GC/35 (2013).

---

140 Universal House of Justice, Letter to the Bahá'ís of the United States, 22 July 2020.

DeGruy, Joy, Ph.D. *Post Traumatic Slave Syndrome: America's Legacy of Enduring Injury and Healing.* Portland: Joy DeGruy Publications Inc., 2005.

Gonzales, Steven. 'Affirmative Action and the Jurisprudence of Equitable Inclusion: Towards a New Consensus on Gender and Race Relations'. *Journal of Bahá'í Studies*, vol. 7, no. 2 (1988). https://bahai-library.com/pdf/g/gonzales_affirmative_action.pdf

Hacker, Andrew. *Two Nations: Black and White, Separate, Hostile, Unequal.* Expanded and updated ed. New York: Ballantine Books, 1995.

Hornby, Helen Bassett, comp. *Lights of Guidance: A Bahá'í Reference File.* 6th ed. New Delhi: Bahá'í Publishing Trust, 1999.

Human Rights Committee. General Comment no. 11. 'Article 20' (1983).

— General Comment no. 34. 'Article 19: Freedoms of Opinion and Expression'. U.N. Doc. CCPR/C/GC/34 (2011).

'Human Rights Council Calls on Top U.N. Rights Official to Take Action on Racist Violence'. *U.N. News.* 19 June 2020. https://news.un.org/en/story/2020/06/1066722

Human Rights Council Resolution 43/1 (2020).

International Convention on the Elimination of All Forms of Racial Discrimination (1965) ('ICERD'). 660 U.N.T.S. 195. https://www.ohchr.org/en/professionalinterest/pages/cerd.aspx

International Covenant on Civil and Political Rights (1966) ('ICCPR'). 999 U.N.T.S. 171. https://www.ohchr.org/en/professionalinterest/pages/ccpr.aspx

Lepard, Brian D. *Customary International Law: A New Theory with Practical Applications.* New York: Cambridge University Press, 2010.

Lepard, Jenina S. 'Obstacles to Interracial Unity: Some Psychological and Spiritual Insights'. *International Journal of Applied Psychoanalytic Studies*, vol. 4, no. 1 (2007), pp. 63–73. https://onlinelibrary.wiley.com/doi/abs/10.1002/aps.124

National Spiritual Assembly of the Bahá'ís of the United States. *The Vision of Race Unity: America's Most Challenging Issue: A Statement by the National Spiritual Assembly of the Bahá'ís of the United States.* 1991. https://www.ibiblio.org/Bahai/Texts/English/The-Vision-Of-Race-Unity.html

Ogletree, Jr., Charles J. *All Deliberate Speed: Reflections on the First Half-Century of Brown v. Board of Education.* New York: W.W. Norton & Co., 2004.

Richie, Beth E. *Arrested Justice: Black Women, Violence, and America's Prison Nation.* New York: New York University Press, 2012.

Rothstein, Richard. *The Color of Law: A Forgotten History of How Our Government Segregated America.* New York: Liveright Publishing Corp., 2017.

Ruhe-Schoen, Janet. *Champions of Oneness: Louis Gregory and His Shining Circle.* Wilmette, IL: Bahá'í Publishing, 2015.

Shoghi Effendi. *The Advent of Divine Justice.* Wilmette, IL: Bahá'í Publishing, 2006.

— *Citadel of Faith: Messages to America 1947–1957.* Wilmette, IL: Bahá'í Publishing Trust, 1995. https://www.bahai.org/library/authoritative-texts/shoghi-effendi/citadel-faith/1# 290165562

— *The Promised Day Is Come.* Wilmette, IL: Bahá'í Publishing Trust, rev. ed. 1980. https://www.bahai.org/library/authoritative-texts/shoghi-effendi/promised-day-come/1

— *The World Order of Bahá'u'lláh: Selected Letters.* Wilmette, IL: Bahá'í Publishing Trust, 1991.

Statute of the International Court of Justice (1945). https://www.icj-cij.org/en/statute

Strossen, Nadine. *Hate: Why We Should Resist It with Free Speech, Not Censorship.* New York: Oxford University Press, 2018.

Tatum, Beverly Daniel, Ph.D. *'Why Are All the Black Kids Sitting Together in the Cafeteria?' and Other Conversations About Race.* Rev. ed. New York: Basic Books, 1999.

Thomas, Richard W. *Racial Unity: An Imperative for Social Progress.* Ottawa: Bahá'í Studies Publications, 1990.

U.N. Charter (1945). 59 Stat. 1031. https://www.un.org/en/charter-united-nations/.

United Nations Office of the High Commissioner for Human Rights. 'Statement on the Protests against Systemic Racism in the United States'. 5 June 2020. https://www.ohchr.org/EN/NewsEvents/Pages/DisplayNews.aspx?NewsID=25927

Universal Declaration of Human Rights. G.A. Res. 217A (III) (1948).

Universal House of Justice. Letter to the Bahá'ís of the United States, 22 July 2020. https://www.bahai.org/library/authoritative-texts/the-universal-house-of-justice/messages/20200722_001/1#870410250

— Letter to the Bahá'ís of the World, 25 March 2007. https://www.bahai.org/library/authoritative-texts/the-universal-house-of-justice/messages/20070325_001/1#126035670

— Letter to the Followers of Bahá'u'lláh in the United States of America, 29 December 1988. https://www.bahai.org/library/authoritative-texts/the-universal-house-of-justice/messages/19881229_001/1#986857639

— 'The Promise of World Peace'. https://www.bahai.org/documents/the-universal-house-of-justice/promise-world-peace

U.S. Constitution. https://www.archives.gov/founding-docs/constitution

Vienna Convention on the Law of Treaties (1969). 1155 U.N.T.S. 331.

7

Toward a New World Tax Order: A Bahá'í Vision for International Tax Law and Policy

Brian D. Lepard[1]

Introduction: A New World Tax Order?

'The OECD Consults on a New Tax World Order' announces the title of an article in a prominent tax journal.[2] From a Bahá'í perspective this headline about the Organization for Economic Cooperation and Development (OECD) signifies major progress in international relations, because of the many references in the Bahá'í writings regarding the need to establish a 'new world order' that fosters economic and social justice, including in matters of taxation.[3]

As this example demonstrates, international taxation, a subject previously of interest mainly to legal and policy experts, now generates headlines and widening public interest. Governments have recently devoted unprecedented high-level attention to making the international tax system more equitable and efficient. They have been compelled to re-examine the foundations of the present system by dramatic changes in the world's economy and the distribution of material resources within and among nations.

In particular, economies have become more interdependent. Capital can now move freely among countries in the blink of an eye. New technologies have upended old economic structures and made national borders obsolete in many areas of commerce. Digital currencies have proliferated, and online services can now be provided across the globe. National governments often have difficulty regulating these new types of transactions, which can easily evade taxation.

---

1   I express my deep appreciation to Richard Weisman for his substantial research assistance and help in the writing of this chapter.
2   Herzfeld, 'The OECD Consults on a New Tax World Order'. The article opens: 'A new world order is emerging from the OECD base erosion and profit-shifting project and U.S. tax reform. Those efforts, combined with larger economic and political forces, have mostly laid waste to the previous international tax regime.' The OECD program mentioned in the article is discussed below.
3   On the concept of a 'new world order' in the Bahá'í teachings, see, e.g. Hatcher and Martin, *Bahá'í Faith*, p. 193.

Compounding the problem, many countries have marketed themselves as so-called 'tax havens' by offering low or zero tax rates to companies organized within their jurisdictions, but operating globally. Meanwhile, many developing countries where Western-based multinational corporations sell or produce their goods and services may be unable fully to tax profits from those sales because of longstanding rules in tax treaties limiting the ability of a 'host country' to tax such business profits unless the multinational corporation has a 'permanent establishment' there, usually requiring a physical presence.[4] In today's world of e-commerce having a permanent establishment can be easily avoided by, for example, undertaking sales through websites and social media.[5]

These and other factors have exacerbated economic inequality between developed and developing countries. Within countries, wealthy individuals can often take advantage of tax preferences implemented by governments ostensibly to encourage economic growth, resulting in them paying little tax compared to poorer individuals. Such tax policies, along with other factors, have increased economic inequality among individuals within nations.[6]

As legal scholars Michael J. Graetz and Anne L. Alstott point out, the current rules of international taxation are antiquated and have contributed to these contemporary problems. They write:

> The system of international taxation that governs transactions in today's modern global economy, which is characterized by instantaneous communication and capital transfers, is in substantial part a relic from the early part of the 20th century, a time that predates both transoceanic flights and telephone calls. Improving this archaic system may well prove the greatest tax policy challenge of our time.[7]

Governments today have at last begun to seriously debate proposals to meet that challenge. These global developments have generated intense political pressure on governments to reform venerable rules and structures.

This pressure has resulted in a call by heads of state of the 'Group of 20' ('G20') industrialized nations for ground-breaking changes to the framework of international taxation. In this connection, the OECD, an intergovernmental organization of primarily developed countries with 38 state members and additional state 'partners',[8] has developed proposals in the early 21st century to restrain certain types of corporate tax planning, resulting in previously unattainable levels of cooperation between national taxing authorities. It has in particular attempted to prevent the artificial shifting of profits by multinational businesses to low-tax countries and to ensure that global corporations pay a minimum amount of corporate tax. Leaders

---

4   See generally OECD, *Preventing the Artificial Avoidance of Permanent Establishment Status*, p. 9.
5   See ibid. p. 10. See also the discussion of permanent establishment rules in treaties below.
6   See e.g. Stiglitz, *Price of Inequality*, especially pp. 89–93.
7   Graetz & Alstott, *Federal Income Taxation*, p. 29.
8   See generally https://www.oecd.org/en/about.html

are also discussing the idea of imposing a minimum annual tax on the wealth of very high net worth individuals (typically those with at least $1 billion in assets).[9]

This chapter explores the strengths and weaknesses of the existing international tax system in general, as well as the significance of these new reform initiatives in light of the Bahá'í teachings. It also investigates what Bahá'í principles suggest about desirable future directions for reform, first by providing an overview of the current international tax system and then by taking a more detailed look at existing rules regarding the taxation of international transactions. Next, the chapter identifies weaknesses in the current system and elaborates on the above-mentioned contemporary efforts to address them. It explores diverse normative perspectives on this system propounded by tax scholars, exemplified by the contrast between views emphasizing national sovereignty and those advocating the need for a global vision. Then it turns to an identification of relevant Bahá'í principles and their implications for reforms of the system to meet the needs of an economically and spiritually interdependent world. Finally, it evaluates the future prospects for these types of reforms.

An Overview of the Existing System of Taxation in the World and the Tension Between National and Global Interests

Most people recognize that taxation is necessary to provide the funds for basic government services. In this connection, Angel Gurría, former Secretary-General of the OECD, wrote:

> Tax is at the heart of our societies. A well-functioning tax system is the foundation stone of the citizen-state relationship, establishing powerful links based on accountability and responsibility. It is also critical for inclusive growth and for sustainable development, providing governments with the resources to invest in infrastructure, education, health, and social protection systems.[10]

Historically, in the current system of sovereign states described in Chapter 1, tax policy has been determined primarily at the state (country) level. In a purely domestic context, a nation's government can make decisions about designing a tax system that ideally seeks to achieve the above goals solely within the borders of the country it rules. These include appropriate attention to providing for the defense of the country, funding a 'social safety net' for the poor, facilitating desirable economic activity, and achieving some distribution of economic resources among people and businesses within the country that the population perceives as 'fair'. Professor Tsilly Dagan writes in this connection:

> The traditional perspective envisions a state ruled by a sovereign that is entrusted with exclusive tax legislative powers, seeking (at least ideally) to

---

9   See the discussion of these initiatives below.
10   OECD, *OECD Work on Taxation, 2018–19.*

maximize welfare (efficiency) and justly (re)distribute it, while reinforcing the underlying normative values shared by its constituents.[11]

National governments usually regard themselves as free to make their own tax policy decisions without regard to the policies or needs of other countries.

However, given the growth of international economic and cultural interchange described earlier, governments can no longer ignore the impact of other countries' tax policies on them, or their policies' impact on other countries. In today's inter-dependent economic environment, many countries have sought to gain competitive advantages regarding economic investment from abroad through their tax policies. Dagan explains that when it comes to the international context governments must thus take many other policy considerations into account. She writes:

> The international context is changing the way in which we generally think about income taxation . . . From the current globalized perspective . . . [each] powerful sovereign is only one of approximately 200 sovereigns competing with one another for investments, residents, and tax revenues. Taxation is the currency of this competition, with states luring investments as well as residents to their jurisdiction with attractive taxing and spending 'deals'. Hence, in conditions of tax competition, tax policies almost inevitably become marketized, as countries attempt to tailor their taxation and benefits packages to the needs and requirements of their most valuable current and potential investors and residents. Mobile capital enjoys lower tax rates; foreign investors benefit from attractive exemptions; and sought-after MNEs [multi-national enterprises] enjoy favorable tax regimes (e.g. favorable regimes for R&D [research and development]). As a result of this marketization, redistribution is increasingly falling by the wayside. State welfare systems are struggling to survive, while the wealth disparities within and between states grow wider. The challenges of income taxation in this globalized competitive setting are substantial, almost overwhelming, leading many to lament the demise of the welfare state and sending policymakers as well as scholars in search of a viable solution for sustaining the efficiency and justice goals of income taxation.[12]

Dagan goes on to emphasize the absence of a central tax authority and the extreme decentralization of the current international tax regime:

> At its base, international taxation is decentralized: there is no central government that sets the rules and tax rates or allocates rights to tax. Despite the considerable recent efforts of cooperation, and notwithstanding views that a customary international law of taxation has emerged and that its rules limit states' choices, every country is still independently making its own tax policy and setting its own

---

11   Dagan, *International Tax Policy*, p. 2.
12   ibid. pp. 2–3.

rules and tax rates. These national policies interact to create the international tax regime. The decentralized nature of international taxation has led to several inconsistencies between systems, producing barriers to cross-border economic activities as well as opportunities for tax avoidance. Decentralization makes the international tax regime not only market-competitive but also highly fragmentized. Sophisticated taxpayers are able to pick and choose among the components of the various tax systems using tax-planning instruments and thereby free-ride states' public goods and services. The fragmentation and marketization of international tax in these conditions of competition have eroded the ability of states both to collect taxes to finance their public fisc and to redistribute wealth. This, in turn, has seriously undermined the legitimacy of states' use of their coercive power to tax.[13]

This new political and economic environment has shaped the recent efforts described at the outset of this chapter to achieve greater equity and harmonization among national tax systems. The weaknesses of the existing system of international taxation deserve a more detailed investigation.

A More Detailed Examination of the Existing System of International Taxation

The current system of international taxation traces its roots back to the 1920s. During this period international trade was growing, and countries began recognizing the need to harmonize national tax rules. The League of Nations, which had been created in 1920 in the aftermath of World War I, appointed panels of experts to study the problem of international tax coordination and particularly that of double taxation (the taxation of the same income by two different countries), which was perceived as unfairly burdening taxpayers.[14]

A hundred years ago countries adopted diverse approaches to tax policy relating to transactions crossing international borders. These differences helped motivate the League of Nations' efforts to achieve some degree of coordination. Despite those historic efforts at harmonization, including through modern organizations such as the United Nations and the OECD, these differences persist today.

For example, a country may claim the right to impose an income tax on legal persons (which could be individuals or companies) residing in it (referred to as 'residents'). Some countries impose tax on the worldwide income of residents, while others tax them only on income from sources within the country. Likewise, a country may claim the right to tax income of persons residing abroad (referred to as 'non-residents') that is in some way related to the taxing country and therefore sourced there, such as income from a business operated by the non-resident in the taxing country, or from a more passive investment (such as in stocks or bonds)

---

13   ibid. p. 3.
14   See Lepard, 'Is the United States Obligated to Drive on the Right?', p. 61.

held in the taxing country. Countries differ in how they source particular types of income and the tax rates they impose on various types of domestic source income as well as on residents versus non-residents.

Of course, many businesses today operate across international borders. Very often they create corporations under the laws of the diverse countries where they operate, all controlled at the 'top' by a single parent corporation. For example, Corporation X, which is incorporated in the U.S., may form a wholly-owned subsidiary, Corporation Y, under the laws of the Republic of Ireland ('Ireland') to operate in Ireland. Corporation X may engage in various business transactions with Corporation Y. To illustrate, Corporation X may have developed computer software in the U.S. that is then licensed (in effect, leased) to Corporation Y for a certain price (known as a 'transfer price') so that Corporation Y can then use the software in its manufacturing activities in Ireland. The payments Corporation Y makes to Corporation X for the use of its software are referred to as 'royalties'.

Now let us assume, as has historically been the case, that the U.S. imposes a comparatively high tax on the income of U.S.-based corporations like Corporation X, and that Ireland imposes a relatively low tax on Ireland-based corporations like Corporation Y (which Ireland may do to try to attract foreign investment). Corporation X, which controls Corporation Y, will have an incentive to set the royalty price as low as possible so as to reduce the amount of income taxed to Corporation X in the U.S. at a high rate, and increase the amount of profit taxed to Corporation Y by Ireland at a low rate. (Corporation Y's profit will be higher because the cost of the royalties paid to its parent Corporation X is reduced.) Chains of controlled corporations, like X and Y, can manipulate transfer prices in this way to reduce their total tax liability owed to all countries where they operate.

In principle, two methods can prevent such manipulation. One is for tax authorities (in either or both countries) to recalculate tax liabilities by ignoring the actual (artificially low) price that was charged (here, the royalty price) and assuming instead that a price was paid equal to what unrelated corporations would agree upon if they were negotiating 'at arm's length' (thus referred to as an 'arm's length price'). Such a recalculation would increase Corporation X's royalty income and thus its tax paid to the U.S., and decrease Corporation Y's profits, thus lowering its tax paid to Ireland. This method is known as the 'arm's length standard' or 'arm's length principle'.[15]

Note that double taxation could occur if Ireland respects the low royalty price in computing Corporation Y's profits, but the U.S. increases the royalty price to what it views as an 'arm's length price' in computing Corporation X's profits. In this case, a portion of the profits of the Corporation X-Y combined group would be taxed by both Ireland and the U.S., thus resulting in double taxation of those profits.

An alternative possible method to prevent manipulation of transfer prices,

---

15 On the arm's length standard, see generally Lepard, 'Is the United States Obligated to Drive on the Right? ', pp. 48–50.

although not currently applied in international tax law, is called 'formulary apportionment'.[16] Under this method, the U.S. and Ireland tax authorities would combine the income of Corporation X and Corporation Y, ignoring the royalty transfer price, and then allocate this total income of the Corporation X-Y group to the U.S. and Ireland respectively using a formula. The formula could be based on some factor, such as the amount of sales made in the U.S. versus Ireland, or the number of employees working in each country, or on a combination of factors. In fact, states within the U.S. currently use such a system to allocate income of multi-state corporate businesses among the different U.S. states for state income tax purposes.[17] There have been proposals to use this system at the international level as well, and to replace the arm's length standard with some version of formulary apportionment.[18]

Importantly, tax treaties between a country and other countries can modify their national taxing rules. Indeed, one of the key recommendations of the League of Nations bodies was to encourage the adoption of treaties between two countries (referred to as 'bilateral treaties') with the goal of reducing the potential 'double' taxation of the same income by the two countries, through agreement on a set of coordinated rules that would supplant the different rules in the countries' national tax laws. In particular, the League of Nations in 1927 approved a model bilateral convention (treaty) for the prevention of double taxation, which was succeeded by various other versions and became the inspiration for modern tax treaties.[19]

The League of Nations ultimately promulgated various model bilateral tax treaties, which have been modified and essentially adopted by its successor, the United Nations ('UN') and by the OECD. Many countries have negotiated treaties with trading partner countries that try to generally follow these models. Today more than 3,000 of these bilateral tax treaties exist.[20] During the League of Nations era and today the treaties sought to achieve a degree of harmonization of rules, and minimization of the risk of double taxation, through a variety of means.

For example, the current version of the OECD Model Convention on Income and on Capital (the 'OECD Model Tax Convention') establishes different rules for business income and non-business investment income (such as dividends on stock or interest on bonds). The country where a business is conducted (regardless of the residence of the person or company owning and conducting it), often referred to as the 'host country', has the primary right to tax that income. However, the host country can only tax the income if the owner of the business has a so-called 'permanent establishment' ('PE') in the host country, traditionally defined as some kind of physical location or office. If the business owner has no PE in a host country, the host country cannot tax the relevant business income. Instead, it will be taxed, if at all, by the country of residence of the owner.[21]

---

16   See generally ibid. p. 50.
17   See ibid.
18   See ibid. pp. 52–6.
19   See ibid. pp. 61–70.
20   See https://www.oecd.org/en/topics/tax-treaties.html (last accessed 28 February 2025).
21   See, e.g. OECD, *Model Tax Convention on Income and on Capital*, arts. 5 and 7.

By contrast, under the treaty, the country of residence of any taxpayer has the primary right to tax passive investment income received by that taxpayer, rather than the 'source country' (the country where the investment is located). The source country is allowed to impose only a modest tax on the investment income, including, for example, dividends, interest, and royalties.[22]

The OECD Model Tax Convention also addresses transfer pricing issues. It essentially endorses the arm's length principle (rather than formulary apportionment) and allows profits to be re-allocated between related businesses to reflect the profits that would have been earned had all dealings between the businesses been on arm's length terms. (For example, it would allow the U.S. to allocate additional profits to Corporation X in the above illustration to reflect a higher arm's length royalty rate.) It also obligates countries to make 'correlative' allocations to avoid double taxation. (That is, in the same illustration, it would require Ireland to correspondingly lower the profits of Corporation Y that it taxes.)[23]

The OECD Model Tax Convention contains a myriad of other rules designed to foster coordination between the countries and the avoidance of double taxation. For example, it defines when a corporation is a 'resident' of a particular country.[24] It also establishes procedures for tax authorities in the two countries to follow to resolve any disputes about how to tax a particular taxpayer and prevent double taxation.[25] Additionally, it requires the exchange of relevant tax information between the taxing authorities of the two countries.[26]

Advances and New Challenges Arising from Tax Competition Among Taxpayers and Countries

So what has been the impact of these treaties and other efforts at tax coordination in the last century? While a lively academic debate continues on their precise effect, scholars generally agree they have led to an expansion of global trade and investment, including some degree of significant foreign direct investment in developing countries.[27]

On the other hand, the persisting patchwork of different national rules on international taxation, supplemented by various bilateral treaties, has opened the door to diverse forms of self-interested 'gamesmanship' to achieve tax savings (on the part of taxpayers) or economic benefits (on the part of governments). These strategies often try to exploit differences in the national rules. For instance, as we have just seen, related corporations will try to set transfer prices and justify them as 'arm's length' under relevant treaties and national laws to achieve global tax savings that

---

22   See, e.g. ibid. arts. 10–12.
23   See ibid. art. 9.
24   See ibid. art. 4.
25   See ibid. art. 25.
26   See ibid. art. 26.
27   See, e.g. Petkova et al. 'On the Relevance of Double Tax Treaties' (finding that tax treaties can increase foreign direct investment by about 18%).

can be obtained because of different countries' tax rates on business profits. They may also try to 'game' the rules to actually achieve zero taxation by falling through 'cracks' between national laws, or abuse treaty rules for their benefit.

Governments continue to try to attract foreign investment and achieve financial benefits at the expense of other countries by, for example, offering low or zero rates of taxation to domestic or foreign corporations – referred to as 'tax competition'.[28] Those countries (and subnational jurisdictions) that offer aggressively low tax rates are often referred to as 'tax havens'.

When businesses incorporate in tax havens they deprive other countries, whether developed or developing, of needed tax revenue. This includes revenue for funding efforts to reduce disparities between the rich and poor, and to create a 'social safety net', such as through social security programs. Both developed and developing countries lose much-needed tax revenue to tax havens, which themselves are often super-wealthy enclaves.

Reuven Avi-Yonah describes this dynamic and the challenges it poses to the ability of countries with social safety net systems to provide economic support for the needy:

> The mobility of capital has resulted in international tax competition, in which sovereign countries aim to attract both portfolio and direct investment by lowering their tax rates on income earned by foreigners. Tax competition, in turn, threatens to undermine the individual and corporate income taxes, which traditionally have generated the largest share of revenue for modern welfare states. The developed countries have responded in two ways: first, by shifting the tax burden from (mobile) capital to (less mobile) labor, and second, when increased taxation of labor has become politically and economically problematic, by reducing the social safety net. Thus, globalization and tax competition lead to fiscal crises for countries that wish to continue to provide social insurance; at the same time, demographic factors and the increased income inequality, job insecurity, and income volatility that result from globalization render such social insurance all the more necessary . . . [M]aintaining both globalization and social insurance will require measures that limit tax competition but preserve each democratic state's ability to determine the size of its public sector.[29]

Avi-Yonah adds that 'likewise, unrestrained tax competition is generally not in the best interest of developing countries'.[30]

---

28   On global tax competition, see, e.g. Avi-Yonah, 'Globalization', pp. 1575–9.
29   ibid. pp. 1575–6.
30   ibid. p. 1675.

Efforts to Address the Harmful Impacts of Tax Competition

In the early 2000s, and especially in the wake of the global financial crisis of 2008, governments around the world began to devote much more attention to the harmful effects of tax competition, calling upon the G20 and the OECD to take new action to combat it. The OECD responded by launching initiatives to tackle a number of related problems. First, it developed an action plan to reverse what it called 'base erosion and profit shifting' ('BEPS') by multinational business enterprises through the techniques described above, such as incorporating businesses in tax havens or using abusive transfer pricing practices that violate the spirit if not the letter of the arm's length standard.[31] Second, the OECD launched an effort to ensure that certain multinational corporations pay a minimum corporate tax on their income.[32] The OECD also created an initiative to encourage the greater sharing of tax information by tax authorities (thereby resulting in 'tax transparency'), referred to as the Standard for Automatic Exchange of Financial Account Information in Tax Matters.[33] Other organizations, including the G20, along with various scholars, have floated the idea of countries agreeing to impose a minimum annual wealth tax on the net worth of billionaires.[34] Let us explore some of these programs and ideas.

The Base Erosion and Profit Shifting ('BEPS') Initiative

In July of 2013 Angel Gurría, then-Secretary-General of the OECD, explained the purpose of the BEPS Initiative at the launch of the G20/OECD Action Plan, stating:

> The joint challenges of tax evasion and tax base erosion lie at the heart of the social contract . . . Our citizens are demanding that we tackle offshore tax evasion by wealthy individuals and re-vamp the international tax system to prevent multi-national enterprises from artificially shifting profits, resulting in very low taxes or even double non-taxation and thereby eroding our tax base.[35]

Double non-taxation occurs when, under the tax rules of two countries or an applicable treaty between them, a taxpayer winds up owing no tax to both countries.
The OECD's website on BEPS further explains (as of 2025) that:

> Domestic tax base erosion and profit shifting (BEPS) relates to tax planning strategies that multinational enterprises use to exploit loopholes in tax rules to artificially shift profits to low or no-tax locations as a way to avoid paying tax. The OECD/G20 BEPS Project equips governments with rules and instruments

---

31 See OECD, 'Base Erosion and Profit-Shifting (BEPS)' and the discussion below.
32 See the discussion below.
33 See OECD. *Standard for Automatic Exchange of Financial Account Information in Tax Matters.*
34 See the discussion below.
35 Quoted in Hargis, 'OECD Proposes Plan to Curb International Tax Avoidance'.

to address tax avoidance, ensuring that profits are taxed where economic activities generating them take place and where value is created.[36]

In 2025 the OECD affirmed that a 'conservative' estimate of the loss of revenue from base erosion and profit shifting was $100 to $240 billion every year. It noted this is equivalent to 4 to 10 percent of all revenue globally from countries' corporate income taxes.[37] The BEPS Initiative sought to encourage cooperation among national tax authorities to eliminate this loss. The OECD emphasized that:

> BEPS practices undermine the fairness and integrity of tax systems because businesses that operate across borders can use them to gain a competitive advantage over enterprises operating at a domestic level. In a broader context, when large corporations are seen to be avoiding income tax, it undermines voluntary compliance by all taxpayers.[38]

According to the OECD, BEPS hurts developing countries the most:

> Although BEPS affects all countries, developing economies suffer disproportionately from the practice due to their heavy reliance on corporate income tax, particularly from multinational enterprises . . . Developing countries participate on an equal footing with OECD and G20 countries in the BEPS project, and work is being carried out to support all countries interested in implementing and applying the rules in a consistent and coherent manner, particularly those for which capacity building is an important issue.[39]

Indeed, the OECD has reported that:

> Under the OECD/G20 Inclusive Framework on BEPS, over 140 countries and jurisdictions are working together to implement 15 measures to tackle tax avoidance, improve the coherence of international tax rules and ensure a more transparent tax environment.[40]

The 15 measures that comprise the BEPS Initiative involve multiple lines of action. They include addressing the digitalization of the world economy and adopting common rules for taxing digital transactions; reducing the incentives of a parent company in a developed country to shift profits to a subsidiary located in a low-tax jurisdiction (as described in the example above involving a U.S. corporation and its Irish subsidiary); countering harmful tax practices by increasing transparency; preventing tax treaty abuse; preventing the artificial avoidance of permanent

---

36   OECD, 'Base Erosion and Profit-Shifting (BEPS)'.
37   ibid.
38   ibid.
39   ibid.
40   ibid.

establishment status to take unfair advantage of tax treaty benefits; providing additional guidance on applying the arm's length principle to transfer pricing; and making dispute resolution procedures under tax treaties between the tax authorities of the parties to the treaty more timely, effective, and efficient.[41] The actions also include adopting a 'Multilateral Convention to Implement Tax Treaty Related Measures to Prevent Base Erosion and Profit Shifting'. This multilateral treaty would allow 'governments to modify existing bilateral tax treaties in a synchronised and efficient manner to implement the tax treaty measures developed during the BEPS Project, without the need to expend resources renegotiating each treaty bilaterally'.[42] These actions, taken together, represent a major effort to reform the existing international tax structure and remedy its most glaring deficiencies. Indeed, the OECD has said that in its view 'the BEPS package represents the first substantial renovation of the international tax rules in almost a century'.[43]

Framework for Global Minimum Taxation of Certain Corporations

Alongside the BEPS project, the OECD adopted a proposal to ensure that certain multinational businesses would pay a minimum corporate income tax rate that could not be avoided through the various devices (including abusive transfer pricing) described above. The OECD explains this project:

> A key part of the OECD/G20 BEPS Project is addressing the tax challenges arising from the digitalisation of the economy. In October 2021, over 135 jurisdictions joined a ground breaking plan to update key elements of the international tax system which is no longer fit for purpose in a globalised and digitalised economy. The Global Anti-Base Erosion Rules (GloBE) are a key component of this plan and ensure large multinational enterprise pay a minimum level of tax on the income arising in each of the jurisdictions where they operate.[44]

The OECD indicates further in a 2021 report that the GloBE rules provide for such a minimum level of corporate tax 'by imposing a top-up tax on profits arising in a jurisdiction whenever the effective tax rate, determined on a jurisdictional basis, is below the minimum rate'.[45] The OECD has now developed complex rules for implementing GloBE.[46] The very fact that so many countries have agreed to implement a global minimum corporate tax rate represents a major achievement and a dramatic development in the recent history of the international tax system.

---

41   See ibid.
42   https://www.oecd.org/en/topics/beps-multilateral-instrument.html
43   OECD, *Tax Challenges*, p. 3.
44   https://www.oecd.org/en/topics/sub-issues/global-minimum-tax/global-anti-base-erosion-model-rules-pillar-two.html
45   OECD, *Tax Challenges*, p. 7.
46   See generally ibid.

A Global Wealth Tax

World leaders have not only expressed deepening concern about, and taken action to combat, abusive tax planning by multinational corporations; they have also begun to address concerns about the ability of wealthy individual taxpayers to avoid both income and wealth taxes by shifting their income and wealth to low-tax jurisdictions – or by moving out of high-tax countries and establishing residence in countries offering very low tax rates. Expatriation for tax purposes, including from the U.S., continues to rise.[47] These tax strategies have helped contribute to the increasing economic inequality among individuals documented in earlier chapters.

The concept of the creation of a global minimum wealth tax, although not yet implemented, has gained increasing support. For example, under some proposals countries would agree that ultra-high-net worth individual taxpayers – often defined as those with a net worth of at least $1 billion – should pay an annual tax of 2% of their wealth. Studies undertaken by economists affiliated with the European Union and the G20 have endorsed such a proposal.[48] In addition, in 2014 French economist Thomas Piketty, in his acclaimed book *Capital in the Twenty-First Century*, proposed a European wealth tax with graduated rates that could rise to 2 percent or more of fortunes exceeding 5 million Euros.[49] He also advocated for a progressive global wealth tax along the lines just described.[50] However, governments have been divided over the desirability of a global wealth tax,[51] and as of early 2025 they had not taken steps to realize it.

Weaknesses of the Existing International Tax System in Light of Generally Accepted Criteria for Evaluating Tax Systems

The existing international tax system that the above-mentioned efforts seek to reform exhibits a number of serious weaknesses. One way of understanding these weaknesses – and the potential impact of various remedies for them – involves examining them through the lens of four generally accepted attributes of an 'ideal' tax system. Tax experts have long recommended that a fair system of income taxation should exhibit (1) horizontal equity; (2) vertical equity; (3) efficiency; and (4) simplicity.[52]

Horizontal equity requires that taxpayers with the same economic income should pay the same amount of tax, without regard to the source and type of the income.[53] Vertical equity requires that a taxpayer with greater income than

---

47   See, e.g. La Torre Jeker, 'Expatriation'.
48   See generally Herzfeld, 'Spotlight on Global Minimum Taxes Shifts to Individuals'; Avi-Yonah, 'A Global Wealth Tax?'.
49   See Piketty, *Capital in the Twenty-First Century*, pp. 680–5.
50   See ibid. pp. 663–80.
51   See, e.g. Herzfeld, 'Spotlight on Global Minimum Taxes Shifts to Individuals', pp. 1719–20 (noting opposition of the U.S. to the idea as of 2024).
52   See generally Graetz and Alstott, *Federal Income Taxation*, pp. 24–9.
53   See ibid. pp. 24–5.

another taxpayer should pay more tax (whether calculated at the same tax rate or at progressively higher rates as income increases).[54] Under the efficiency criterion, a tax system should minimize interference with the economic decisions that taxpayers would otherwise make under a given ideal economic system (whether capitalism or some other) so as not to hamper achievement of that system's goals.[55] For example, in a system that gives people the freedom to choose work they want, and is premised on the idea that individuals and society will be better off when everyone has this freedom, a tax system that penalizes income from some types of work compared to others would violate the efficiency criterion. Finally, the simplicity criterion requires that a tax system achieve the above goals as simply as possible. In particular, the rules of a tax system should be simple and comprehensible to taxpayers; compliance with the tax law should be relatively straightforward without the need for complex recordkeeping and expensive professional tax advice; and taxpayers should not have incentives to create highly complex transactions in order to take advantage of tax rules that treat economically similar transactions in different ways for tax purposes.[56]

The current system plainly violates all of these criteria. Taking advantage of the ability to manipulate transfer pricing rules and to source income in or move their residence to tax havens, both multinational businesses and individuals with similar levels of economic income can pay vastly different amounts of tax, thus violating horizontal equity. Using the same strategies a business or individual with huge income can pay the same, or less, total tax (calculated on a global basis) than a much poorer business or individual, thus violating vertical equity. The system in place now is rife with inefficiencies, incentivizing individuals and businesses to shift income-producing activities to tax havens rather than engage in them where they can be most economically productive or contribute to building a social safety net for the less fortunate there. The existing system, hobbled by extraordinary complexity and unjust disparities in tax liabilities among similarly situated taxpayers, allows tax advisers to wealthy individuals and multinational corporations to devise ever-more-byzantine asset ownership and corporate structures to profit from the vast disparities in tax rules around the world.

The significant international tax reforms launched during the last two decades go some way towards remedying these deficiencies and moving the system closer to realizing fair tax policy ideals. However, even under the most optimistic of scenarios they still fall short. The BEPS initiative begins to address some of the worst abuses by enhancing cooperation among tax authorities, but exploitable discrepancies will still remain even when it is fully implemented. This is also true of the global minimum tax concept. Even when implemented fully, it will simply ensure that multinational corporations cannot avoid income tax altogether and will pay a *minimum* level of tax. Corporations with the same income may still

---

54   See ibid. p. 25.
55   See ibid. pp. 25–6.
56   See ibid. pp. 26–8.

pay quite different tax amounts. A global wealth tax on individuals, which today appears unlikely due to controversy and political pressure, would merely serve to mitigate persistent disparities in the taxation of individuals and claw back some of the huge tax savings wealthy individuals can currently enjoy through sophisticated international tax planning.

Critiques of Recent Reforms

Indeed, for these and other reasons, tax experts have critiqued the G20 and OECD-led reform efforts described above. For example, Professor Wendy Herzfeld has alleged that the BEPS project papered over continued disagreements between countries about tax policy and did not fundamentally change the current system anchored in tax competition. She writes:

> Without a re-examination of underlying principles to formulate goals for an international tax system that take into account both global inequalities and the benefits countries obtain from tax competition, it will be difficult for any coordination effort to make substantive progress that could achieve widespread acceptance in fixing the system. The BEPS project – which ostensibly was not about fixing the system, but only about addressing certain perceived abuses – generated unsatisfactory outcomes because different countries had varying objectives.[57]

Herzfeld remains pessimistic about the future of global tax coordination because of countries' divergent interests and the lack of consensus on fundamental principles:

> While the international tax system is broken, there is no ready mechanism to fix it, because the ability of a small group of like-minded countries to coordinate global rules does not exist today as it did in the early twentieth century. Attempts at coordination led by developed countries – of which BEPS represents the most obvious example – are doomed to be unsuccessful because they lack full participation from non-OECD global economic players, are based on incoherent principles, and fail to take account of strong nationalist interests. The BEPS project was inherently problematic precisely because it masked deep underlying differences between countries in the interest of claiming success on achieving consensus . . . Moving forward on a coordinated basis will require a re-examination of fundamental principles and broad agreement on such principles.[58]

If Herzfeld's diagnosis is correct, what is the appropriate response? Should we respect the right of countries to pursue their 'nationalist interests' or should we

---

57   Herzfeld, 'The Case Against BEPS', p. 59.
58   ibid.

continue encouraging them to strive for greater international cooperation based on commonly accepted principles?

National Sovereignty Versus a Global Cooperation Perspective

As Herzfeld notes, despite the efforts to mitigate harmful tax competition and create coordinated rules to achieve greater equity and other tax policy goals, including the BEPS initiative, countries continue to chafe at agreeing to a new set of rules and seek to benefit their own economies by exploiting weaknesses in the existing system. For example, in early 2025 the U.S. government, after a change of administration, signalled its intention to oppose the OECD initiative for a global minimum corporate tax.[59] So should reforming the system be reconsidered? Which direction could function best from a moral or ethical standpoint?

On the one hand, many scholars of tax law have supported the adoption of nationalist tax policies based on a limited conception of the self-interest of states and an expansive interpretation of national sovereignty. One of them is Professor Michael Graetz, an eminent American tax expert. He writes:

> We naturally give primacy to our own citizens in setting national policy, including tax policy. This is both a matter of historical circumstance – some would say accident – and, more importantly, of political organization. In our democratic society, we the people have organized a national government to protect our safety and security, to maintain our liberty, and to promote the well-being of our citizens and residents. By assigning the task of improving the lot of the nation's citizens, including those who are least advantaged, to our government, we have made both economic growth and redistribution of income or wealth a matter of national, rather than worldwide, concern. Likewise, the education of the nation's children and protection of our citizens from economic losses due to ill health, disability, or unemployment, along with ensuring economic security during retirement, are core functions of our national and state governments. Throughout the world, the substance of these protections varies from country to country, depending in democracies like ours ultimately on what the voters say.[60]

Graetz stresses the persisting importance of the nation-state in matters of taxation:

> National governments assign tax burdens and provide benefits. No function is more at the core of government than its system of taxation. It is no accident that the economic and political unification of Europe has stumbled over issues of taxation. Taxes are imposed by national governments (or their subdivisions); the power to tax is rarely delegated to multi-national organizations.[61]

---

59 See 'Despite Fears of a Global Tax War, Donald Trump Has a Chance to Make Peace'.
60 Graetz, 'The David R. Tillinghast Lecture', p. 277.
61 ibid.

Graetz also argues that, notwithstanding the praiseworthy development of international legal norms in such areas as human rights, which require a global approach, it is appropriate for national (and particularly U.S.) tax policy to be determined based on national interests and the interests of citizens rather than global interests:

> Since World War II, international law has become more protective of fundamental human rights of people throughout the world, even when it limits a nation's internal sovereignty. But I have found no one who argues for grounding U.S. international income tax policy on worldwide economic efficiency . . . who also proposes assessing the fairness of U.S. income tax policy on a worldwide basis. More importantly, no nation has ever made a genuine commitment to worldwide equity. We often take quite seriously our obligations to foreigners and show respect for their rights, but we regard our obligation for the well-being of our fellow citizens as more pressing than for people in need elsewhere in the world.[62]

Graetz regards with skepticism the notion that wealthy countries have any obligation to prevent poverty or malnutrition worldwide: 'The responsibility of rich nations to ensure any baseline of resources for all humanity is a controversial idea. And few observers contend that our obligations to people abroad are similar to those within our borders.'[63] He rejects 'utopian . . . ambitions for worldwide harmony implied by those who urge taking a "one-world view"', instead agreeing 'with those political philosophers who insist that a world government – a political entity exercising the powers now held by national governments – would likely live in a constant state of civil unrest, as various populations and regions contest for freedom, autonomy, and self-government'. A 'world government', he maintains, 'would likely become a dictatorship'.[64]

By contrast, many other philosophers and experts today have called for a re-evaluation of purely nationalistic approaches in favor of a vision of all nations working together as part of a global community of nations, and people of all backgrounds supporting one another as part of a worldwide human family. This vision advocates global 'unity in diversity' because it also respects and cherishes differences of race, nationality, culture, religion, and opinion among nations and people.[65] For example, philosopher Peter Singer has argued that we 'should make "one world" a moral standard that transcends the nation-state'.[66] This global outlook has obvious implications for decisions about how to allocate the world's economic resources, including tax revenues, more justly among nations and more equitably among individuals within nations.

---

62   ibid. pp. 277–8.
63   ibid. pp. 300–1.
64   ibid. p. 278.
65   See generally Lepard, *Customary International Law*, pp. 78–81.
66   Singer, *One World*, p. 153.

In the field of international tax law, Professor Reuven Avi-Yonah has advocated for a more global perspective in evaluating nations' tax policies. He has
supported 'global governance' in the area of taxation, and has argued for building
an international tax system that looks at both the needs of developed countries
for sufficient tax revenue to fund 'an adequate social safety net' and the needs of
developing countries for tax revenues sufficient to help them advance economically and socially. He has contended further that 'inter-nation equity indicates that
tax structures should' give preference to the revenue needs of developing countries
over developed countries, thus implying the existence of some obligation of richer
countries to help poorer ones.[67]

How does a Bahá'í perspective view both the existing system and these new
initiatives and concepts? What vision does it set out for the future evolution of the
international tax order?

Foundational Bahá'í Principles

The phrase 'New World Order' in a Bahá'í context refers to the replacement of the
collective political norms and values of the current era, characterized largely by the
pursuit of self-interest by individuals and nations, with a new system of worldwide
governance that incorporates the Bahá'í ideals of unity and justice for all nations
and people of all races, religions, and classes.

Broadly, two separate categories of Bahá'í teachings have particular relevance
to international taxation. The first category focuses on the individual's world view,
including values that affect his or her attitudes toward taxation. In this connection,
the Bahá'í teachings promote the cultivation of a global perspective grounded in
values such as generosity toward others. The second category of Bahá'í teachings
relates more specifically to governance, economics, and taxation.

A Global Vision Anchored in Generosity Toward All Members of the Human Family

First, the Bahá'í writings emphasize the importance of each individual cultivating
a global vision anchored in the principle of the unity of the human family, and in
implementing in his or her personal life values such as generosity toward every
other member of this family. The Bahá'í teachings clearly promote the adoption by
every person of a global perspective. In the words of Bahá'u'lláh, 'Let your vision
be world-embracing, rather than confined to your own self.'[68]

The Bahá'í outlook also emphasizes concern for the welfare of others above
one's own – though it acknowledges a legitimate place for caring for oneself.

---

67 Avi-Yonah, 'Globalization', pp. 1675–6. Avi-Yonah states in this connection: 'When a choice is
    presented between two otherwise comparable alternative rules, one of which has progressive and the
    other regressive implications for the division of the international tax base between poorer and richer
    countries, the progressive rule should be explicitly preferred to the regressive one.' ibid. p. 1650.
68 Bahá'u'lláh, *Gleanings*, p. 106.

Bahá'u'lláh praises a 'pure, kindly, and radiant heart'.[69] The Bahá'í writings call upon each person to undertake altruistic and selfless acts for the well-being of everyone. For example, 'Abdu'l-Bahá says that some of the 'attributes of perfection' include being 'high-minded and magnanimous, and to have regard for the rights of others'.[70] At the same time, the Bahá'í writings indicate there is a place for ensuring also the well-being of one's own self and one's family. Bahá'u'lláh wrote: 'The beginning of magnanimity is when man expendeth his wealth on himself, on his family and on the poor among his brethren in his Faith.'[71]

Bahá'í teachings affirm that these attributes should also characterize the outlook and actions of governmental leaders. Thus, 'Abdu'l-Bahá said that elected leaders must be 'high-minded' and 'incorruptible'.[72] He praised just rulers who are 'powerful champions of the people's rights' and who 'take no pride in gold and silver, but rather in their enlightenment and their determination to achieve the universal good'.[73] These teachings suggest that governments, taxpayers, and other actors should not only look after their own self-interests, but strive to have regard for the welfare of other residents of their nation as well as all nations in the world.

One key aspect of this global welfare, which the Bahá'í teachings urge all governments and peoples to promote, involves the provision of sufficient material benefits to every human being, so that no one lacks the necessities of life and is condemned to poverty. The provision of the necessary means of subsistence to everyone implies that individuals should shun the pursuit of excessive wealth for its own sake, recognizing that our true wealth comes from the cultivation of spiritual qualities and service to others.

'Abdu'l-Bahá critiques the over-emphasis on materialism and the acquisition of wealth for ourselves. He invites us to look beyond our own passing material comfort and welfare, and to strive to help the needy:

> Soon will your swiftly-passing days be over, and the fame and riches, the comforts, the joys provided by this rubbish-heap, the world, will be gone without a trace . . . Be ye loving fathers to the orphan, and a refuge to the helpless, and a treasury for the poor, and a cure for the ailing . . . Think ye at all times of rendering some service to every member of the human race.[74]

'Abdu'l-Bahá also describes justice and impartiality as attributes of perfection:

> This means to have no regard for one's own personal benefits and selfish advantages, and to carry out the laws of God without the slightest concern for

---

69   See Bahá'u'lláh, *Hidden Words*, Arabic no. 1 ('My first counsel is this: Possess a pure, kindly and radiant heart, that thine may be a sovereignty ancient, imperishable and everlasting.').
70   'Abdu'l-Bahá, *Secret of Divine Civilization*, p. 40.
71   Bahá'u'lláh, *Tablets of Bahá'u'lláh*, p. 156.
72   'Abdu'l-Bahá, *Secret of Divine Civilization*, p. 17.
73   ibid. p. 20.
74   'Abdu'l-Bahá, *Selections*, p. 3.

anything else . . . It means to consider the welfare of the community as one's own. It means, in brief, to regard humanity as a single individual, and one's own self as a member of that corporeal form, and to know of a certainty that if pain or injury afflicts any member of that body, it must inevitably result in suffering for all the rest.[75]

Accordingly, as individuals we must also be concerned with the welfare of others, and this affects our views about taxation and fairness – leading us to consider the impact of taxation on others and not just our own wealth.

'Abdu'l Bahá explains that the world of humanity is like a family, and that it would not be morally acceptable for some family members to be rich and others poor; indeed, the law must step in to prevent the suffering of our fellow brothers and sisters:

> Although the body politic is one family, yet, because of lack of harmonious relations some members are comfortable and some in direst misery; some members are satisfied and some are hungry; some members are clothed in the most costly garments and some families are in need of food and shelter. Why? Because this family lacks the necessary reciprocity and symmetry . . . Therefore, a law must be given to this family by means of which all the members of this family will enjoy equal well-being and happiness.[76]

This global, all-embracing vision, incumbent on all individuals, has profound implications for governance, economics, and taxation.

Principles of Governance, Economics, and Taxation Based on the Unity of Humankind

The Bahá'í writings also directly address certain principles of governance, economics, and taxation. First of all, regarding principles of governance, they envision the history of humanity as a process of gradual collective maturation, with humanity now passing through a turbulent period of adolescence, preparing to assume the responsibilities of adulthood. The Bahá'í teachings affirm that this emerging stage of adult maturity will be characterized by an evolving global perspective and the building of institutions that foster cooperation among all peoples and nations.

Bahá'u'lláh announces the moral foundation for this vision in affirming that: 'The earth is but one country, and mankind its citizens.'[77] This goal – world citizenship for all human beings – suffuses the consciousness of the global Bahá'í community and underlies all of its plans and aspirations. Regarding the process of

---

75   'Abdu'l-Bahá, *Secret of Divine Civilization*, p. 39.
76   From a talk delivered by 'Abdu'l-Bahá on 3 September 1912, in 'Abdu'l-Bahá, *Promulgation of Universal Peace*, p. 312.
77   Bahá'u'lláh, *Tablets of Bahá'u'lláh*, p. 167.

the maturation of humankind, Shoghi Effendi, the Guardian of the Bahá'í Faith, wrote in 1936 in *The World Order of Bahá'u'lláh*:

> Unification of the whole of mankind is the hall-mark of the stage which human society is now approaching. Unity of family, of tribe, of city-state, and nation have been successively attempted and fully established. World unity is the goal towards which a harassed humanity is striving.[78]

Shoghi Effendi also wrote that the global society of nations must establish institutions limiting unfettered national sovereignty and promoting unified action for the common good:

> Nation-building has come to an end. The anarchy inherent in state sovereignty is moving towards a climax. A world, growing to maturity, must abandon this fetish, recognize the oneness and wholeness of human relationships, and establish once for all the machinery that can best incarnate this fundamental principle of its life.[79]

Shoghi Effendi explained that this machinery must include a global federation of nations:

> The unity of the human race, as envisaged by Bahá'u'lláh, implies the establishment of a world commonwealth in which all nations, races, creeds and classes are closely and permanently united, and in which the autonomy of its state members and the personal freedom and initiative of the individuals that compose them are definitely and completely safeguarded.[80]

In connection with that world commonwealth, Shoghi Effendi stated that:

> Some form of a world super-state must needs be evolved, in whose favor all of the nations of the world will have willingly ceded every claim to make war, *certain rights to impose taxation* and all rights to maintain armaments, except for purposes of maintaining internal order within their respective dominions.[81]

This passage suggests that the state members of this world federation would continue to have fundamental sovereignty, including the right to fashion their own national tax laws, while also ceding 'certain rights to impose taxation' to the federation. Shoghi Effendi goes on to explain that one institution of this global federation would be 'a world parliament whose members shall be elected by the

---

78   Shoghi Effendi, *World Order*, p. 202.
79   ibid.
80   ibid. p. 203.
81   ibid. p. 40 (emphasis added).

people in their respective countries and whose election shall be confirmed by their respective governments'.[82]

Shoghi Effendi also says that under the supervision of this world federation:

. . . the economic resources of the world will be organized, its sources of raw materials will be tapped and fully utilized, its markets will be coordinated and developed, and the distribution of its products will be equitably regulated.[83]

This Bahá'í charter of a nascent global system of governance also asserts that:

. . . economic barriers and restrictions will be completely abolished, and the inordinate distinction between classes will be obliterated. Destitution on the one hand, and gross accumulation of ownership on the other, will disappear.[84]

Shoghi Effendi explains that:

The enormous energy dissipated and wasted on war, whether economic or political, will be consecrated to such ends as will extend the range of human inventions and technical development, to the increase of the productivity of mankind, to the extermination of disease, to the extension of scientific research, to the raising of the standard of physical health, to the sharpening and refinement of the human brain, to the exploitation of the unused and unsuspected resources of the planet, to the prolongation of human life, and to the furtherance of any other agency that can stimulate the intellectual, the moral, and spiritual life of the entire human race.[85]

Second, other Bahá'í teachings also set forth various principles regarding economics. For example, because they emphasize the promotion of the well-being of all people and all nations, rather than just that of citizens of a single nation-state,[86] they consequently call for the alleviation of global indigence and the elimination of the extremes of wealth and poverty. In the words of 'Abdu'l-Bahá:

Nobody should die of hunger; everybody should have sufficient clothing; one man should not live in excess while another has no possible means of existence . . . Let us try with all the strength we have to bring about happier conditions, so that no single soul may be destitute.[87]

How might the world achieve these Bahá'í teachings on just economics? The

---

82   ibid. pp. 40–1.
83   ibid. p. 204.
84   ibid.
85   ibid.
86   On these teachings, see Bahá'í International Community, *A Governance Befitting*, pp. 1–2.
87   'Abdu'l-Bahá, *Paris Talks*, p. 132.

Bahá'í writings endorse both institutional reforms as well as individual, voluntary acts of generosity. 'Abdu'l-Bahá explains:

> It is evident that under present systems and conditions of government the poor are subject to the greatest need and distress while others more fortunate live in luxury and plenty far beyond their actual necessities. This inequality of portion and privilege is one of the deep and vital problems of human society. That there is need of an equalization and apportionment by which all may possess the comforts and privileges of life is evident. The remedy must be legislative readjustment of conditions. The rich too must be merciful to the poor, contributing from willing hearts to their needs without being forced or compelled to do so.[88]

In a letter to the world's Bahá'ís of 1 March 2017, the Universal House of Justice elaborated on these principles of economic justice grounded in a global outlook:

> The welfare of any segment of humanity is inextricably bound up with the welfare of the whole. Humanity's collective life suffers when any one group thinks of its own well-being in isolation from that of its neighbours or pursues economic gain without regard for how the natural environment, which provides sustenance for all, is affected. A stubborn obstruction, then, stands in the way of meaningful social progress: time and again, avarice and self-interest prevail at the expense of the common good. Unconscionable quantities of wealth are being amassed, and the instability this creates is made worse by how income and opportunity are spread so unevenly both between nations and within nations. But it need not be so. However much such conditions are the outcome of history, they do not have to define the future, and even if current approaches to economic life satisfied humanity's stage of adolescence, they are certainly inadequate for its dawning age of maturity. There is no justification for continuing to perpetuate structures, rules, and systems that manifestly fail to serve the interests of all peoples.[89]

Third, regarding the required 'legislative readjustment of conditions' referred to by 'Abdu'l-Bahá in the quotation above and the necessary restructuring of economic life referred to by the Universal House of Justice, the Bahá'í writings contain certain principles relevant specifically to taxation. They endorse, among other reforms, a progressive income tax system.[90] Under such a system, those with higher incomes would pay proportionately more of their income in tax. This progressive system of taxation accords with a general emphasis in the Bahá'í teachings on justice and

---

88   From a talk delivered by 'Abdu'l-Bahá on 7 May 1912, in 'Abdu'l-Bahá, *Promulgation of Universal Peace*, p. 107.
89   Universal House of Justice, Letter to the Bahá'ís of the World 1 March 2017.
90   See e.g. a discussion of 'Abdu'l-Bahá's teachings on a progressive income tax in 'Abdu'l-Bahá, 'Economic Happiness for the Human Race', pp. 228–9.

fairness. For example, Bahá'u'lláh has declared that 'the best beloved of all things in My sight is Justice'.[91] Moreover, 'Abdu'l-Bahá explicitly indicates that at least a portion of the revenues raised under such a progressive system of tax should be used to reduce extreme poverty and ensure that no one is destitute.[92]

The Bahá'í writings, in addition to calling for a progressive income tax system within nations, endorse the establishment of a tax system at the global level, with the larger goal of ensuring the equitable distribution of the world's products and resources. In particular, the Bahá'í writings envision the 'willing ceding' by states of 'certain rights to impose taxation' to some future form of world federation, suggesting broad principles relevant to envisioning reforms of the current international tax system, but obviously not specific details of the structure of that system.

However, at the same time the Bahá'í teachings prescribe a fair tax system, as well as other societal mechanisms to alleviate the plight of the poor, they encourage each individual to engage in personal acts of charity and to make charitable donations as a means of eliminating extremes of wealth and poverty.

Toward a Bahá'í Vision for the Future of International Tax Law and Policy

What do the Bahá'í writings suggest about the desirable future of international tax law and policy? First, they indicate that at some point in the future there will need to be a fundamental shift in the world order that would lead to a much more global approach to taxation rather than a nationalist one that emphasizes unlimited state sovereignty. We have just seen that Shoghi Effendi called for the establishment of a world federation in which states would still retain a significant degree of autonomy – including, we can presume, in adopting appropriate laws and policies regarding taxation – while also allowing the federation itself to exercise certain rights of taxation for the benefit of the whole global community of nations and people.

In particular, passages from Shoghi Effendi's writings suggest that this global tax system might be used to alleviate the extremes of wealth and poverty that impede the realization of a just economic order, and more broadly assist in funding all activities that will benefit 'the intellectual, the moral, and spiritual life of the entire human race'. In this connection, a global tax system might help ensure a more equitable distribution of resources between countries with developed economies and those with developing economies. However, the Bahá'í writings also suggest that the purpose of this redistribution to countries with developing economies is to assist them in development that benefits the less fortunate, and to allow them to redress gross inequalities of wealth among their people – not just to enrich the bank accounts of wealthy leaders. To the extent the system also ensures that even developed countries obtain a fair amount of tax revenue by eliminating the

---

91   Bahá'u'lláh, *Hidden Words*, Arabic no. 2.
92   'Abdu'l-Bahá, 'Economic Happiness for the Human Race', p. 227.

types of tax competition strategies discussed earlier in this chapter, these countries too must use these revenues to alleviate gross inequalities in the economic fortunes of their own residents, and ensure that everyone has an adequate standard of living.

Clearly, the Bahá'í writings specifically endorse a progressive income tax system as a means to this end. Countries might agree to adopt such a system in their national tax laws (a system that most already have), but there also might be a supplemental global progressive income tax used to fund projects that benefit all nations as well as the whole of humanity. These could include not only projects aimed at eliminating poverty, but also those aimed at safeguarding the natural environment.[93] This is an idea not currently being discussed among world leaders.

The Bahá'í writings also endorse implicitly the goals of an ideal tax policy described earlier, and their application to the international economic system, including the international tax system. For example, the progressive income tax itself represents an effort to institute horizontal equity – holding that taxpayers with the same incomes should pay the same tax, and vertical equity – holding that a taxpayer with greater income than another should pay proportionately more tax. Shoghi Effendi's discourses on world order also refer to the goal of effectuating an 'equitable' distribution of the world's products, which by extension suggests they would support an equitable distribution of tax revenues among nations. Shoghi Effendi's guidance implies, too, that the international tax system should strive to implement this goal of equitably apportioning tax revenues in the most efficient manner possible by referring to the 'coordination' of markets. Clearly, we can imagine that one of the purposes of a global federation designed to facilitate world-wide economic coordination would also be to simplify the complex tax laws that currently exist in the absence of a central guiding authority.

Of course, any mention of a global federation today may feed fears of a world dictatorship, as the comments of tax scholar Michael Graetz indicate. However, the Bahá'í writings make clear that such a federation must guarantee the fundamental autonomy of member nations, and also ensure the human rights and freedoms of every individual on the planet. Its constituent organs would be democratically accountable. Indeed, the world parliament foreseen in the Bahá'í writings would be democratically elected by the world's people. We already have seen successful experiments with this type of global governance, including the development and expansion of the European Union.

The Bahá'í-inspired vision for international tax law and policy summarized above would signify a marked departure from the current system of taxation. Historically, governments as well as taxpayers have sought primarily to achieve what they understand as their own economic self-interest, often being motivated by the prospect of short-term selfish financial gain rather than taking into account the

---

93   In this connection, the Bahá'í International Community stated in 2020 that 'Strengthening the legal framework relating to the natural world would lend coherence and vigor to the biodiversity, climate, and environmental regimes and provide a robust foundation for a system of common stewardship of the planet's resources.' Bahá'í International Community, *A Governance Befitting*, p. 7.

long-term impact of their policies on sustainable human well-being as a whole. In contrast, the Bahá'í teachings call for a new focus on the welfare of every person, every business, and every country that complements an appropriate consideration of both short-term and long-term well-being for oneself – whether a nation, corporation, or individual.

We have seen that in addition to endorsing 'legislative readjustment of conditions', which can include a progressive income tax, the Bahá'í writings praise and encourage individual acts of charity. Many national tax systems give tax benefits for charitable donations, as Kathryn Moore's chapter points out, and thus we can infer that both national tax systems as well as a new global tax system implemented by a world federation ought to encourage such giving. More generally, apart from international tax law, the Bahá'í writings call for a significant change in individuals' thinking and orientation with respect to their material means, leading to them being happy to share those means with others in need.

In short, the system advocated by the Bahá'í teachings would strike a balance between the legitimate needs of states to determine their own tax policies to achieve a just distribution of resources among people within them, and the requirement of ensuring a global minimum level of subsistence, and indeed, enhanced economic prosperity, through global cooperative mechanisms. This integrative vision can help provide guidance for new initiatives designed to create a more just international tax system at both the national and global levels.

A Bahá'í Perspective on Recent Reform Efforts

A Bahá'í vision for the future of international tax law and policy certainly would approve of the reform efforts undertaken in recent years, since they aim to make the international tax system more equitable, fair, and efficient. Most importantly, these steps towards global cooperation can help humanity achieve the laudable goals of ensuring that every country receives sufficient tax revenue to address urgent public needs, including narrowing the gap between rich and poor.

The Bahá'í teachings related to tax policy consist of general, overarching spiritual and material principles, and as such are not sufficiently detailed to engage in a careful evaluation of these reform efforts. For example, they have nothing particular to say about how the profits of multinational businesses should be allocated, whether by the arm's length principle or formulary apportionment. Nor do they address the idea of a global minimum corporate tax or a global wealth tax on individuals. However, they do suggest that these collaborative global efforts should be pursued vigorously and not abandoned because of claims to protect national tax sovereignty. The Bahá'í teachings also imply that these measures should be tailored to achieve the ethical goals emphasized in the Bahá'í writings, including the alleviation of poverty within countries, limitations through some form of taxation on the unfettered and extreme accumulation of wealth by any one individual, and the devotion of adequate resources to the protection of the environment and other public goods necessary for human beings to live together in dignity, in peace, and in unity. Finally, Bahá'í principles relating to global cooperation and the establishment of a world federation suggest that mechanisms for open consultation among nations on how best to achieve these goals should be strengthened, ideally with opportunities for democratic input from ordinary citizens.

The Prospects for Reform of International Tax Law and Policy in Line with a Bahá'í Vision

What are the prospects for nations moving toward some of the above reforms consistent with a Bahá'í-inspired vision of international tax law and policy? On the one hand, we see a variety of discouraging signs. Many countries still devote themselves to a program of securing economic benefits by engaging in blatant tax competition. Of course, both corporate and individual taxpayers continue to seek ways to exploit divergent national tax rules, as well as treaty rules, for their own benefit.

Legal scholar Tsilly Dagan foresees such challenges in achieving effective coordination on tax matters, writing:

> Countries differ in their economic and political characteristics as well as in their expectations of their tax systems. Their decisions regarding tax rates – in particular in relation to redistribution – are strongly anchored in the divergent characteristics and beliefs (and, sometimes, simply the means) of their citizenry and leadership. The variety of interest groups within each country complicates the picture even further. Countries can therefore be expected to diverge and even conflict in terms of their positions and interests vis-à-vis a multilateral accord, and the prospects of arriving at a collective agreement on a single solution seems problematic at best.[94]

Dagan also stresses that even if countries can reach accord on a particular common set of tax rules (like the global corporate minimum tax) they will have an incentive to 'defect' from this agreed-upon framework in their own self-interest:

> Furthermore, even if such coordination were to be achieved, sustaining it would be difficult given the possible incentives of individual countries to defect. As with cooperative efforts in general, any given country could derive greater economic benefits from defecting even if the overall world welfare increases due to the cooperation. Defection can take the form of imposing taxes that are lower than what was cooperatively agreed upon, in order to attract residents and investors (as is the case of a tax haven).[95]

---

94   Dagan, *International Tax Policy*, p. 131.
95   ibid. pp. 131–2.

Dagan points out how difficult tax coordination is. She notes:

> For multilateral coordination to be truly effective in preventing tax competition, states would have to agree on the common basic building blocks of their tax systems (specifically defining who should be taxed, on what income, and when). This would enable them to close the loopholes that arise from the inconsistencies between different jurisdictions and facilitate tax avoidance. Moreover, to curb the race to the bottom, states must coordinate not only their tax rules but also their tax rates (at least with regard to taxes collected beyond the value of the state-provided public services), so as to prevent price-based competition for residents and investments.[96]

On the other hand, we have seen more positive trends that are simultaneously at work. The BEPS and global minimum corporate tax initiatives underscore that many countries see it as in their own self-interest to enhance coordination of tax policies. Many taxpayers, too, recognize that coordination among tax authorities helps them avoid the burdens of double taxation by multiple countries.

At least some governments seem motivated in part by the ethical goal of ensuring that all countries obtain sufficient revenue through such tax coordination to fund needed public works and social welfare programs. Businesses, too, have begun to pay more attention to the ethical impacts of their activities, including on the enjoyment of universal human rights for their workers, customers, and members of the communities where they operate. This is reflected, for example, in the efforts of businesses to implement the 'Guiding Principles on Business and Human Rights' adopted by the United Nations General Assembly in 2011.[97]

The Bahá'í writings, while encouraging reforms in the international tax order, do not provide guidance on their likelihood of acceptance or when we might expect these types of new initiatives. However, we can surmise that eventually, even if only as a result of severe tribulations, leaders will come around to establishing the type of federation foreseen in the Bahá'í teachings, accompanied by new mechanisms of global cooperation on international tax issues.

The Bahá'í vision of a just and coherent international tax system encourages governments to adopt an ethical framework that acknowledges the spiritual as well as the economic interdependence of nations and peoples. Through the promulgation of an ethos that recognizes the value of global unity and the right of everyone to a minimum standard of living, countries may be motivated to build on the positive trends apparent in recent years and create a fairer, more equitable, more efficient, and simpler international tax system that promotes global, national, and individual prosperity – constituting, indeed, a new world tax order.

---

96   ibid. p. 129.
97   See United Nations, *Guiding Principles on Business and Human Rights*.

Bibliography

'Abdu'l-Bahá. 'Economic Happiness for the Human Race'. *Star of the West*, vol. XIII, no. 9 (December 1922), pp. 227–32.

— *Paris Talks: Addresses Given by 'Abdu'l-Bahá in Paris in 1911–1912*. 11th ed. London: Bahá'í Publishing Trust, 1969.

— *The Promulgation of Universal Peace: Talks Delivered by 'Abdu'l-Bahá During His Visit to the United States and Canada in 1912*. Compiled by Howard MacNutt. 2nd ed. Wilmette, IL: Bahá'í Publishing Trust, 1982. Online edition at https://www.bahai.org/ library/authoritative-texts/abdul-baha/promulgation-universal-peace/1#820079356

— *The Secret of Divine Civilization*. Translated from the Persian by Marzieh Gail. Wilmette, IL: Bahá'í Publishing Trust, 1970.

— *Selections from the Writings of Abdu'l-Bahá*. Compiled by the Research Department of the Universal House of Justice and Translated by a Committee at the Bahá'í World Centre and by Marzieh Gail. Haifa: Bahá'í World Centre, 1978.

Avi-Yonah, Reuven S. 'A Global Wealth Tax?' 183 *Tax Notes Federal* 2299, 16 September 2024.

— 'Globalization, Tax Competition, and the Fiscal Crisis of the Welfare State'. 113 *Harvard Law Review* 1573 (2000).

Bahá'í International Community. *A Governance Befitting: Humanity and the Path Toward a Just Global Order* (2020). https://www.bic.org/sites/default/files/print_pdf/ un75_20201020.pdf

Bahá'u'lláh. *Gleanings from the Writings of Bahá'u'lláh*. Translated by Shoghi Effendi. Wilmette, IL: Bahá'í Publishing Trust, 1983.

— *The Hidden Words*. Translated by Shoghi Effendi with the assistance of some English friends. Wilmette, IL: Bahá'í Publishing Trust, 1993.

— *Tablets of Bahá'u'lláh Revealed after the Kitáb-i-Aqdas*. Compiled by the Research Department of the Universal House of Justice and translated by Habib Taherzadeh with the assistance of a Committee at the Bahá'í World Centre. Wilmette, IL: Bahá'í Publishing Trust, 1988.

Dagan, Tsilly. *International Tax Policy: Between Competition and Cooperation*. Cambridge: Cambridge University Press, 2018.

'Despite Fears of a Global Tax War, Donald Trump Has a Chance to Make Peace'. *The Economist*, 30 January 2025. https://www.economist.com/leaders/2025/01/30/despite-fears-of-a-global-tax-war-donald-trump-has-a-chance-to-make-peace

Graetz, Michael J. 'The David R. Tillinghast Lecture: Taxing International Income: Inadequate Principles, Outdated Concepts, and Unsatisfactory Policies'. 54 *Tax Law Review* 261 (2001).

— and Anne L. Alstott. *Federal Income Taxation: Principles and Policies*. 9th ed. St. Paul, MN: West Academic, 2022.

Hargis, Cydney. 'OECD Proposes Plan to Curb International Tax Avoidance'. *Inter Press Service*, 19 July 2013. https://www.globalissues.org/news/2013/07/19/17105

Hatcher, William S. and J. Douglas Martin. *The Bahá'í Faith: The Emerging Global Religion*. New ed. Wilmette, IL: Bahá'í Publishing, 2002.

Herzfeld, Mindy. 'The Case Against BEPS: Lessons for Tax Coordination'. 21 *Florida Tax Review* 1 (2017).

— 'The OECD Consults on a New Tax World Order'. *Tax Notes*, 18 February 2019, p. 730.

— 'Spotlight on Global Minimum Taxes Shifts to Individuals'. 183 *Tax Notes Federal* 1715, 3 June 2024.

La Torre Jeker, Virginia. 'Expatriation: New Forms, More Government Scrutiny, Bigger Stakes'. *Forbes*, 3 December 2024. Accessed 1 March 2025. https://www.forbes. com/sites/virginialatorrejeker/2024/12/03/expatriation-new-forms-more-government-scrutiny-bigger-stakes/

Lepard, Brian D. *Customary International Law: A New Theory with Practical Applications*. New York: Cambridge University Press, 2010.

— 'Is the United States Obligated to Drive on the Right? A Multidisciplinary Inquiry into the Normative Authority of Contemporary International Law Using the Arm's Length Standard as a Case Study'. 10 *Duke Journal of Comparative & International Law* 43 (2000).

OECD. 'Base Erosion and Profit-Shifting (BEPS)'. Accessed 15 February 2025. https://www.oecd.org/en/topics/policy-issues/base-erosion-and-profit-shifting-beps.html

— *Model Tax Convention on Income and on Capital: Condensed Version 2017*. Paris: OECD Publishing, 2017. https://doi.org/10.1787/mtc_cond-2017–en

— *OECD Work on Taxation, 2018–19*. https://www.readkong.com/page/taxation-oecd-work-on-1678377

— *Preventing the Artificial Avoidance of Permanent Establishment Status, Action 7 - 2015 Final Report*. OECD/G20 Base Erosion and Profit Shifting Project. Paris: OECD Publishing, 2015. https://doi.org/10.1787/9789264241220-en

— *Standard for Automatic Exchange of Financial Account Information in Tax Matters*. 2nd ed. Paris: OECD Publishing, 2017. https://doi.org/10.1787/9789264267992-en

— *Tax Challenges Arising from the Digitalisation of the Economy – Global Anti-Base Erosion Model Rules (Pillar Two): Inclusive Framework on BEPS*. Paris: OECD Publishing, 2021. https://doi.org/10.1787/782bac33-en

Petkova, Kunka; Andrzej Stasio, and Martin Zagler. 'On the Relevance of Double Tax Treaties'. 27 *International Tax and Public Finance* 575 (2020). https://link.springer.com/article/10.1007/s10797-019-09570-9

Piketty, Thomas. *Capital in the Twenty-First Century*. Translated by Arthur Goldhammer. Cambridge, MA: Harvard University Press, 2014.

Shoghi Effendi. *The World Order of Bahá'u'lláh: Selected Letters*. Wilmette, IL: Bahá'í Publishing Trust, 1974.

Singer, Peter. *One World: The Ethics of Globalization*. New Haven: Yale University Press, 2002.

Stiglitz, Joseph E. *The Price of Inequality: How Today's Divided Society Endangers Our Future*. New York: W.W. Norton and Co., 2013.

United Nations. *Guiding Principles on Business and Human Rights: Implementing the United Nations 'Protect, Respect and Remedy' Framework*. New York and Geneva: United Nations Publications, 2011. https://www.ohchr.org/sites/default/files/Documents/Publications/GuidingPrinciplesBusinessHR_EN.pdf

Universal House of Justice. Letter to the Bahá'ís of the World, 1 March 2017. https://universalhouseofjustice.bahai.org/involvement-life-society/20170301_001

PART THREE

CONCLUSION

8

The Prospects for Reforming the Global Legal Order to Achieve Justice

Brian D. Lepard

What are the prospects for reforming the global legal order to achieve justice in line with Bahá'í principles, and realizing the visions for legal reform sketched by the authors of the preceding chapters based on those principles? To answer that question, this chapter first summarizes some key elements of the Bahá'í vision for a justice-centered world legal order as highlighted by the authors, and then suggests various ways Bahá'í principles can help global law address the contemporary social problems highlighted in the book more effectively and justly.

The entire Revelation of Bahá'u'lláh is transformational. At one level, it stands above and apart from any existing system of law, whether national or international. As Bahá'u'lláh has written, 'Mankind's ordered life hath been revolutionized through the agency of this unique, this wondrous System – the like of which mortal eyes have never witnessed.'[1] His Revelation thus is no mere continuation of past revelations, or refinement of them; it seeks to revolutionize every aspect of the life of each individual and the functioning of every society.

Furthermore, the laws Bahá'u'lláh revealed in His sacred Book of Laws, the Kitáb-i-Aqdas, constitute no simple refinement and updating of the laws of former Dispensations, nor a religious version of the secular laws reviewed in this volume. Bahá'u'lláh declares at the very beginning of the Kitáb-i-Aqdas:

> Think not that We have revealed unto you a mere code of laws. Nay, rather, We have unsealed the choice Wine with the fingers of might and power. To this beareth witness that which the Pen of Revelation hath revealed. Meditate upon this, O men of insight![2]

In addition, while the essays in this volume have attempted to gain insight into the unique character of Bahá'u'lláh's Revelation and its implications for the global

---

1   Bahá'u'lláh, *Gleanings*, p. 136.
2   Bahá'u'lláh, *Kitáb-i-Aqdas*, para. 5.

legal order by comparing and contrasting its central features with various characteristics of contemporary legal orders, whether national or global, Bahá'u'lláh's
teachings clearly transcend any existing legal concepts. Bahá'u'lláh Himself counsels in the Kitáb-i-Aqdas:

> O leaders of religion! Weigh not the Book of God with such standards and
> sciences as are current amongst you, for the Book itself is the unerring Balance
> established amongst men. In this most perfect Balance whatsoever the peoples
> and kindreds of the earth possess must be weighed, while the measure of its
> weight should be tested according to its own standard, did ye but know it.[3]

Of course, Bahá'u'lláh's laws cannot be judged by contemporary standards because
they have a divine source, rather than a human one. As the essays in this book have
demonstrated, we can glean insights into Bahá'u'lláh's laws and principles through
comparing them with human laws, and, indeed, we can and should reflect on how
to reform existing human laws and institutions in a way that accords with Bahá'í
laws and principles. Nevertheless, Bahá'í laws and principles will always, and
should always, retain their own sacred character and distinctiveness.

Looking a little more carefully at the nature of Bahá'u'lláh's laws as explored
by the preceding chapters, it becomes evident that many of the laws brought by
Bahá'u'lláh are intended to apply only to those individuals who have recognized
His Revelation. Although that circle of individuals is ever-expanding, it does not
encompass the entire planet. We might refer to this subset of Bahá'u'lláh's laws as
'Bahá'í law'. Bahá'í law would include, for example, the Law of Ḥuqúqu'lláh, as
explored by Kathryn Moore, as well as the laws of Bahá'í administration. While
some aspects of Bahá'í law bear certain resemblances to existing 'secular' laws,
as Prof. Moore has also shown, Bahá'í law is fundamentally different in its origin,
and indeed, its spirit.

However, as we explored in Chapter 1, other principles taught by Bahá'u'lláh
are intended to apply to the entire planet. These include the achievement of peace
through the establishment and strengthening of institutions of global governance,
the promulgation of universal education, the full realization of equality of women
and men, the eradication of prejudices of all kinds, the fulfillment of racial justice,
and the protection of freedom of religion or belief, all of which the preceding chapters have touched upon. The critical question this book explores asks how we can
best implement these Bahá'í principles in national and global legal systems today.

One consistent theme of the reflections in the preceding chapters is that the
global legal order must ultimately be transformed not only through a multitude of
institutional and legal reforms, but by a revolution in the outlook of every single
individual – and especially those responsible for the legal system in every country
– toward a personal commitment to divinely-ordained principles of justice. As
Bahá'u'lláh underscores in *The Hidden Words*:

---

3   ibid. para. 99.

O Son of Spirit! The best beloved of all things in My sight is Justice; turn not away therefrom if thou desirest Me, and neglect it not that I may confide in thee. By its aid thou shalt see with thine own eyes and not through the eyes of others, and shalt know of thine own knowledge and not through the knowledge of thy neighbor. Ponder this in thy heart; how it behooveth thee to be. Verily justice is My gift to thee and the sign of My loving-kindness. Set it then before thine eyes.[4]

One of the critical points this book emphasizes is that all of those involved with the law must 'see with their own eyes' by developing a keen sense of justice, setting aside time-worn ways of thinking about law, and boldly seeking to align laws and legal institutions with the urgent needs of our time. As Kiser Barnes pointed out in his chapter, Bahá'u'lláh's teachings also stress the role that all members of society must play in transforming their inner characters and striving to build bonds of unity, grounded in principles of justice, with neighbors, associates, and fellow citizens.

However, the global legal order must undergo a transformation at the institutional level as well. The substance of laws, and the agencies that implement them, must be completely reexamined and re-thought to ensure their consonance with the overarching principle of human unity and the equality of people of all races, ethnicities, religions, and cultures. Open-minded consultation is also an essential tool that must be cultivated, refined, and implemented at countless levels to effectuate these reforms.

What are some implications, then, of the trenchant analyses of the contributors to this volume for the many social problems reviewed in Chapter 1? What are some key elements of global justice relating to these problems that they identify? What Bahá'í-inspired visions for legal reform do the contributors sketch in order to achieve global justice?

At the broadest level, it seems clear that the critical prerequisite for solving these social problems, achieving global justice, and reforming the global legal order is the cultivation of an awareness of the ideal, and reality, of human oneness. As the Bahá'í International Community affirmed in a statement issued in 2020 on the occasion of the 75th anniversary of the creation of the United Nations:

The human family is one. This is a truth that has been embraced by multitudes around the world. Its profound implications for our collective behavior must now give rise to a coordinated movement toward higher levels of social and political unity. As Bahá'u'lláh declared over a century ago, 'True peace and tranquility will only be realized when every soul will have become the well-wisher of all mankind.' The perils of a global community divided against itself are too great to countenance.[5]

---

4   Bahá'u'lláh, *Tablets of Bahá'u'lláh*, p. 36.
5   Bahá'í International Community, *A Governance Befitting*, p. 1.

We have seen throughout this volume that the global legal order constitutes one field where humanity must achieve 'higher levels of social and political unity'. The task of Bahá'ís engaged in the field of law includes helping to promote this unity. In a broader context, the Universal House of Justice has stated, with reference to the particular challenge of racism:

> Whether through deeds or words, the merit of your every contribution to social well-being lies, first, in your *resolute commitment to discover that precious point of unity* where contrasting perspectives overlap and around which contending peoples can coalesce.[6]

Each of this book's contributors has explored the powerful impact that the concept of unity can have on the way we understand the failings of our existing national and international legal orders, and how they can be remedied.

Intimately connected with the principle of unity is love – a love for all humanity that transcends national boundaries and embraces the whole of the planet. Lawyers and jurists are not used to thinking of law as related to 'love'. However, the Bahá'í perspective discloses that one of the deficiencies of existing legal orders is their detachment from love, and one of the prerequisites for reforming them to achieve justice is to reexamine them in light of the principle and virtue of love for all. Many of the chapters have explored this theme in relation to the legal problems they have addressed, including my own chapter on racial justice. Bahá'u'lláh Himself draws this connection between law and love in the Kitáb-i-Aqdas, declaring: 'The Tongue of My power hath, from the heaven of My omnipotent glory, addressed to My creation these words: "Observe My commandments, for the love of My beauty."'[7]

Simultaneously, the Bahá'í teachings emphasize, as Kiser Barnes' chapter points out, that humanity must strive not for unity around just any ideal, but rather unity of thought and action in implementing divinely-ordained principles of justice, including racial and gender equality. All of the chapters in the book have explored the multiple dimensions of justice grounded in Bahá'í principles – dimensions that accord with, and yet transcend, existing conceptions of justice reflected in the current legal order. Perhaps most importantly, they have investigated Bahá'u'lláh's unique teaching that the very purpose of justice is unity among all human beings. In Bahá'u'lláh's own words: 'The purpose of justice is the appearance of unity among men.'[8] Thus, we see a dynamic circle, with unity as a prerequisite for justice, while the purpose of justice is unity – an intimate relationship that suggests the yin and yang of reciprocity and mutuality.

As all the contributors have emphasized, in this new day law must no longer be used as an instrument of oppression, or to pursue man-made ideologies, but rather

---

6   Universal House of Justice, Message to the Bahá'ís of the World, 25 November 2020 (emphasis added).
7   Bahá'u'lláh, *Kitáb-i-Aqdas*, para. 4.
8   Bahá'u'lláh, quoted in Shoghi Effendi, *Advent of Divine Justice*, p. 28.

must be transformed into a powerful means for promoting unity and justice among all members of the human family, and an instrument for improving their well-being and happiness. To recall the words of Shoghi Effendi:

> . . . legal standards, political and economic theories are solely designed to safeguard the interests of humanity as a whole, and not humanity to be crucified for the preservation of the integrity of any particular law or doctrine.[9]

A search for unity in the quest for justice through law must characterize all elements of the multi-faceted global legal order. Bahá'ís can contribute significantly to this process as part of the evolution of the 'Lesser Peace', even if that chiefly political peace among nations will be brought about directly through the efforts of leaders who are not Bahá'ís. The many essays in this volume have suggested ways in which Bahá'ís can make a contribution to discourses affecting these efforts. However, Bahá'ís must also labor, based on Bahá'í law, to build up the Most Great Peace, that eventual state of true harmony and unity toward which a beleaguered humanity must continue to strive. Kathryn Moore's chapter points to the critical role of this parallel process in providing long-lasting solutions to the social problems of our time, such as gross economic injustice, through the more widespread implementation of Bahá'í law as the Bahá'í community expands and develops.

Toward that end, the three lines of action described by the Universal House of Justice as central to the activities of the Bahá'í community over the last quarter century provide crucial elements in reforming the global legal order through these twin processes of the Lesser Peace and the Most Great Peace. Thus, through community-building, local communities in every part of the globe can begin to cultivate a shared vision of justice and a commitment to act to achieve it, including through their various ways of participating in the legal system. They can contribute to relevant discourses relating to the legal order, as described in many of the chapters. They can undertake relevant social action in the field of legal reforms, which many of the authors have touched upon.

This book's contributors offer many insights into how the global legal order can better address the social problems highlighted in the first chapter and achieve justice. As they all underscore, the only solution to the political and social turmoil gripping the globe, and challenging longstanding legal norms and institutions, is the evolution of a common vision of justice consonant with Bahá'í principles and in turn achieved through open-minded consultation and a desire for unified action.

As Kiser Barnes and others stress, a prerequisite for transformation of the global legal order is a reaffirmation of foundational personal virtues such as trustworthiness, truthfulness, and commitment to the improvement of the lives and well-being of others. The corruption infecting legal, political, and social institutions today cannot be solved by any purely procedural safeguards, but only by a

---

9   Shoghi Effendi, *World Order*, p. 42.

moral transformation. Likewise, a commitment to the rule of law at every level of society must be rooted in such a shared moral perspective, including an emphasis on human equality and developing inclusive legal institutions, as Aaron Emmel explores in his chapter. Otherwise, the concept of the rule of law will remain an empty slogan.

This is true as much at the international level as it is at the national or local levels. As we saw in Chapter 6, the Bahá'í International Community has emphasized:

> Respect for international law, upholding fundamental human rights, adherence to treaties and agreements – only to the extent that such commitments are honored in practice can the United Nations and its Member States demonstrate a standard of integrity and trustworthiness before the people of the world. Barring this, no amount of administrative reorganization will resolve the host of long-standing challenges before us.[10]

The uprisings we have witnessed against governmental oppression reveal the symptoms of peoples' yearning for true justice. The Bahá'í teachings assert the imperative of ensuring the protection of the human rights of all, including Black people and racial minorities, on a footing of equality. At the same time, Bahá'í principles reject violent extremism and revolution, upholding, as Emanuel Towfigh notes in the context of religious liberty, a principle of loyalty to authorities in whichever country one lives – albeit a conditional loyalty that can brook no compromise with one's most cherished religious and philosophical beliefs. Bahá'u'lláh's emphasis on unity, and the importance of sacrifice for the good of the whole, counsels in favor of respectful and nonviolent protest. In this connection, 'Abdu'l-Bahá said:

> Each and every one is required to show obedience, submission and loyalty towards his own government . . . For while all sects and races . . . are absorbed in promoting their own interests and only obey their governments either with the hope of reward or from fear of punishment, the Bahá'ís are the well-wishers of the government, obedient to its laws and bearing love towards all peoples. Such obedience and submission is made incumbent and obligatory upon all by the clear Text of [Bahá'u'lláh]. Therefore the believers, in obedience to the command of the True One, show the utmost sincerity and goodwill towards all nations; and should any soul act contrary to the laws of the government he would consider himself responsible before God, deserving divine wrath and chastisement for his sin and wrongdoing.[11]

Unfortunately, as this book highlights, not all citizens and voters have yearned for a

---

10   Bahá'í International Community, *A Governance Befitting*, pp. 7–8.
11   'Abdu'l-Bahá, *Selections*, p. 293.

system of universal human rights; rather, in recent years we have seen the election of leaders who have brazenly promoted an agenda of suppression of the rights of some groups. Clearly, this problem can only be solved through the promulgation among the mass of the people, including voters, of moral ideals of equality and unity. Aaron Emmel makes this point in his close examination of the rise of intolerant and corrupt leaders around the globe.

Similarly, the extremist, racist, and discriminatory policies of many governments today can in part be limited by certain legal reforms, including implementing constitutional protections of equality for all, and adopting laws ensuring the accountability of government officials who violate human rights. However, these legal measures are insufficient without a fundamental change in the outlook of government leaders themselves, and the acquisition by them of civic virtues.

In this connection, the Bahá'í writings emphasize that political leaders must acquire these virtues, and also ensure the adoption and implementation of laws that accord with divinely-revealed principles of justice, without being sectarian or favoring one religion over another. Thus, 'Abdu'l-Bahá affirmed that the elected members of parliaments should be:

> . . . righteous, God-fearing, high-minded, incorruptible . . . They must be fully cognizant, in every particular, of the laws of God, informed as to the highest principles of law, versed in the rules which govern the management of internal affairs and the conduct of foreign relations, skilled in the useful arts of civilization, and content with their lawful emoluments.[12]

'Abdu'l-Bahá further encouraged 'the setting up of just legislation, in accord with the Divine laws which guarantee the happiness of society and protect the rights of all mankind'.[13] He said that these Divine laws 'are an impregnable proof against assault',[14] and he asserted that just secular laws consistent with Divine Law will ensure 'the integrity of the members of society and their equality before the law'.[15]

One of the most acute challenges facing the world today – the rise of extremist religious policies by governments, including the oppression of Bahá'ís in Iran – must be remedied through the adoption of policies of freedom of religion or belief and nondiscrimination. We can accomplish this important step by adhering to the teachings of religious concord brought by the founders of the great religions themselves, and by respecting the need for every government to harmonize competing claims and strive to achieve social unity, as aptly analyzed by Emanuel Towfigh in his chapter. As the passages above demonstrate, 'Abdu'l-Bahá urges legislators to consider laws that accord with the essence of Divine Law common to all religions, which includes principles of both unity and equality.

---

12 'Abdu'l-Bahá, *Secret of Divine Civilization*, p. 14.
13 ibid.
14 ibid.
15 ibid.

The chapters relating to tax law raise the important problem of how to establish a just system of taxation – one that not only supports civil society but helps eliminate the extremes of wealth and poverty. Professor Moore's chapter shows how Bahá'u'lláh's law of the Right of God fulfills many goals of economic justice that are only imperfectly achieved by existing methods of taxation. Mine demonstrates the imperative, according to Bahá'í teachings, of governments collaborating to establish both national and international tax systems that reflect the economic reality of interdependence among the world's peoples, as well as the spiritual truth of human unity, and therefore help achieve a more just distribution of economic resources and tax burdens among the peoples of the world.

We have also explored in this book how the glaring deficiencies in national and global legal orders have been exacerbated by larger societal forces of disunity. Bahá'í principles underscore the imperative of overcoming these forces with a powerful vision of global unity, and indeed, with profound universal love. No effort to patch up problems in existing laws or legal institutions will achieve success in the long run without these more profound societal transformations.

As many of the contributors have pointed out, justice requires that people of all backgrounds be educated, from earliest childhood, to appreciate the oneness of the human family, the beauty of diversity, and the imperative of achieving fairness and equity for every member of the human family. These principles must be taught in schools, inculcated by parents in the home, and of course internalized by children, junior youth, and youth through the activities associated with the community building process described earlier – and they must be advocated by leaders of nongovernmental organizations as well as enlightened political leaders.

The more these justice-centered principles permeate societies bombarded by contrary voices advocating extreme nationalism, factionalism, racial hatred, white supremacy, religious exclusivism, and isolationism, the more likely it is that political leaders will find it possible to implement legal reforms in keeping with them. Those who support the Bahá'í teachings on unity and justice can counter the advocates of virulent racial hate with appeals to the truth of racial oneness and a willingness to engage with others in humble consultation rather than confrontation. To recall the advice of the Universal House of Justice to American Bahá'ís in addressing systemic racial injustice:

> Your approach, instead, will be distinguished by maintaining a humble posture of learning, weighing alternatives in the light of His teachings, consulting to harmonize differing views and shape collective action, and marching forward with unbreakable unity in serried lines.[16]

The world's experience with combating racial discrimination in law in the last hundred years has amply demonstrated this imperative of transforming human hearts as well as laws and legal institutions.

---

16   Universal House of Justice, Letter to the Bahá'ís of the United States, 22 July 2020.

Many of this book's contributors have also examined how gross economic inequalities that trigger social unrest can be remedied with a recognition of the right of everyone to the basic needs of life, and a commitment by all social actors, including governments, to ensure that these needs are met. Bahá'í principles reject extreme economic ideologies. They emphasize instead integrating creativity and initiative in the economy with a societal responsibility to ensure a minimal level of well-being for all[17] – in the words of a title given to a talk of 'Abdu'l-Bahá, 'economic happiness for the human race'.

One element of the vision of a new 'divine economy' brought by Bahá'u'lláh is a commitment on the part of private businesses themselves to help all individuals enjoy minimal economic rights. Bahá'í teachings on economics suggest that businesses must ensure that their workers are fairly compensated and indeed, share in profits generated.[18] We saw in Kiser Barnes' chapter that Shoghi Effendi calls on Bahá'ís to exhibit the highest standard of conduct in, among other spheres of activity, their 'business dealings'.[19] More broadly, Bahá'í principles indicate that businesses must uphold all human rights and make these rights a focal point of their activities, including those involving supply chains, interactions with their customers, or engagement with the local population of the places in which they operate. Also, they must ensure that they protect the rights of women, helping them to rise to positions of leadership on a footing of equality with men, and guaranteeing that they are free of sexual harassment by superiors or co-workers.

At the global level, the Bahá'í teachings resolutely reject isolationism, instead advocating the need for worldwide collaboration among otherwise independent states and all peoples to solve the many social problems we have explored. They call, as well, for the fortification of international law and the international institutions dedicated to solving these problems, and ultimately foresee the need for and the formation of a global federation of nations. Just as at the national level, these reforms must be motivated by the evolution of a new ethical and spiritual perception on the part of the leaders of the world of humanity's organic wholeness. As 'Abdu'l-Bahá declares:

> True civilization will unfurl its banner in the mid-most heart of the world whenever a certain number of its distinguished and high-minded sovereigns – the shining exemplars of devotion and determination – shall, for the good and happiness of all mankind, arise, with firm resolve and clear vision, to establish the Cause of Universal Peace. They must make the Cause of Peace the object of general consultation, and seek by every means in their power to establish

---

17 See, e.g. 'Abdu'l-Bahá, *Some Answered Questions*, p. 316, para. 4 (affirming that 'one must therefore enact such laws and regulations as will moderate the excessive fortunes of the few and meet the basic needs of the myriad millions of the poor').

18 See, e.g. ibid. (stating that 'laws and regulations should be enacted which would grant the workers both a daily wage and a share in a fourth or fifth of the profits of the factory in accordance with its means, or which would have the workers equitably share in some other way in the profits with the owners').

19 Shoghi Effendi, *Advent of Divine Justice*, para. 41.

a Union of the nations of the world. They must conclude a binding treaty and establish a covenant, the provisions of which shall be sound, inviolable and definite. They must proclaim it to all the human race.[20]

Thus, the Bahá'í writings stress the importance of strengthening international law, including norms designed to maintain international peace and security. This view lends impetus to efforts to implement and improve the peace and security machinery established by the United Nations, and ensure that parties to the U.N. Charter faithfully observe that treaty's binding provisions. In its Riḍván 2022 message, referring to the war in Ukraine, the Universal House of Justice reaffirmed the importance of global leaders applying Bahá'u'lláh's principles of collective security and global governance, saying:

We pray that, if the recent outbreak of war in Europe is to yield any lessons for the future, it will serve as an urgent reminder of the course that the world must take if it is to attain genuine and enduring peace.[21]

Bahá'í principles also reinforce the imperative of strengthening international treaties and customary international law relating to universal human rights. During His visit to North America in 1912, for example, 'Abdu'l-Bahá declared that 'an equal standard of human rights must be recognized and adopted',[22] thus foreseeing the adoption of the Universal Declaration of Human Rights less than 40 years later. The Bahá'í teachings make clear that the protection of human rights, so fundamental to preserving the dignity of all members of the human family, can never be compromised in the name of protecting state sovereignty. The sovereignty of each nation, while entitled to a certain minimal respect, cannot be unrestricted and must instead be carefully limited in the interest of protecting fundamental human rights as well as the basic interests of humanity, including the cessation of war and a just distribution of economic resources. This theme is also taken up by the Bahá'í International Community in *A Governance Befitting*:

Whatever benefits have accrued from past conceptions of state sovereignty, present conditions demand a far more holistic and coherent approach to analysis and decision-making. What will be the global implications of domestic policies? What choices contribute to shared prosperity and sustainable peace? What steps foster nobility and preserve human dignity? As awareness of the oneness of humanity is increasingly woven into processes of decision-making, nations will find it easier to see each other as genuine partners in the stewardship of the planet and in securing the prosperity of its peoples.[23]

20   'Abdu'l-Bahá, *Secret of Divine Civilization*, p. 64.
21   Universal House of Justice, Ridván Message 2022.
22   'Abdu'l-Bahá, *Promulgation of Universal Peace*, p. 182.
23   Bahá'í International Community, *A Governance Befitting*, p. 4.

As this statement also emphasizes, governments must undertake new efforts to find peaceful solutions to conflicts and ensure that everyone enjoys fundamental human rights. The Bahá'í teachings clarify that the enjoyment of these human rights must be extended to refugees and internally displaced persons as well as those residing in their home country and region. It is also essential, according to Bahá'í principles, for the nations of the world to develop coordinated policies and laws on migration that seek not only to eliminate prejudice against refugees and ensure their human rights, but also alleviate the poverty and conflicts that lead them to flee their home countries.[24]

Regarding human trafficking, Bahá'í principles, including the equality of women and men, and an emphasis on the education of and promotion of the rights of girls and women, imply that both national and international laws on trafficking must be strengthened. They must aim at protecting women and children from trafficking, recognizing their status as victims, and ensuring that perpetrators are punished and would-be traffickers deterred. As the Bahá'í International Community has underscored, it is important to change the social structures that facilitate trafficking, including 'laws, regulations and policies'.[25] Yet it is equally important to educate women and girls so that they will be aware of their rights, and to educate men and boys so that they will be less likely to commit crimes against women and girls. This also requires strong parenting, including by educated mothers aware of their dignity and self-worth. All of these efforts reinforce each other, 'resulting in a tipping point at which the society will no longer tolerate the oppression of its girls and women'.[26]

The world needs new mechanisms for resolving global disputes peacefully, in keeping with the Bahá'í vision of the Lesser Peace and of the eventual establishment of a global commonwealth. This vision incorporates a world court able to take binding decisions, which would draw on the experience of the present-day ICJ, and the evolution, through cooperation, of a global legal order able to effectively guarantee both the security of nations and the human rights of individuals. Many of the contributions in this book have explored how we can begin to reform the existing global legal order to move toward the greater legal cohesion and cooperation implied by this vision.

One conclusion becomes clear from the essays in this volume: the existing global legal order as it now stands is woefully inadequate to address the multidimensional problems facing national societies and world society today – and to achieve justice. That order will continue to be deficient without a transformation grounded in a recognition of humanity's fundamental oneness.

As the chapters in this book have explored, the principle of the oneness of

---

24 See in this connection Bahá'í International Community, 'Viewing the Movement of Populations in the Larger Context of Humanity's Collective Life' (affirming that global policy on migration 'needs to include a genuine reflection on how [the current] order can be redesigned to ensure an adequate response to the needs of masses of the world's population living in situations of war, poverty and oppression').
25 Bahá'í International Community, 'Women's Health and Human Rights'.
26 See ibid.

the human race, as well as many other Bahá'í principles, provide guideposts for needed reforms to the existing legal order. Those principles, when implemented, will better promote the inseparable goals of justice and unity. While the immediate prospects for these reforms are unknowable, if lawyers, judges, and lawmakers can be convinced through social and professional discourses of the verity of these principles, and resolve to implement them in national and international legal systems, humanity can undoubtedly achieve great progress in realizing global justice. Bahá'u'lláh envisioned just such a transformative process, affirming: 'Soon will the present-day order be rolled up, and a new one spread out in its stead.'[27]

Bibliography

'Abdu'l-Bahá. *The Promulgation of Universal Peace: Talks Delivered by 'Abdu'l-Bahá During His Visit to the United States and Canada in 1912*. Compiled by Howard MacNutt. 2nd ed. Wilmette, IL: Bahá'í Publishing Trust, 1982.

— *The Secret of Divine Civilization*. Translated from the Persian by Marzieh Gail in consultation with Ali-Kuli Khan. Wilmette, IL: Bahá'í Publishing Trust, 1990.

— *Some Answered Questions*. Collected and translated from the Persian by Laura Clifford Barney. Newly translated ed. Haifa: Bahá'í World Centre, 2014.

Bahá'í International Community. *A Governance Befitting: Humanity and the Path Toward a Just Global Order* (2020). https://www.bic.org/sites/default/files/print_pdf/un75_20201020.pdf

— 'Viewing the Movement of Populations in the Larger Context of Humanity's Collective Life'. Intergovernmental Conference on the Global Compact for Migration, Marrakech, Morocco – 10 December 2018. https://www.bic.org/statements/viewing-movement-populations-larger-context-humanitys-collective-life

— 'Women's Health and Human Rights: The Case for Comprehensive and Sustainable Development'. The Bahá'í International Community's Contribution to the 44th Session of the UN Commission on Population and Development, 18 January 2011. https://www.bic.org/statements/womens-health-and-human-rights-case-comprehensive-and-sustainable-development

Bahá'u'lláh. *Gleanings from the Writings of Bahá'u'lláh*. Translated by Shoghi Effendi. Wilmette, IL: Bahá'í Publishing Trust, 1976.

— *The Kitáb-i-Aqdas: The Most Holy Book*. Wilmette, IL: Bahá'í Publishing Trust, 1993.

— *Tablets of Bahá'u'lláh Revealed after the Kitáb-i-Aqdas*. Translated by Habib Taherzadeh. Compiled by the Research Department of the Universal House of Justice at the Bahá'í World Centre. Wilmette, IL: Bahá'í Publishing Trust, 1998.

Shoghi Effendi. *The Advent of Divine Justice*. Wilmette, IL: Bahá'í Publishing, 2006.

— *The World Order of Bahá'u'lláh: Selected Letters*. Wilmette, IL: Bahá'í Publishing Trust, 1991.

Universal House of Justice. Letter to the Bahá'ís of the United States, 22 July 2020. https://www.bahai.org/library/authoritative-texts/the-universal-house-of-justice/messages/20200722_001/1#870410250

---

27   Bahá'u'lláh, *Gleanings*, p. 7.

— Message to the Bahá'ís of the World, 25 November 2020. https://www.bahai.org/library/authoritative-texts/the-universal-house-of-justice/messages/20201125_001/1#300076430

— Message to the Bahá'ís of the World, Riḍván 2022 ('Riḍván Message 2022'). https://universalhouseofjustice.bahai.org/ridvan-messages/20220421_001

www.ingramcontent.com/pod-product-compliance
Lightning Source LLC
Chambersburg PA
CBHW050042220326
41599CB00045B/7250